# This Will Make a Man of Me

# This Will Make a Man of Me

*The Life and Letters of a Teenage Officer in the Civil War*

By James M. Scythes

LEHIGH UNIVERSITY PRESS
Bethlehem

Published by Lehigh University Press
Copublished by The Rowman & Littlefield Publishing Group, Inc.
4501 Forbes Boulevard, Suite 200, Lanham, Maryland 20706
www.rowman.com

Unit A, Whitacre Mews, 26-34 Stannary Street, London SE11 4AB

Copyright © 2016 by James M. Scythes

*All rights reserved.* No part of this book may be reproduced in any form or by any electronic or mechanical means, including information storage and retrieval systems, without written permission from the publisher, except by a reviewer who may quote passages in a review.

British Library Cataloguing in Publication Information Available

**Library of Congress Control Number: 2016943906**

ISBN 978-1-61146-218-0 (cloth : alk. paper)
ISBN 978-1-61146-219-7 (electronic)

∞™ The paper used in this publication meets the minimum requirements of American National Standard for Information Sciences Permanence of Paper for Printed Library Materials, ANSI/NISO Z39.48-1992.

Printed in the United States of America

For Isabella Rose

# Contents

| | |
|---|---|
| List of Figures | ix |
| Acknowledgments | xi |
| Preface | xiii |
| Introduction | 1 |
| **Part I: "The Rough Life of a Soldier"** | **17** |
| **Part II: "Hot Work Soon Enough"** | **71** |
| Conclusion | 141 |
| Bibliography | 163 |
| Index | 169 |
| About the Author | 181 |

# List of Figures

*Figure 1.1* Letter from Col. George W. Taylor to Gov. Charles Olden requesting Thomas Howell's commission as a second lieutenant. In this letter, Taylor refers to Howell as "Charles W. Howell."    19

*Figure 1.2* Photograph of 2nd Lt. Thomas James Howell taken in Philadelphia shortly before his departure from Camden to Virginia in February 1862.    21

*Figure 1.3* Map of the forts around Alexandria, Virginia, 1862. The arrow is pointing to the location of Fort Worth.    23

*Figure 1.4* Photograph of Lt. Col. Henry W. Brown.    28

*Figure 1.5* Photograph of Capt. Daniel Penrose Buckley.    30

*Figure 2.1* Photograph of the *John A. Warner*.    72

*Figure 2.2* Map of the movement of the New Jersey Brigade up the peninsula (The dashed line indicates the movement of the brigade).    76

*Figure 3.1* Map of the Battle of Gaines's Mill, June 27, 1862.    142

*Figure 3.2* Map of the placement of Taylor's command along Boatswain's Swamp during Battle of Gaines's Mill.    144

*Figure 3.3* Photograph of the Woodbury-Alexander Bridge.    149

*Figure 3.4* Photograph of Dr. Edward Welling, assistant surgeon of the Third New Jersey.    151

*Figure 3.5* Photograph of Tom Howell's prayer book and epaulettes.    152

*Figure 3.6* Photograph of Annie Howell from 1862.    156

# Acknowledgments

A number of people have helped me throughout the process of writing this book, far too many for me to name here, but I would like to point out some people who have played an instrumental role in helping this book come to fruition. First I would like to thank the Lehigh University Press Editorial Board and Dr. Kate Crassons, the director of Lehigh University Press, for their patience and guidance throughout this process. I would also like to thank Tommy Moore, the managing editor of Lehigh University Press, for always replying quickly to my numerous e-mails. I am very appreciative of the valuable advice and guidance given by the two readers of my manuscript on ways to improve the work. I am also grateful for all of the assistance I received from Zachary Nycum, Laura Chappell, and Brooke Bures from Rowman & Littlefield. A special thanks goes to my copyeditor, Jill R. Hughes, for everything she did to help me complete my manuscript.

    The staff and trustees of the Gloucester County Historical Society (past and present) have been very supportive and helpful during this process, and I am indebted to them. My family, especially my parents, Mervin and Virginia Scythes, and my in-laws, Gary and Antoinette Garton; my sister, Lisa Duffield; my buddy, Dolly Scythes; Bill Parton and Kim Miner; and my friends have been very helpful and supportive during this process, listening to me talk about Tom Howell or helping me track down information about his life. My cousin Donald Kwasnicki has been a great help to me in my efforts to retell Tom Howell's story, and I will be forever grateful. My colleagues in the History Department of West Chester University, especially our chairperson, Dr. Wayne Hanley, have also been very supportive during this process. I want to thank Dr. Charles Hardy, who read an early draft of this work and offered suggestions on improving it. Dr. Steve Gimber, who was my Civil War professor at Rowan College (now Rowan University) and is now my colleague at West Chester University, has helped me immensely with this project (reading drafts of the work, helping me find material to fill some of the gaps I had in the manuscript, listening to me complain), and I will forever be in his debt. I also want to thank Robert E. L. Krick for giving me a personal tour of the Gaines's Mill battlefield, showing me where the Third New Jersey was positioned during the battle, and answering my numerous questions. Mr. Krick was also kind enough to read my section on the Battle of Gaines's Mill and gave me valuable insight into the fighting in the woods along Boatswain's Swamp on that bloody Friday. John W. Kuhl was instrumental in helping me find some of the photographs I used in this book and was very kind in allowing me to publish one from his personal collection. A special thanks goes to Jon Bozard and Joanne Nestor from the New Jersey State Archives for helping me search for material on Tom Howell and for answering all of my e-mail questions.

Lastly, I want to thank the people who have been the most important to me during this process and in my life. The first person is my late wife, Valerie Garton Scythes, who listened to my stories of Tom Howell more times than I can count and accompanied me to the Gaines's Mill battlefield on numerous occasions. Tom Howell became such an important part of our lives that we even considered naming our firstborn after Howell if we had a boy. Val, I hope Tom was there to meet you as you entered the gates of heaven. The next two people are my fiancée, Chere Parton and stepson, Brady William Smith. Chere, you have given me the love and support that I thought I would never experience again. You have brought so much love and happiness into my life. Brady, you are a fun and intelligent young man and I am so proud to be your dad. I am so fortunate to have you both as a part of my family. The last person is my wonderful daughter, Isabella Rose Scythes. Isabella, you amaze me every day. I never thought I could love another person as much as I love you. You make me want to be a better person each day, and I cannot imagine my life without you.

# Preface

*This Will Make a Man of Me* is the story of seventeen-year-old 2nd Lt. Thomas James Howell during Maj. Gen. George B. McClellan's Peninsula Campaign. I first became aware of Tom Howell in 2000 when I was a volunteer in the library of the Gloucester County Historical Society. The librarian, the late Edith Hoelle, showed me Howell's thirty-one wartime letters, his epaulettes, and his prayer book in the boxes containing the Howell Family Collection. She told me he was a seventeen-year-old officer who died early in the Civil War. I immediately became intrigued by his story, knowing there were not that many teenage officers in the war, so I decided to do a little research and possibly write an article on Howell.

As I started researching, I saw that someone on eBay was selling transcribed copies of all of Tom Howell's letters, including thirty-four letters that were not part of the Gloucester County Historical Society's collection. All but two of these thirty-four transcribed letters were ones that Tom Howell had written to his sister Anna (Annie) and his brother Joshua during the Civil War. I found out later that these transcribed letters had been sold at an estate sale after the death of Sarah Draper in 2000. Mrs. Draper was a descendant of Howell's sister Annie, and in 1977 she donated most of the Howell family documents, including the thirty-one original letters written by Tom Howell (thirty of these letters were written by Howell to his mother) that are in the Gloucester County Historical Society Library. I was able to purchase the transcribed letters, but I have not been able to find the original letters.

At the end of the last transcribed letter, Mrs. Draper, who must have transcribed the letters in the 1960s or early 1970s, wrote that she was leaving the original letters Tom Howell wrote to Annie and Joshua to a family member named Morris Lloyd, but she did not explain why she was separating the collection. The collection, with some minor exceptions, seems to have been divided between letters Howell wrote to his mother and those he wrote to his siblings. After doing some research, I found out that Morris Lloyd died in 1986, so I contacted his descendants. One of them, Thomas Lloyd, has letters from other family members, but none from Tom Howell. Eleanor Lloyd, the widow of Morris Lloyd Jr., told me in an email that her late husband did not have Howell's letters and that the letters may have been thrown out when her mother-in-law died.[1] Although I cannot locate the rest of the original letters, I have no doubt that these transcriptions were made from the originals. It is clear to me that the prose of the transcribed copies matches that of the originals, and I see no reason why a member of the family in the 1960s or 1970s would create "fake" letters about Howell's service in the Civil War. The material in the transcribed letters does not indicate anything unusual or counter to the language used by Tom Howell in the original letters in the collection of the Gloucester County Historical Society.

With the addition of these transcribed letters, I now had sixty-five of Howell's wartime letters—thirty-one original letters and thirty-four transcribed letters—and transcriptions of four letters he wrote before the war. As I did more research on Tom Howell, another of the Howell descendants, Esther Ravinus, donated Annie Howell's diary to the Gloucester County Historical Society. The diary describes how Annie and her husband, Malcolm Lloyd, traveled to Virginia to search for Tom Howell's body around the Gaines's Mill battlefield in 1890. I was also able to find an original letter from one of the Howells' Camden neighbors (also found on eBay), which commented on Tom Howell's death in the summer of 1862. With all of the sources I was able to gather related to Tom Howell, along with letters from other soldiers from Tom's regiment, the Third New Jersey Volunteer Infantry, I decided to publish a narrative of Lt. Howell's experiences in the Army of the Potomac during the first half of 1862. Although the collection of Howell's sixty-five letters covers a short period of time, it is an important account of soldier life in the Army of the Potomac during the spring and summer of 1862 and provides a rare look at the experiences of a teenage officer in the Civil War.

## NOTE

1. Mrs. Eleanor Lloyd, email message to author, July 6, 2015.

# Introduction

During the last week of June 1862, Maj. Gen. George B. McClellan's Army of the Potomac stood just a few miles from the Confederate capital, Richmond, Virginia, and was ready to begin the final stages of besieging the city. McClellan's arrival at the outskirts of Richmond was the culmination of a three-month campaign that saw the Union Army transported from the defenses around Washington, D.C., to the Virginia Peninsula between the York and James rivers, and a march up the peninsula. Over the course of these three months, the Confederate Army, first under the command of Gen. Joseph E. Johnston and by June 1862 under the leadership of Gen. Robert E. Lee, delayed McClellan's progress, but the Union commander seemed poised to take the rebel capital before the end of summer.

One young soldier in McClellan's army in June 1862 was a teenage lieutenant named Thomas James Howell. The seventeen-year-old Howell served as a second lieutenant in Company I, Third New Jersey Volunteer Infantry Regiment. He was just one of the thousands, and possibly tens of thousands, of young men under the age of eighteen that took up arms to fight during the war. Many teenagers got caught up in the patriotic fervor that swept through the North in the weeks after the firing on Fort Sumter in April 1861 and volunteered to "save the Union." These boys, just like the men over eighteen, believed it was their duty to join the army.[1] If a young man remained a civilian during time of war, his actions were regarded as being unmanly, but if a young man volunteered for service and went to war, he accepted his responsibility of defending his home and country, which was seen as a sign of coming into manhood.[2]

In the mid-nineteenth century, the period of transition from boyhood to manhood varied in length because there was no standard pattern for a young man to chart his course through this phase of life.[3] Working-class boys came of age earlier than those in the middle and upper classes. Typically, these lads between the ages of twelve and seventeen entered the workforce and provided valuable income to their families.[4] Boys growing up in middle- and upper-class families were usually able to further their education because the family did not need the extra income and could delay their transition into adulthood. But this was not always the case in the mid-nineteenth century, as events such as leaving school, entering the labor force, leaving home, getting married, and having children were not as clearly structured as they are today and did not always represent major turning points in life that led to adulthood.[5] Many youths shuttled between school, work, and home during their teenage years, depending on the season and the economic needs of the family, and some continued to live at home well into their twenties.[6] The Civil War offered young people an opportunity to establish their independence from their parents. For these young men, the war would serve as the major life event that would aid them in their transition into manhood.

Although some historians refer to the American Civil War as "The Boys' War," they debate the number of boys under the age of eighteen who served during the war. The numbers range from 10,000 to 800,000, but the higher estimate seems greatly exaggerated.[7] According to Benjamin Gould's *Investigations in the Military and Anthropological Statistics of American Soldiers*, which was originally published in 1869, there were 10,413 soldiers in the Union Army who were under the age of eighteen, but Gould's work only covered approximately one million of the two million soldiers who fought for the Union so it is likely that the number of soldiers under the age of eighteen is higher.[8] In an examination of 14,330 soldiers, historian Bell I. Wiley reveals that 1.6 percent of the troops were boys under the age of eighteen.[9] Works by two other historians, George Langdon Kilmer's "Boys in the Union Army" and Dennis M. Keesee's *Too Young to Die*, have attempted to address the deficiencies of Gould's study and to estimate the number of boys who fought in the Civil War.[10] Both authors believe that Gould's statistics are inaccurate because his calculations were based on the ages recorded on enlistment forms, but many soldiers overstated their ages by as much as one or two years. Therefore, the number of soldiers under the age of eighteen who fought in the war could be much higher. Although it is impossible to know the true number of boys who fought in the Civil War, a good estimate would place the figure around 100,000, but the number could be higher.

The role these young men played in the army varied. Some of them became drummers and fifers. These young men were unarmed noncombatants who sometimes acted as orderlies to officers or stretcher-bearers and hospital attendants after battles.[11] Most of the boys under the age of eighteen, though, were soldiers in the ranks, usually privates, who carried guns and fought alongside the other men of the regiment during skirmishes and battles. But a small number of these youths, like Tom Howell, served as officers during the Civil War, although the likelihood of one receiving a commission before his eighteenth birthday was rare.

According to Benjamin Gould's study of Civil War soldiers, only eleven of the 10,413 soldiers under the age of eighteen were officers.[12] Gould wrote that relatively "few officers were commissioned under the age of legal maturity," and his statistics show that only five of the 37,183 officers in his study were seventeen years old.[13] Since his study looked at approximately half of the soldiers that served in the Union Army, it can be assumed that a dozen, maybe a little more, officers were seventeen years of age and that the total number of officers below the age of eighteen would have been no more than twenty-five.

It is apparent that there may have been more "boy" officers in the Union Army than Gould stated, but neither Kilmer nor Keesee offer any statistics on that particular subject in their works on young soldiers. Keesee does mention in his book three young men who served as commissioned officers in the Union Army, but they seem to be the only examples he gives of men under the age of eighteen serving in that capacity. Also, these men were promoted from the ranks, not commissioned as officers when they joined the regiment, as was the case with Tom Howell. According to Keesee, "Some soldiers were not easily persuaded to place their trust in young officers. Older recruits attached to a regiment displayed misgivings."[14]

At the age of seventeen, Tom Howell was not the youngest officer to serve during the American Civil War. The youngest officer to serve in the war was the Confederate E. G. Baxter, who was commissioned as a second lieutenant in the Seventh Kentucky in June 1862 at the age of thirteen.[15] In the Union Army, Edward R. Geary, the son of John W. Geary, received a commission in 1861 as a second lieutenant shortly after his sixteenth birthday and joined Capt. Joseph M. Knap's battery of artillery.[16] Geary may have been the youngest officer to serve in the Union Army. In August 1862, Ellis Hamilton of the Fifteenth New Jersey also received a commission at the age of sixteen as a second lieutenant.[17]

It is clear that a very small number of officers that served during the Civil War were under the age of eighteen, but most of their experiences and contributions have been limited to a few lines in a book. Although Edward Geary's experiences were the subject of a seven-page article written by Bell I. Wiley in *Civil War Times Illustrated* in 1980, there is a void in the literature describing the experiences of teenage officers during the Civil War. A number of historians have written about "boy soldiers" in the Civil War, but these are mostly limited to the experiences of boys who served as musicians or privates in the army. With the exception of Arthur MacArthur, who received a commission as a first lieutenant in the Twenty-fourth Wisconsin Volunteer Infantry Regiment at the age of seventeen, little is known of the role of teenage officers. But even MacArthur did not give his age accurately when he received his commission. MacArthur's father lied, stating that Arthur was nineteen so that his son could receive his commission.[18] The dearth of information on the role that teenage officers played in the Civil War represents how rare it was for someone, like Tom Howell, to receive a commission before his eighteenth birthday.

Thomas James Howell was born at six o'clock in the morning on Thursday, October 10, 1844, in Camden, New Jersey.[19] He was the seventh child born to Richard Washington Howell and Mary Tonkin Carpenter Howell and was named after two of his mother's brothers, Thomas Preston Carpenter and James Stratton Carpenter.[20] Rev. Joseph M. Lybrand of St. Paul's Episcopal Church in Camden baptized him on Sunday, January 19, 1845.[21]

The Howell and Carpenter families were among the largest and best known in South Jersey and Philadelphia. By the time of Tom's birth the Howells had acquired hundreds of acres of land along the Delaware River and the West Point Fishery. The Carpenters were importers, whose ships docked at Carpenter's Landing in New Jersey as well as Baltimore and Philadelphia.[22]

The Carpenter family had emigrated from England to Barbados and then to Pennsylvania shortly after the arrival of William Penn. Samuel Carpenter built "one of the finest houses of the day" just north of Philadelphia and started building docks and mills along the Delaware River.[23] Descendants of Samuel Carpenter moved to New Jersey shortly before the American Revolution and built a mansion at Carpenter's Landing, which is in present-day Mantua, New Jersey. Mary Tonkin Carpenter, Tom Howell's mother, was born at Carpenter's Landing on September 14, 1805, to Edward and Sarah Carpenter.[24]

The Howell family emigrated from Wales to Philadelphia in 1697. As a young boy Tom Howell no doubt learned the history of his country by listening to stories about his forefathers. His great-grandfather John Ladd Howell was a deputy quartermaster general for the Continental Army during the American Revolution. In 1776, by order of the Committee of Safety, he inspected the powder mills in the Delaware Valley that supplied the Revolutionary forces, and in 1778 and 1779, under the direction of the Board of War, he engaged in collecting and forwarding supplies to the troops.[25] Tom's grandfather Joshua Ladd Howell was very active in the political and military affairs of New Jersey. He was involved in state politics, supporting the Federalist candidates. In 1811, Joshua Ladd Howell purchased West Point Fishery, which was located on the New Jersey side of the Delaware River opposite the lower part of Philadelphia.[26] During the War of 1812 he served as colonel of the Second Regiment, Gloucester Brigade, New Jersey Militia.

Tom Howell's father, Richard Washington Howell, was born on December 15, 1799, at "Candour Hall," near Woodbury, New Jersey, to Joshua Ladd and Anna Blackwood Howell. Richard had been named "by request of Gov. Richard Howell, an intimate friend of his father, after himself. Gen. Washington's death occuring [sic] about that time, his name was also adopted."[27] He was described as a shy, sincere, and gentle man, who was known by his kin as the scholar of the family.[28] Richard had a longing to attend the College of New Jersey (known today as Princeton University), but that was out of the question, since his family was hopelessly in debt. In addition to the West Point Fishery, his father had purchased an iron furnace called the Etna Furnace, which had failed, and much of the family fortune was lost by 1817.[29] After working odd jobs to earn money, Richard was given the opportunity to study law under Richard Wood of Philadelphia. By 1827 he had become a lawyer and started his own practice in Camden. With his professional life stable, Richard Howell settled down, marrying Mary Tonkin Carpenter on March 24, 1830.[30]

In 1831, shortly after the birth of their first child, Richard and Mary purchased a home at 308 Market Street in Camden so that Richard could be close to his mother, who was living at the Howell family estate, known as "Fancy Hill."[31] During this time, both were very active in the church and other causes of the time. Richard was a vestryman of St. Paul's Episcopal Church in Camden, and Mary was also active in church affairs and Sunday school. The two devoted themselves to the Episcopal Church in Camden and Philadelphia, usually attending services in both cities every Sunday.[32]

As mentioned above, Richard W. Howell was active in a number of causes during the 1820s and 1830s. He started Bible societies all over the state of New Jersey and lauded the numerous Bible societies that had been established around the country; he was proud that the state of New Jersey had played an active part in the "improvement of the moral condition of the community."[33] "Show *us a nation* that has *rejected* the Bible," he said in a speech in 1827, "and we will prove to you that she has either sunken into torpor & debasement or that her soil has been died [sic] with the blood of her own children."[34] The Howells were very pious and their strong religious beliefs would be instilled in their children.

Richard W. Howell was also very critical of President Andrew Jackson, especially Jackson's Indian removal policy. In a speech he wrote in February 1830 but never delivered, Howell, speaking from the perspective of the Native Americans, asked, "Wither shall we emigrate? You have driven us from the land of our birth—from the land over which, long before the white man's foot prints were seen on these shores, our mighty forefathers roamed free as the winds of Heaven . . . wither shall we turn and not be in the white man's way?"[35] Howell continued to criticize Jackson's administration, and by 1834, believing the country was "in the midst of political strife," he became active in the anti-Jacksonian, or Whig, movement.[36]

Richard W. Howell was also involved with the American Colonization Society, an organization that had as its goal the emancipation of American slaves and their settlement in Africa. He believed colonization was "the only way in which the abolition of slavery can be accomplished with safety to the country & justice to the blacks."[37] In addition, he was a vocal figure in the temperance movement, which gained a large following during the 1830s, delivering a speech on temperance on February 26, 1833.[38] The strong religious and moral ideals of Richard and Mary had a significant impact on the character of their children and laid the foundation for the interest in religion and implicit faith that marked their lives.[39]

Tom Howell sought to embody the traits of a "Christian Gentleman," a nineteenth-century ideal of manhood that wanted to "maintain moral order at a time when communal values had lost their force and individualism threatened to run unchecked."[40] This ideology stressed love, kindness, and compassion, but also included philanthropy, church activities, self-sacrifice, and a deep involvement in family life.[41] A "Christian Gentleman" was taught to avoid temptations of vices such as sex and liquor, which would divert a man's attention from more productive efforts in life, and instead to direct his attention to the needs and concerns of others. This ideology would have a significant impact on Howell's experiences during this Civil War, as he encountered many men he perceived to be "immoral" and "ungentlemanly."

In December 1850 the last of Richard and Mary Howell's ten children, Sarah "Sallie" Carpenter Howell, was born. The decade, though, would prove to be a tragic one for the family. Early in 1850 a streptococcus infection swept through the entire household. On January 3, the couple's fifth child, Richard, who was almost ten years old, died. At the end of 1851 the same disease hit the family again. This time it took the youngest child, Sallie. Others in the family suffered from the effects of the infection for the rest of their lives. Anna, who the family called Annie, suffered damage to her heart; Frank was left with damaged kidneys; and Charles (Charley) experienced enduring chest trouble.[42] Tom Howell was fortunate and did not experience any lasting effects of the infection, except the loss of one of his closest brothers. Only four years separated Richard, Joshua, and Tom, and the three boys were inseparable. These losses also took their toll on their mother, who became terrified by every illness.[43]

The end of the decade brought more tragedy. On May 13, 1859, Richard Washington Howell died of pneumonia. As he was dying, he told his wife to marry someone who could help her with the kids. She replied, "'Oh no, Richard. Never.'"[44] After Richard's death the family had sufficient wealth to survive, but there was not enough money to provide the younger children—Tom, Annie, and Frank—with the same private education that their older siblings had received. In order to have the necessary funds for schooling, a considerable part of the family silver and furniture was sold off.[45] However, the older sons, Samuel, Charley, and Joshua, started pursuing their own careers after their father's death. Samuel, who became a physician after graduating from the University of Pennsylvania, moved with his wife, Maria (Minnie), to Minersville, Pennsylvania, to practice medicine. Charley graduated from the College of New Jersey (Princeton University) in 1858 and temporarily moved to the Colorado Territory to stay with relatives, but he later returned to Camden to live with his mother. In 1862, he received a job as the music and entertainment director at the Institute of Pennsylvania Hospital.[46] Joshua remained at home in Camden and began studying law with his uncle, Judge Thomas Preston Carpenter.

Born on April 19, 1804, Thomas Preston Carpenter was Mary Howell's older brother. He studied law in Woodbury and became an attorney in September 1830. Carpenter developed into one of the most respected lawyers in New Jersey, and on February 5, 1845, he was appointed by his uncle, Gov. Charles Stratton, as one of the associate justices of the Supreme Court of New Jersey, with his circuit comprising Camden, Burlington, and Gloucester counties.[47] In his seven years on the state supreme court, Judge Carpenter "was held in high esteem by his associates and by the bar of the State for his ability, learning and for the uniform good judgment which he brought to the consideration of cases. In the counties where he presided at circuits, and which he visited during his term of office at regular periods, his genial manners and kindly intercourse with the people made him very popular."[48] After retiring from the judgeship, Carpenter continued to practice law in Camden, remained active in local groups, and played an important role in the lives of the Howell children after the death of their father.[49]

Another man who played an important role in shaping Tom Howell's character was his teacher William Fewsmith. Fewsmith had a classical school for boys at 1008 Chestnut Street in Philadelphia and lived just a few doors from the Howell family on Third Street in Camden with his wife, Catharine, and their four children.[50] Born in Philadelphia in 1826, Fewsmith was educated at Yale University and graduated from that institution in 1844. While at Yale, he was considered to be the best Latin and Greek scholar in his class.[51] Fewsmith taught ancient languages and English grammar for several years at the Philadelphia Academy before starting his own school, the Fewsmith Classical and Mathematical School, originally located at Tenth and Arch in Philadelphia.[52] In 1860 the school moved to 1008 Chestnut Street.

During his time as a student in Fewsmith's school, Tom learned the history of the United States, along with a number of other subjects, and was most likely influenced by his textbooks. The books children read in antebellum America had a great impact on the development of their character and, by glorifying warfare, may have led to the romanticized view of war, a notion which was shared by many who became soldiers during the Civil War.[53] The space devoted to war in these textbooks and the colorful descriptions they gave of battles were "much more appealing to the mind of the child, and much more easily grasped."[54] Historian Earl Hess contends that "antebellum schoolbooks thus inadvertently prepared young men to accept and even to embrace the idea of going to war."[55] Many young men of that generation must have thought it was exciting to be a soldier and that dying for one's country was glorious and admirable. As a student in Fewsmith's school, Tom wrote a paper on chivalry that seemed to support this idea. In this short essay he said that chivalry was still present "both in public and private life," which was evident "when men . . . surrender[ed] their lives and means . . . for the benefit of their fellow men."[56] Clearly he believed one's sacrifice for the greater good was appropriate and truly noble.

Tom Howell received a "gentleman's education" from Fewsmith. Teachers who offered a classical education believed studying past civilizations offered students a better understanding of the progress of civilization by demonstrating how "they" became "us" and would ultimately provide the student with a sense of culture.[57] With a classical education, Howell would become a "refined" man, ready to enter the "realm of high culture."[58]

Fewsmith did not teach Tom Howell everything he would need to know to become a "gentleman." It is also apparent that Howell learned many other elements of cultural refinement at home, because his father wanted the children to have the advantages that he himself had been denied. The Howell children were all taught to play the piano, to draw, and to speak French.[59] In the evenings Richard and the family would select books to read from his vast library—one favorite was the atlas.[60] Other nights the family would spend singing or playing charades with their neighbors, the Brownings, Woodhulls, and Potts families.[61]

After the death of his father, Tom Howell spent the next year and a half either in Minersville with his brother Sam or with his mother and other siblings in Camden. From his pre–Civil War letters it appears that he and Annie alternated spending weeks at a time in Minersville with Sam. Tom seems to have enjoyed his time with his brother, learning new things. In one letter from Minersville he described his first long horse ride. He illustrated in great detail the events of the day and told his sister that Sam said he was a very good rider, although he disclosed that he was so sore the next morning that he could hardly sit down.[62] While at home in Camden, Howell continued his studies and helped his mother in their garden.[63] He was also aware that he was maturing, as he made clear in a letter to his sister in early 1860 to "tell Sam that I have put on a coat and vest. I tell you, I feel more like a man."[64]

As the fifteen-year-old Howell began feeling like he was becoming a man in early 1860, the country that his forefathers fought to establish and defend started to come apart over the issue of slavery. In the decades since Howell's father's activity in the American Colonization Society, the opposition to the South's "peculiar institution" became more organized with the American Anti-Slavery Society. Also, after the end of the Mexican-American War in 1848, the debates in Congress became more heated over the expansion of slavery into the new territories acquired as a result of that war. Throughout the 1850s, tensions continued to rise between the free and slave interests in the United States over issues such as the Kansas-Nebraska Act, Bleeding Kansas, and John Brown's Raid on Harper's Ferry.[65]

In Philadelphia in early 1860, opponents to the Fugitive Slave Act of 1850 attempted to prevent the return of a runaway slave to his master in

Virginia. The slave, Moses Honnor, fled to Pennsylvania in August 1859 but was captured. A hearing was held in March 1860 in Philadelphia to determine if Honnor should be sent back to his owner, Charles T. Butler, in Virginia. On March 28, 1860, the judge ruled that Honnor should be transported back to Virginia. As police transported Honnor to prison in a carriage, a crowd attempted to rescue the runaway slave. Two black men grabbed the heads of the horses that were pulling the carriage, and the carriage ran against the curb in front of Independence Hall, snapping the axle. Police officers surrounded the carriage and kept the crowd from rescuing Honnor. Ten men, nine black and one white, were arrested and imprisoned in Eastern Penitentiary.[66]

In a letter to his sister, who was staying in Minersville, Tom Howell asked if his brother Sam had "heard about the fuss in Philadelphia about the attempt to rescue the slave."[67] He informed Annie that on March 31, 1860, a man had come to their house in Camden and talked to his brother Charley for about twenty minutes. According to Howell, Charley and the man left after the conversation to attend a meeting to help those who had attempted to rescue Honnor;[68] all of the men were released by July 1860. Although Tom did not give his personal opinion of slavery in any of his prewar letters, it seems quite clear that Charley Howell's support of the rescuers of Moses Honnor demonstrates that the Howell children were influenced by their father's view on slavery.

Shortly after Abraham Lincoln's victory in the election of 1860, South Carolina seceded from the Union. By the beginning of February 1861, six other Southern states left the Union. These seven states formed the Confederate States of America. On April 12, 1861, the American Civil War started when Confederate forces began firing on Fort Sumter, a federal fort in Charleston Harbor. Two days later the defenders of the fort surrendered. President Lincoln called for seventy-five thousand three-month volunteers to put down the rebellion on April 15, 1861, which led to the secession of four more Southern states from the Union.

On April 16, 1861, just two days after the surrender of Fort Sumter, a number of citizens in Camden, New Jersey, including Joshua Howell, signed a declaration in which they pledged to "maintain the honor, the integrity, and the existence of our National Union, and the perpetuity of the popular Government."[69] A large crowd gathered for a meeting at the Camden Court House on April 18. The room was decorated with flags and patriotic mottos, such as "The Union Must and Shall Be Preserved" and "Liberty And Union, One And Inseperable [sic], Now And Forever."[70] Thomas Preston Carpenter headed a committee that drafted a series of resolutions. Carpenter told those in attendance:

> It is the imperative duty of one Government and of the nation in order to preserve our nationality which our heroic ancestors established by so much labor and of blood. . . . We solemnly pledge ourselves to stand

by our national flag, to bear our share of the sacrifices and perils of the hour, and to support the government by whomsoever administered, both against those who stand with arms in hands, to assail its integrity, and against those who give traitors their aid and comfort."[71]

As a result of this meeting, the men of the city began enlisting into military service over the next few weeks, filling the ranks of the state's three-month regiments, and by the middle of May they began enlisting for three years' service in the First, Second, and Third New Jersey Regiments.

There is no evidence to indicate whether Tom Howell attended the meeting at the Camden Court House on April 18. If he did not, he surely would have heard about the event from his uncle, since Howell was studying law with him when the Civil War started.[72] Since he was only sixteen, Howell was too young to join any of the regiments that were forming in New Jersey in April and May 1861, but as he saw friends and neighbors leave for war, he likely got caught up in the patriotic fervor. Throughout the year, news of the war no doubt distracted him from his studies, but he made no attempt to enlist.

In October 1861 Tom celebrated his seventeenth birthday. Within two months, he sought a commission into the army as an officer, although he was still under the required age of eighteen.[73] Why did he suddenly begin seeking a commission at the end of 1861? As mentioned earlier, Tom Howell was likely swept up in the spirit of patriotism that followed the attack on Fort Sumter, but this was not enough to compel him to join the army. His family was opposed to the institution of slavery, but there is nothing in his prewar letters to suggest that this served as a motive to enlist. After a careful analysis of the letters Howell wrote while in the army and those written by his family, it seems that there were two major factors that influenced him in his decision to join the army.

First, Tom believed it was his duty to enlist, serving as a rite of passage from boyhood to manhood. He wrote in one of his early letters home: "This will make a man of me."[74] Howell believed his experiences in the military would be best for him in the long run. Like many young men of his generation, he had spent his boyhood preparing "for the tests and responsibilities of manhood. And there could be no sterner test than war. It quite literally separated men from boys."[75] According to historian Reid Mitchell in his study of Civil War soldiers: "Fighting was a man's responsibility—if one did not fight one was less than a man. Men may very well have fought during the Civil War for reasons having less to do with ideology than with masculine identity."[76] After joining the army, Howell explained in a letter to his mother, "I did not come to play soldier."[77] He added in a later letter, "When duty calls, I shall not think of danger."[78] Tom Howell was determined to prove himself a man.

Second, it seems that money was a major motivator for Tom. After the death of his father, the family experienced some financial difficulties, and his maternal uncle, Thomas Preston Carpenter, stated that his young nephew entered the service with the "desire to aid his mother whose means were limited."[79] At least five times in his letters home, Howell mentioned sending money or wanting to send money to his family. In fact, he wrote twice that it gave him pleasure to be able to support his loved ones. With the pay for a second lieutenant at $105.50 a month, Howell would be able to contribute significantly to the support of his mother and siblings. Determined to join the army, all he needed to do was secure a commission as an officer.

The story that follows describes Tom Howell's experiences in the Army of the Potomac during the first half of 1862. This narrative is divided into two parts, plus a conclusion. Part I traces Howell's military career from January 12, 1862, to April 15, 1862, which is the period between his first trip to Virginia to secure a commission and the movement of his regiment to join the rest of the Army of the Potomac on the Virginia Peninsula. This section focuses on his experiences in camp and his relationship with some of the officers and men in his regiment, including his disagreements with the regiment's lieutenant colonel, who seemingly disliked Howell. The twenty-seven letters that Howell wrote to his family during these three months are included at the end of this section. Notations are used to identify people, places, and any unclear words or phrases that appear in Howell's letters. Howell's letters are presented in this book with their original grammar, punctuation, and spelling. Changes that have been made for clarification or to facilitate readability appear in brackets.[80]

Part II concentrates on Howell's experiences during Maj. Gen. George McClellan's Peninsula Campaign from April 15, 1862, to June 26, 1862. In this section Howell marches with the rest of McClellan's army up the Virginia Peninsula toward Richmond. During this two-month period, Howell saw firsthand the destruction caused by a battle, and his romantic view of war began to disappear. He wrote to his mother and siblings about his frustrations, and he described the moral and mortal perils he faced as a soldier. The thirty-eight letters that Howell wrote to his family during this time are included at the end of this section. Also in both of these sections, the history of the Third New Jersey, his regiment, and the movements of McClellan's army are retold through the words of Lieutenant Howell, along with comments from other soldiers in the regiment.

The Conclusion concentrates on the Battle of Gaines's Mill and Howell's death. He performed with "distinguished merit" during the battle but was killed at the end of the engagement when a cannonball struck him in the abdomen and tore him nearly in two. His body was left on the battlefield and never recovered. This section also focuses on how the young man's death affected his family, particularly his younger sister

Annie, who traveled to Virginia in 1890 with her husband to search for Howell's body.

The story of Tom Howell and the sixty-five letters he wrote during his time in the army gives us a rare look at the war through the eyes of a teenage officer. His letters describe the experiences of a youth coming of age in the army and the challenges he faced as a young officer seeking to earn the respect of both the men he commanded and his superiors. Despite these trials, Howell believed that it was his duty to serve and that the experience would aid in his transition to manhood. Unfortunately, Tom Howell never reached his eighteenth birthday, as his life ended tragically along the banks of the Chickahominy River.

## NOTES

1. The term "boy" is used in this book to reference anyone under the age of eighteen.
2. Reid Mitchell, *The Vacant Chair: The Northern Soldier Leaves Home* (New York: Oxford University Press, 1993), 12.
3. E. Anthony Rotundo, *American Manhood: Transformations in Masculinity from the Revolution to the Modern Era* (New York: Basic Books, 1993), 56.
4. Joseph F. Kett, *Rites of Passage: Adolescence in America, 1790 to the Present* (New York: Basic Books, 1977), 169.
5. Tamara K. Hareven, "The Last Stage: Historical Adulthood and Old Age," in *Adulthood*, ed. Erik H. Erikson (New York: W. W. Norton, 1978), 206.
6. Ibid.
7. Jack Rudolph, "The Children's Crusade: Youth in the Civil War," *Civil War Times* 21, no. 3 (1982): 10.
8. Benjamin Apthorp Gould, *Investigations in the Military and Anthropological Statistics of American Soldiers* (New York: U.S. Sanitary Commission, 1869; rprt. New York: Arno Press, 1979), 38.
9. Bell I. Wiley, *The Life of Billy Yank: The Common Soldier of the Union* (Baton Rouge: Louisiana State University Press, 2008), 299.
10. George Langdon Kilmer, "Boys in the Union Army," *Century* 70 (June 1905): 269–75; Dennis M. Keesee, *Too Young to Die: Boy Soldiers of the Union Army, 1861–1865* (Huntington, WV: Blue Acorn Press, 2001), chapter 1.
11. Willard A. Heaps, *The Bravest Teenage Yanks: True Stories of Extraordinary Heroism in the Civil War* (New York: Duell, Sloan, and Pearce, 1963), 5.
12. Gould, *Investigations in the Military and Anthropological Statistics of American Soldiers*, 38, 57.
13. Ibid., 56–57.
14. Keesee, *Too Young to Die*, 209.
15. Albert A. Nofi, *The Civil War Notebook: A Collection of Little-Known Facts and Other Odds-and-Ends about the Civil War* (New York: Da Capo, 1993), 65.
16. Bell I. Wiley, "Boy Lieutenant in Blue," *Civil War Times Illustrated* 19, no. 6 (1980): 25.
17. Bradley M. Gottfried, *Kearny's Own: The History of the First New Jersey Brigade in the Civil War* (New Brunswick, NJ: Rutgers University Press, 2005), 76.
18. Kenneth Ray Young, *The General's General: The Life and Times of Arthur MacArthur* (Boulder, CO: Westview Press, 1994), 21.
19. Howell Family Bible, *Genealogical Charts, Lineage Papers, Notes and Letters Regarding the Howell Families of Gloucester County, New Jersey*, Bertha McGeehan Collection [FC Ho], Historical Society of Pennsylvania (hereafter cited as HSP). This is actually a

## Introduction

folder of genealogical material collected by Bertha McGeehan, not a book. This source is a transcription of the contents of the family Bible, which was done by Malcolm Lloyd, Jr. on February 2, 1943. According to the transcription, the original Bible was in possession of Esther Lloyd Morton, the daughter of Anna Howell Lloyd.

20. Richard W. and Mary Howell would have a total of ten children, but only six would survive to adulthood. The children were, in order of birth, John Paschall Howell, Edward Carpenter Howell, Samuel Bedell Howell, Charles Stratton Howell, Richard Holmes Offley Howell, Joshua Ladd Howell, Thomas James Howell, Anna Howell, Francis Lee Howell, and Sarah Carpenter Howell.

21. Howell Family Bible, *Genealogical Charts, Lineage Papers, Notes and Letters Regarding the Howell Families of Gloucester County, New Jersey*, Bertha McGeehan Collection [FC Ho], HSP.

22. Edward Carpenter and Louis Henry Carpenter, *Samuel Carpenter and His Descendants* (Philadelphia: J. B. Lippincott, 1912), 95–97. Additional information came from "Richard Washington Howell," unpublished paper, Howell Family Collection, Gloucester County Historical Society (hereafter cited as GCHS), Woodbury, New Jersey.

23. Anna Howell Lloyd Hayward, "The Carpenters," as appears in her recollections, author's collection. The recollections of Anna Howell Lloyd Hayward, Annie Howell's daughter, are a series of typed pages in which she recorded her memories of various family members and family history.

24. Carpenter and Carpenter, *Samuel Carpenter and His Descendants* , 68.

25. Ibid., 96.

26. Ibid., 95.

27. Francis Howell, *The Book of John Howell and His Descendants* (New York: Francis Howell, 1897), 418.

28. "Richard Washington Howell," unpublished paper, Howell Family Collection, GCHS.

29. The Etna Furnace was located about four miles west of the town of Tuckahoe, New Jersey. For more information on the Etna Furnace, refer to Thomas T. Lubin's unpublished paper "Colonel Joshua Ladd Howell Letters, 1762–1818," Stewart Collection, Campbell Library, Rowan University, Glassboro, New Jersey.

30. The two were married at Carpenter's Landing by Rev. Norman Nash. Howell Family Bible, *Genealogical Charts, Lineage Papers, Notes and Letters Regarding the Howell Families of Gloucester County, New Jersey*, Bertha McGeehan Collection [FC Ho], HSP.

31. There are no remains of Richard and Mary Howell's house today. It is now a parking lot for the U.S. District Court in Camden. "Fancy Hill" was located along the Delaware River just below the West Point Fishery. Nothing of "Fancy Hill" remains either. The house burned down in a fire in 1909 and is now the site of the Sunoco Logistics Eagle Point terminal in Westville, New Jersey.

32. Sarah H. Draper, *The Howells of Fancy Hill* (Stonington, CT: Draper, 1978), 81.

33. Richard W. Howell, "An Address delivered before the Gloucester County Bible Society at St. Peter's Church," January 30, 1827. Richard W. Howell Collection, Camden County Historical Society, Camden, New Jersey.

34. Ibid.; emphasis in the original.

35. Richard W. Howell, "Hasty sketch of an address to have been delivered at the meeting relative to the removal of the Indians," February 25, 1830. Richard W. Howell Collection, Camden County Historical Society, Camden, New Jersey.

36. Richard W. and Mary Howell to James Carpenter, October 13, 1834. Richard W. Howell Collection, Camden Historical Society, Camden, New Jersey.

37. Richard W. Howell to James Carpenter, July 13, 1830. Richard W. Howell Collection, Camden County Historical Society, Camden, New Jersey.

38. A copy of the speech is in the Richard W. Howell Collection, Camden County Historical Society, Camden, New Jersey.

39. "Anna Howell," *Genealogical Charts, Lineage Papers, Notes and Letters Regarding the Howell Families of Gloucester County, New Jersey*, Bertha McGeehan Collection [FC Ho],

HSP. This article about Anna Howell was most likely written by her daughter Anna Howell Lloyd Hayward.

40. A. Anthony Rotundo, "Learning about Manhood: Gender Ideas and the Middle-Class Family in Nineteenth-Century America," in *Manliness and Morality: Middle-Class Masculinity in Britain and America, 1800–1940*, ed. J. A. Mangan and James Walvin (New York: St. Martin's, 1987), 38.

41. Ibid.

42. All of these are described in "Richard Washington Howell," unpublished paper, Howell Family Collection, GCHS.

43. According to her granddaughter, "Mary had jewelry made of the hair of all her dead children and spent the rest of her life mourning over the dead and fussing over the living." Anna Howell Lloyd Hayward, recollections, author's collection.

44. Anna Howell Lloyd Hayward, recollections, author's collection.

45. "Anna Howell," *Genealogical Charts, Lineage Papers, Notes and Letters Regarding the Howell Families of Gloucester County, New Jersey, Bertha McGeehan Collection* [FC Ho], HSP.

46. "Richard Washington Howell," unpublished paper, Howell Family Collection, GCHS.

47. Geo. R. Prowell, *The History of Camden County, New Jersey* (Philadelphia: L. J. Richards & Co., 1886), 206.

48. Ibid.

49. "Anna Howell," *Genealogical Charts, Lineage Papers, Notes and Letters Regarding the Howell Families of Gloucester County, New Jersey, Bertha McGeehan Collection* [FC Ho], HSP. In this article Mrs. Hayward writes that Mary Howell had the advice and encouragement of her brother Thomas Preston Carpenter and that he played an important part in the family councils.

50. According to the 1860 Camden City Directory, the Fewsmiths lived on Third Street above Market Street, close to the Howells. The 1860 census lists William and Catharine Fewsmith along with their four children. It also includes two other females who lived with them: Jessie Brown, from Edinburgh, Scotland, and Annie Devilly from Galway, Ireland, who was their servant.

51. Obituary, William Few Smith, 1900 (source unknown). Newspaper clipping from Few Smith file, Alice B. Doughten Collection, Camden County Historical Society. Later in life Mr. Fewsmith (sometimes spelled Few Smith) became superintendent of Camden's public schools; the two textbooks he authored, *Grammar of the English Language* and *Elementary Grammar*, were widely used at the time.

52. Prowell, *History of Camden County*, 335–36.

53. Ruth Miller Elson, *Guardians of Tradition: American Schoolbooks of the Nineteenth Century* (Lincoln: University of Nebraska Press, 1964), chapter 11.

54. Ibid., 334.

55. Earl J. Hess, *The Union Soldier in Battle: Enduring the Ordeal of Combat* (Lawrence: University Press of Kansas, 1997), 2.

56. "Chivalry," by Thomas James Howell, April 20, 1860. Malcolm Lloyd Collection (#1618), HSP.

57. Caroline Winterer, *The Culture of Classicism: Ancient Greece and Rome in American Intellectual Life, 1780–1910* (Baltimore: Johns Hopkins University Press, 2002), 134–35.

58. Ibid., 144.

59. Draper, *The Howells of Fancy Hill*, 79.

60. Ibid.

61. Ibid.

62. Tom Howell to Annie Howell, August 13, 1860. Transcribed copy, author's collection.

63. Tom's niece later recalled in her diary that her grandmother had a "big garden with fruit trees and raspberries and currant bushes." Anna Howell Lloyd Hayward, recollections, author's collection.

64. Tom Howell to Annie Howell, 1860 [exact date unknown]. Transcribed copy, author's collection.

65. The Kansas-Nebraska Act, created in 1854, divided the Nebraska territory into two separate territories—Kansas and Nebraska—and repealed the 36° 30' line, which was established by the Missouri Compromise. By repealing the Missouri Compromise line, the entire Louisiana Territory was open to the expansion of slavery. This angered abolitionists in the North who did not want to see the expansion of slavery into any territory. The Kansas-Nebraska Act led to the eventual destruction of the Whig Party, as Northern Whigs broke from the party and formed the Republican Party, which opposed the expansion of slavery into any territory. As a result of the Kansas-Nebraska Act, the citizens of Kansas could determine through popular sovereignty whether the territory would become a free or slave state. Unfortunately, settlers from Missouri, a slave state, crossed the Kansas border and voted in the Kansas territorial election. Proslavery candidates won the election and began drafting a proslavery constitution for Kansas—the Lecompton Constitution. In 1855, antislavery and proslavery forces began battling in Kansas, as the territory became engulfed in its own civil war, known as "Bleeding Kansas." This event led to a debate in Congress, in which Massachusetts Senator Charles Sumner delivered a speech entitled "The Crime against Kansas." Sumner denounced the Kansas-Nebraska Act and criticized several members of Congress for giving into the slave-holding interests in the country, including South Carolina Senator Andrew P. Butler, who was absent from the Senate at the time. Two days later, Congressman Preston Brooks, a cousin of Butler, viciously beat Sumner with a cane over the head thirty times on the Senate floor. The incident became a symbol of Southern irrationality and violence in defense of slavery and strengthened Northern public opinion against slavery.
On October 16, 1859, John Brown led eighteen followers in a raid on the federal arsenal and armory at Harper's Ferry, Virginia. Brown, an abolitionist from New England, planned to start an armed slave revolt in Virginia. Brown seized control of the arsenal but was unsuccessful in starting a slave uprising, as he was captured by federal troops. He was executed on December 2, 1859. The news of Brown's raid sent a wave of shock and rage through the South. As a result of the raid, Southerners became convinced that they could no longer live safely in the Union. For more information on the "Crisis of the 1850s" see David M. Potter, *The Impending Crisis: America Before the Civil War, 1848–1861* (New York: Harper & Row, 1976) and James M. McPherson, *Battle Cry of Freedom: The Civil War Era* (New York: Oxford University Press, 1988), chapters 2–7.

66. "The Fugitive Slave Case Hearing Concluded," *The Press–Philadelphia,* March 29, 1860. This article gives details of the hearing and of the attempted rescue.

67. Tom Howell to Annie Howell, 1860 [exact date unknown]. Transcribed copy, author's collection.

68. Ibid. A meeting was held on July 13, 1860, at the Masonic Hall on Eleventh Street in Philadelphia, in which two of the men arrested in the attempted rescue spoke. The details of this meeting were published in the July 14, 1860, edition of the *Philadelphia Inquirer.*

69. "Camden, New Jersey, April 16th 1861, To the President of the United States," *West Jersey Press,* April 17, 1861.

70. "Immense War Meeting," *West Jersey Press,* April 24, 1861.

71. Ibid.

72. Deposition of Thomas Preston Carpenter, December 11, 1862. Thomas Howell Pension Records, National Archives, Washington, D.C.

73. In Anna Howell Lloyd Hayward's recollections, she stated that Tom falsely gave his age as eighteen when he enlisted. There is no evidence to support this claim.

74. Tom Howell to Mother, January 12, 1862. Howell Family Collection, GCHS.

75. James M. McPherson, *For Cause and Comrades: Why Men Fought in the Civil War* (New York: Oxford University Press, 1997), 25.

76. Reid Mitchell, *Civil War Soldiers* (New York: Viking, 1988), 17–18.

77. Tom Howell to Mother, March 5, 1862. H-41, Howell Family Collection, GCHS.
78. Tom Howell to Mother, March 22, 1862. H-41, Howell Family Collection, GCHS.
79. Deposition of Thomas Preston Carpenter, December 11, 1862. Thomas Howell Pension Records, National Archives, Washington, D.C.
80. Letters from other sources also appear in their original forms.

*Part I*

# "The Rough Life of a Soldier"

In early January 1862 Tom Howell learned of an upcoming vacancy in the Third New Jersey Volunteer Infantry Regiment. The position of second lieutenant of Company I was to become vacant, because the current second lieutenant, Lewis Spencer, accepted a position as first lieutenant of Company C. It is unclear how Howell heard about this vacancy. He could have found out through his uncle Thomas Preston Carpenter, who traveled a few times to Washington, D.C., and Alexandria, Virginia, to visit Union camps and may have used his influence to obtain a commission for Howell.[1] It is also possible that he learned of the vacancy through one of the officers of the regiment on recruiting duty in New Jersey during that winter, or perhaps he learned through a friend in the regiment. Nothing in the correspondence of Tom Howell or his family members offers any answer, so one can only speculate.

Tom Howell traveled to the camp of the Third New Jersey near Alexandria, arriving on January 12, 1862. Upon his arrival at the camp, he met with the commander of the regiment, Col. George W. Taylor. The fifty-three-year-old Taylor was from Clinton, New Jersey, and had served as a captain in the Mexican-American War. On the eve of the Civil War, he was engaged in mining and the manufacturing of iron, and when the war began, he became colonel of the Third New Jersey.[2] During the meeting between Howell and Taylor, Tom likely inquired about an upcoming vacancy in the regiment and asked the colonel to recommend him for the position.

Tom stayed at the camp of the Third New Jersey for a few days before traveling back to his home in Camden. During his stay in the camp he was serenaded by the regimental band and took some time to write his mother a letter to reflect on the possibility of living a soldier's life. He knew that leaving his family would be difficult, but he believed joining the army would be the best thing for him in the long run. The rigors he would face in the service of his country would make him a man. After his brief stay in Virginia, he returned to New Jersey to await word of his appointment.

On January 30, 1862, Colonel Taylor wrote to Charles S. Olden, the Governor of New Jersey, to recommend Tom Howell for the position of second lieutenant of Company I, Third New Jersey Regiment (fig. 1.1). Taylor wrote: "I have seen him once for a short time but conclude he is one of the [sic] kind. We should not fail to secure, as he seems above the common standard of applicants—a young man of education and spirit— and of excellent habits."[3] The colonel explained to the governor that he (Taylor) was departing from the established rule of making all promotions to second lieutenant from the ranks of sergeants of the regiment because there was a lack of "good material."

Strangely, in this letter Colonel Taylor refers to Tom as "Charles W. Howell." However, there is no doubt that this letter refers to Tom's commission, since his appointment is dated January 30, 1862. Nevertheless, this name confusion leaves us with a few questions. Was this commission originally offered to Tom's brother Charles (Charley)? That seems unlikely, since there is no evidence in any of the family records that Charles sought a commission. Plus, Charles's middle initial was S, not W. Another question then emerges: did Tom lie and give his name as Charles when he inquired about the vacancy in the Third New Jersey? Tom Howell was only seventeen, and army policy stated that men had to be at least eighteen to be mustered into service. One of his relatives later wrote that Tom had lied about his age so that he could join the army, but this is questionable, since every reference to the young man during his time in the army mentions his age as seventeen, not eighteen. It also seems doubtful that Tom posed as his brother when inquiring about the lieutenancy. The most likely explanation is that Colonel Taylor simply made an error and wrote the wrong first name in his letter to the governor. The governor received the letter on February 3, and within a few days Tom received word that the governor had approved his commission.

Howell's cousin, Louis Henry Carpenter, who was serving with the Sixth U.S. Cavalry, was astonished that Tom received a commission so quickly. "I am surprised to hear that Lieut. Tom Howell has succeeded in obtaining a commission so rapidly," he wrote in a letter to his mother. "I rather imagine that he would have found more difficulty if his ambition had led him in the direction of the regular service."[4] Writing to another cousin, Carpenter elaborated on Howell's commission:

> I am very glad to hear of Tom Howell's appointment as 2nd Lieutenant in the New Jersey Volunteers. Before long, if they keep on and the war lasts[,] a goodly number of our family will be in the service; it is not unlikely however that some of us will never return. Time will tell. These that fall in this war will meet an honorable death and be remembered hereafter, as our forefathers of Revolutionary fame are, as men who were not afraid to lose their lives in defence of their country.[5]

"The Rough Life of a Soldier"

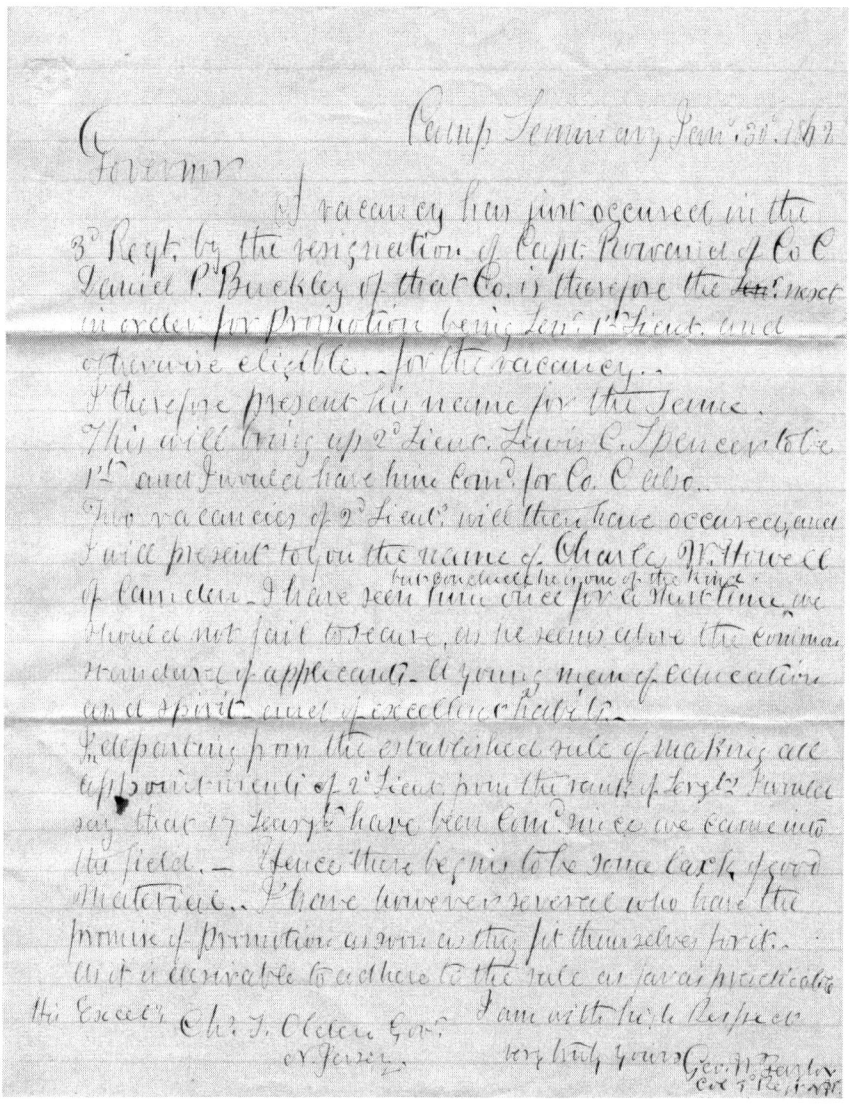

**Figure 1.1** Letter from Col. George W. Taylor to Gov. Charles Olden requesting Thomas Howell's commission as a second lieutenant. In this letter, Taylor refers to Howell as "Charles W. Howell." *Source*: Courtesy of the New Jersey State Archives; Department of State.

As Louis Henry Carpenter noted, many of Tom Howell's relatives served in the Union Army. Carpenter entered the service as a private in the Sixth U.S. Cavalry and by the end of the war would rise to the rank of brevet colonel of volunteers.[6] James Edward Carpenter, Louis's brother, joined the Eighth Pennsylvania Cavalry and rose to the rank of brevet major by 1865.[7] Howell's uncle Joshua Blackwood Howell was also actively serving in the army. Born on September 11, 1806, Joshua Blackwood Howell had studied law in Philadelphia and started his own practice in Uniontown, Pennsylvania. Prior to the outbreak of the Civil War he was a brigadier general in the Pennsylvania militia, but when the war commenced, he raised the Eighty-fifth Pennsylvania Volunteer Infantry Regiment and became its colonel in August 1861.[8] It was not uncommon for families to use their political ties to obtain commissions during the Civil War.[9] With many of Tom's relatives holding commissions in the army, the political ties of the Howell and Carpenter families are quite clear.

After receiving his commission, Tom Howell began making preparations to join his regiment in Alexandria. Since officers in volunteer regiments were required to provide their own uniforms, he had a new uniform made in Philadelphia. Before he left for Virginia, the six-foot-tall teenage lieutenant had his photograph taken in uniform at Broadbent & Co., located at 814 Chestnut Street in Philadelphia. The photo (fig. 1.2) shows the boyish, clean-shaven Howell holding his kepi in his left hand and resting his right arm on a column. It is interesting that he does not have a sword around his waist or a pistol in his hand in this photograph, since many soldiers posed for their photographs with a weapon.

On his last night with his family, Howell and his younger brother, Frank, who was twelve years old, went to Thomas Preston Carpenter's law office in Camden so that Howell could say his good-byes and see his brother Joshua. After spending some time there, the three Howell brothers went to Philadelphia to visit other family members and close friends before Tom Howell's departure to the seat of war. The young men stopped to visit Dr. Caspar Wistar and his family on Arch Street. After a brief visit, they walked to Chestnut Street to see Tom's former teacher William Fewsmith and converse with him and some of Tom's schoolmates. Joshua remembered that everyone there that night hoped Tom's separation from them "would be short and that he would soon come home laden with honors and covered with glory. To all of which Tom answered, 'Thank you Sir' with many warm handshakes."[10] After leaving Fewsmith's school and having dinner at their aunt Sarah Stratton's house on Locust Street, the brothers returned to Camden. As Tom bid his family farewell on the morning of February 8, 1862, his sister Annie gave him a prayer book to carry with him through his campaigns. On the front cover of the prayer book she signed, "Thos. James Howell / From his loving sister / Anna Howell / Feb. 8, 1862."[11] The young lieutenant left Camden for the journey to Alexandria to join his regiment, the Third New Jersey.

The Third New Jersey Volunteer Infantry Regiment was organized on May 4, 1861, after President Abraham Lincoln issued a call for additional

*Figure 1.2* Photograph of 2nd Lt. Thomas James Howell taken in Philadelphia shortly before his departure from Camden to Virginia in February 1862. *Source*: Courtesy of the author.

troops the previous day. The regiment was mustered into service on June 4, 1861. The Third New Jersey, along with the First and Second New Jersey Regiments, formed the First New Jersey Brigade.[12] After the men were equipped and armed, the brigade left New Jersey and arrived in Washington, D.C., on June 29, 1861.[13] The brigade was placed under the command of Brig. Gen. Theodore Runyon, and along with the four regiments of New Jersey militia, which were three-month units, they became the Fourth Division of Brig. Gen. Irvin McDowell's army.[14] The Third New Jersey did not see action during the Battle of Bull Run on July 21, 1861, but the regiment was involved in a skirmish with Confederate troops on August 31, 1861, at Munson's Hill, Virginia, where two of its men were killed and three wounded.[15] Earlier that month, on August 7, the New Jersey Brigade received a new brigade commander, Philip Kearny, who molded them into one of the "finest fighting brigades in the Union army."[16]

Philip Kearny was born in New York City on June 2, 1815. He served as a second lieutenant in the First U.S. Dragoons during the Mexican-American War and lost his left arm at the Battle of Churubusco. After that war he resigned his commission from the army to settle down in New Jersey, but in 1859 he went to France and served in Napoleon III's Imperial Guard during the Italian War of Independence. He saw action at Magenta and Solferino, where it is said he led his men with his reins clenched in his teeth. When the Civil War broke out in 1861, Kearny hurried home to offer his services and was given command of the First New Jersey Brigade.[17] On October 15, 1861, the Army of the Potomac was reorganized and the New Jersey Brigade was attached to the division under the command of Brig. Gen. William B. Franklin.[18] The action at Munson's Hill was the last contact the brigade would have with the rebels in 1861 before the Jerseymen went into winter quarters at Camp Fort Worth near Alexandria, Virginia.

Tom Howell arrived in Virginia on February 10, 1862, and joined the Third New Jersey at Camp Fort Worth.[19] He noted that the fort was "on the top of a hill and commands the country for miles around."[20] Fort Worth (fig. 1.3), which was part of the defenses of Washington, was located on Seminary Heights near Alexandria about one and a half miles west of Fort Ellsworth.[21] Construction of the fort started around September 1, 1861. Its perimeter was 463 yards, which was defended by eight 24-lb. guns, five 12-lb. howitzers, five 4.5-inch Rodmans, two 20-lb. Parrotts, two 12-lb. Whitworth rifles, four 10-inch mortars, two 24-lb. mortars, and one 100-lb. Parrott.[22] According to a soldier from the Third New Jersey, the New Jersey Brigade helped in the construction of the earthwork: "The Brigade whent to work and in a short time had finished the Formidable Earth Work known as Fort Worth and the Brigade had the Honor of Building it themselves."[23]

Upon his arrival at Fort Worth, the men of the regiment warmly received Tom. He mentioned in one of his early letters to his family that he was pleased with how he was received by Colonel Taylor, who had not expected the young lieutenant to arrive so promptly. Within a few days the colonel issued an order announcing Tom Howell's commission to the regiment.

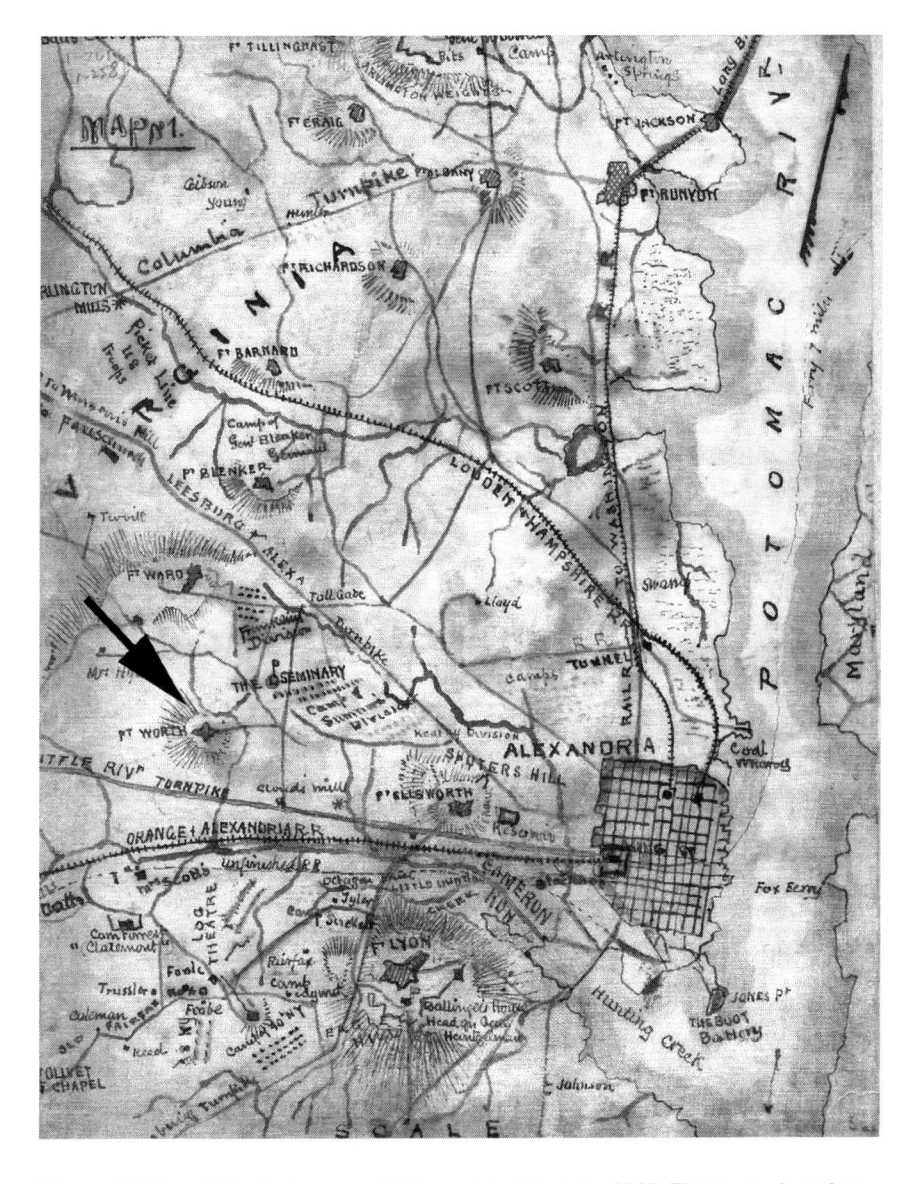

*Figure 1.3* **Map of the forts around Alexandria, Virginia, 1862. The arrow is pointing to the location of Fort Worth.** *Source*: **Courtesy of the Library of Congress.**

Fort Worth VA
Feb. 13, 1862
Special Order No. 21

The following appointment is made in the 3rd Regiment N.J. Vols. Thos. J. Howell of Camden N.J. to be 2nd Lieut. of Co. I having been commissioned Jan. 30, 1862. He will be obeyed and respected accordingly.

By order of
George W. Taylor
Col. Com. 3 Reg't[24]

His commission as lieutenant was also announced in the newspaper in Camden three days later:

> Military Appointment:
> We learn that Thomas Howell, son of the late Richard Howell, Esq., of this city, has been appointed a Lieutenant in Company I, Third New Jersey Regiment.[25]

Lieutenant Howell had to quickly get accustomed to the strict and monotonous schedule of military life. He also had to familiarize himself with the different exercises that were to be practiced during the drilling of the troops. On February 18, after being in the regiment for less than two weeks, Howell had command of his company, Company I, since 1st Lt. Archibald S. Taylor was sick and Capt. Leonard H. Regur was on recruiting duty in Plainfield, New Jersey. Howell apparently had no problem handling his duties and put the men through two hours of bayonet exercises.[26] He learned during this day, however, that it was necessary for every officer to possess a watch, and he asked his mother to send him one.

Tom Howell was growing up far away from home in the service of his country. From his early letters it is clear that he missed his family dearly. He longed for letters and packages from his loved ones at home. Once, after receiving a package of food from his mother, he explained that she had no idea how much it lifted his spirits. Like most soldiers who served in the military during the Civil War, he worried about his family at home, and they, of course, worried about him. As the only member of the family bringing in a steady income, he knew his mother and siblings relied on the money he sent home, and he reassured them on numerous occasions that he would not do anything foolish that would put himself in harm's way.

During his first few weeks in camp, Tom Howell not only had to get used to the routines and rigors of military life, but he also had the added pressure of proving himself in order to gain the respect of both the men he commanded and his superiors. Although he never said it, his actions demonstrate that he worried that the men of his company thought he was not qualified or deserving of his commission. As a result, he sought to earn their respect and acceptance. Civil War historian James M. McPherson explains that the "most important criteria for a good officer were concern for the welfare of his men and leadership by example—that is, personal courage and a willingness to do anything he asked his men to do."[27] It is apparent that Howell was determined to lead by example and show his men that he was not afraid to face the same hardships as the rest of the troops. He also did not want to bring shame or dishonor to himself or his family by seeming like a coward to the other soldiers. Since he was from a family with a rich history, he felt obligated to uphold its honor.

In his correspondence with family members Tom frequently inquired about friends or news from home, but in letters to his brother Joshua and sister Annie he quite often asked for news about or descriptions of two young ladies: Mary Harbert and Gertrude (Gert) Browning. Mary Harbert was fifteen years old and lived a few blocks from the Howells on Cooper Street in Camden. Her father, Samuel, was the regimental quartermaster of the Fourth New Jersey. Tom mentioned Mary seven times in his letters home, which was the most of any of the young ladies he inquired about. He even asked Annie to ask Mary if she would exchange photographs with him. Gert Browning was fifteen and lived one block from the Howell family. Her father, Abraham Browning, was a lawyer in Camden and the best friend of Howell's father, Richard. It is not clear if either young lady was Tom's girlfriend or just someone he was interested in. There is no evidence that he corresponded with either of them while he was in the army, so it seems that the members of his family kept him apprised of their actions. In a letter to Joshua, Tom wrote, "I supposed Gert is rushing around pretty generally or is she more of a lady now?"[28] He apparently had heard something about how she had conducted herself, and he disapproved; he told Annie a few weeks later to "remember me to all my young lady friends with the exception of Gert Browning. I don't want to be remembered to her."[29] Gert appears to have acted too unladylike for this "Christian Gentleman." Howell, like most young men, was very interested in members of the opposite sex and frequently told his siblings to "remember me to the ladies." As he and the rest of the army prepared to move south in the spring of 1862, he even asked his mother to send him some white handkerchiefs so that "when the young ladies appear I want to appear more than so, so."[30]

Tom Howell's correspondence did not offer a positive description of camp life. He thought that for some the experience of camp life made "beasts out of the men, instead of making men."[31] He was disgusted by the fact that many of the officers of the regiment did not act as gentlemen: "In their intercourse with each other and with those *outside* of *themselves* they do not show themselves to be the polished gentlemen; they have given me no cause for *this feeling; it is only* what I have seen, everything is so coarse, it is not what I have been brought up to."[32] Another officer in the regiment felt the same way as Tom, explaining: "The worst feature of the service is the absence of good society, though the officers are generally good hearted obliging fellows, there is an awful want of refinement."[33] Officers were expected to conduct themselves with a certain amount of class and culture when interacting with other "gentlemen."

Howell believed officers should set a good example for the enlisted men. He was horrified that most officers spent their Sundays swearing and reading novels instead of attending church services. This practice extended to the other men, and only a dozen or so soldiers would be present at services on Sunday. Article Two of the Rules and Articles of War "earnestly recommended to all officers and soldiers diligently to attend divine service."[34] The young lieutenant believed if the officers had set a good example in the beginning, then more men would attend service. Tom wrote his mother, saying, "I shall use all my influence and by good example get my men to go, and by these means get everything straight again."[35] His actions were typical of many Christian officers in the army who used their positions of leadership to encourage spirituality. These men reached out to those individuals around them in an attempt to stamp out immorality in the army and create moral regiments.[36]

Howell was also appalled at how much the men, including the officers, smoked and drank, and he told his sister to reassure his mother "that she need not be afraid of my breaking those resolutions which I made about drinking and smoking."[37] A week later, after explaining the activities of other officers to his mother, he set her mind at ease by telling her, "You may be certain that your son *Thomas* is not among that crowd. I have not sworn neither have I smoked nor had strong drink in my mouth since I have been here."[38] It is clear that the lessons taught by his parents had a great impact on his character. This "Christian Gentleman" would practice self-restraint and would not indulge in vulgarity and drunkenness, for those traits would lead him toward eternal damnation and earthly failure as well.[39]

Less than a week after arriving at Camp Fort Worth, Tom Howell began having problems with Lt. Col. Henry W. Brown (fig 1.4). Brown, born in 1816 in Boston, was actually born with the name Henry W. Barnes, but he changed his last name to Brown after abandoning his wife in April 1839 and joining the Fourth U.S. Artillery. After being discharged in 1844, Brown, now married to another woman, took up residence in Philadelphia. When the Civil War broke out in 1861, he became captain of Company A, Third New Jersey, but shortly after that he was named lieutenant colonel of the regiment.[40] It is apparent from Howell's letters, and from others in the regiment, that Lieutenant Colonel Brown was a mean-spirited, habitual drunkard and was clearly not a refined gentleman as Tom expected officers to be.

Lieutenant Howell described how Brown became hostile when he had too much to drink and would take it out on the men of the regiment. Howell recounted to his mother one such instance of Brown's practices: "When he gets drunk he always makes a fuss. Once at Fort Worth being 'under the weather,' as it is called, he went out and watching his opportunity ran up [surprised the camp guard], seizing the musket from a guard took it off with him, next day he gave the sentry four hours extra."[41] Another officer of the regiment summed up his feelings about Brown: "He is a miserable specimen, an ex policeman.... The officers all unite in despising him. We are on the watch for him, and should he slip as he frequently did at Fort Worth (intoxication) we'll send his heels a kicking to the sky."[42] Most officers considered a vice such as intoxication to be incompatible with gentlemanly behavior and a violation of the Eighty-third Article of War for conduct unbecoming an officer and a gentleman.[43] It was clear that some officers in the regiment, especially Howell, did not get along very well with Lieutenant Colonel Brown and did not think very highly of him, but Tom assured his brother Joshua that he could hold his own "against Brown or any other man like him no matter who he is."[44]

Although Tom Howell had problems getting along with Lieutenant Colonel Brown, he did make some close friends while in the army. Among those he befriended were Archibald S. (Arch) Taylor and Robert T. (Bob) Dunham. Arch Taylor was born on June 1, 1842, near High Bridge, Hunterdon County, New Jersey. He had just finished his schooling at Hartwick Seminary when the Civil War started. He volunteered as a private in the Fifth New York "Duryea's Zouaves" and traveled with the regiment to Fort Monroe in Virginia in April 1861. In June of that year Arch Taylor was recommended by his uncle Col. George W. Taylor, the commander of the Third New Jersey, for a commission as first lieutenant of Company I.[45] The colonel described his nephew as a "young man of education and promise, and excellent habits, all of which is within my own personal knowledge."[46] Arch Taylor's appointment was approved and he joined the regiment as it formed in Trenton. Tom and Arch became close friends from the moment Tom arrived in Virginia. The two young lieutenants bunked together, exchanged photographs with each other's families, and were left to command the company, since the captain of the company, Leonard Regur, was on recruiting duty in New Jersey and never returned, due to a case of erysipelas.[47]

Twenty-two-year-old Bob Dunham was from Camden and had been one of Tom's friends before the war. When the war began, Dunham was a law student in James B. Dayton's office in Camden.[48] On May 30, 1861, Dunham—who believed one of the best traits of a young man, next to honesty, was ambition—wrote Governor Olden regarding an appointment as adjutant of the Third New Jersey.[49] The following day Colonel Taylor, who was also Dunham's uncle, wrote the governor recommend-

*Figure 1.4* Photograph of Lt. Col. Henry W. Brown. *Source*: Courtesy of the New Jersey State Archives; Department of State.

ing Dunham for the position of adjutant of the regiment, after Capt. David Vickers of Company A declined the appointment to remain with his company.[50] Dunham was mustered in as adjutant on June 27, 1861.

Tom Howell befriended another officer from the regiment, Capt. Daniel Penrose Buckley (fig. 1.5) of Company C. In a letter home to his mother, Howell described why he liked Captain Buckley:

> There is one officer in the regiment who I like and admire quite a good deal. (his name is Capt. Buckley) [H]e is from Philadelphia[,] is and was quite a promising young lawyer; he reads his Bible every morning and often through the day when not having anything else to read in the shape of newspapers, besides he is not ashamed to be seen by others[;] I like that. I should choose such a man for a friend. I like him more than any other officer in the regiment just upon that account.[51]

The twenty-five-year-old Buckley, called "Pen" by his friends, seemed to be a "Christian Gentleman" like Tom. As Tom stated, Buckley was an attorney; his office was located on 619 Walnut Street in Philadelphia.[52] When the war began, Buckley mustered into service in Burlington as first lieutenant of Company C on May 25, 1861, with his cousin Edward Burd Grubb, who was the second lieutenant. Buckley became captain of the company on January 30, 1862, the same day Tom received his commission as a lieutenant.

Tom Howell also had a servant while in the army. Pvt. Louis Loeb of Company I was detailed as his waiter on February 1, 1862. Loeb was born in Darmstadt, Germany, in 1838. He and his family left Germany for the United States in 1842, arriving in New York City on May 23, 1842. The Loebs moved to Camden, New Jersey, and settled in a house on Front Street. Prior to the Civil War, Louis had been employed as a butcher. In September 1861, he enlisted as a private in the Third New Jersey. According to a letter written in October 1861, Loeb seemed happy with the pay he was receiving from the government but mentioned that his mother drew the $6.00 a month he received from the state.[53] The need for additional money may explain why he became Tom Howell's servant. The extra duty earned Loeb $24.50 a month, along with his regular monthly pay of $13.00.[54]

After spending all of February 1862 at Camp Fort Worth getting accustomed to army life and drill, Tom readied himself as he and his regiment prepared to move during the first week of March. He explained to his mother that he had exchanged his sword for a cavalry saber and was almost prepared for any advance. The young lieutenant realized, though, that he needed another weapon in addition to his sword. According to one of Tom's letters, Arch Taylor had "three [guns] and a knife in his boot besides his sword," so he asked his mother to send him a revolver, saying it was important for an officer to have one.[55] With this extra weapon he

*Figure 1.5* Photograph of Capt. Daniel Penrose Buckley. *Source*: Courtesy of John W. Kuhl Collection.

would be equipped for whatever action he may face during the upcoming campaign.

By early March 1862 rumors began to circulate throughout the Army of the Potomac that the Confederate Army under the command of Gen. Joseph E. Johnston was withdrawing from its lines around Manassas.[56] To determine if these rumors were true, Brigadier General Kearny, acting without orders, decided to move his brigade forward toward Sangster's Station. During the afternoon of March 7, 1862, the day the Confederate Army began its march away from Manassas toward Fredericksburg, Tom Howell's regiment and the entire New Jersey Brigade broke camp about 4:00 p.m. after three hearty cheers for the Union proposed by Kearny and marched westward. After a twelve-mile march, the men rested for the night and continued on toward Fairfax Station the next morning.[57] The troops marched along the Orange and Alexandria Railroad line, but enemy soldiers were spotted about a mile before they reached their destination. These were Confederates acting as rearguard to cover the retreat from Manassas. Company I, Howell's company, was placed on a hill along the railroad, just a quarter mile from the enemy. The young lieutenant got his first look at the enemy and ordered his men to keep quiet so they did not alert the rebels. He later recalled, "I had made up my mind that if we were attacked I would show my men and also the enemy what I was and what I was made of and that they had Howell blood to contend with."[58] Although no battle ensued and the brigade reached Fairfax Station unmolested, Howell's statement proves he was determined to show his men that he was a brave and fearless officer, worthy of his commission.

The next day, March 9, Colonel Taylor took seven companies of the regiment, along with a detachment of the First New York Cavalry, about seven miles to Sangster's Station, where enemy pickets were again discovered.[59] A group of eighteen cavalrymen, led by Lt. Henry Hidden, charged the Confederate troops. Kearny, who witnessed Hidden's charge, ordered another group of the First New York Cavalry to attack.[60] Tom and the men of his regiment watched as this brief fight between the Union's First New York Cavalry and the Confederates from the First Maryland unfolded. The New Yorkers won the engagement and captured fourteen Southerners but lost its lieutenant, Henry Hidden. This was the first combat Howell had witnessed since joining the army, and he was very impressed, describing it as "a most brilliant affair."[61]

After a march to Union Mills on March 10, the Third New Jersey continued its advance toward Manassas on March 11 at 4:00 a.m. One soldier described the events of the march:

> The 3rd Regt with Col. G. W. Taylor a head started down the rail road to see if they could finde any secesh[,][62] so we went on to Bull Run ware the rebels had burnt the bridg so our pioneers soon constructed a

rude bridge and the boys passed oaver and on they went[,] and at 9 o clock we run up the Colors of the 3rd Regt on the Ramparts of the great Sebastapol of Secesia ware a few hours before the reble rag had floated.[63]

The men discovered items such as knives, guns, swords, clothing, and tobacco that had been discarded by the withdrawing Confederate troops. General Kearny, who arrived shortly after the Third New Jersey, told his soldiers to help themselves to the items left behind, which also included a number of Confederate flags "of different sizes and shapes."[64]

Three hours later the men of the regiment received an order to march to Centreville, where they arrived shortly before sunset.[65] According to Tom, many of the men were "almost tired to death" from the day's long march.[66] He wrote that he did not give out once during the march but at times had felt like falling behind and resting on the side of the road. He added, "Then I thought that the officers should set the men a good example, that if I gave out the men would think that they had an equal right so I kept on and did not think of fatigue but only when we would stop for the night."[67] The young lieutenant, who had only been with the regiment for one month, wanted to make a good impression on his men and prove that he was a good officer. Over the next three days, the regiment retraced its steps back to its camp at Fort Worth, where it arrived at 1:00 a.m. on March 15, 1862, rejoining the rest of the army. The commander of the Army of the Potomac, Maj. Gen. George B. McClellan, had ordered the entire army back to the vicinity of Alexandria as he prepared for the upcoming campaign.[68]

George Brinton McClellan was born in Philadelphia on December 3, 1826, and graduated second in the West Point class of 1846. He served on the staff of Maj. Gen. Winfield Scott during the Mexican-American War and remained in the army until he resigned his commission in 1857 to become the chief engineer of the Illinois Central Railroad.[69] When the Civil War began in 1861, McClellan volunteered his services to the federal government, and that July he became commander of the Army of the Potomac and General-in-Chief in November 1861.[70]

The men in the Army of the Potomac greatly admired McClellan, who some called "Little Mac" or the "Young Napoleon." McClellan never dismissed comparisons between himself and the great French general; he even allowed himself to be photographed in the traditional Napoleonic pose, with one arm folded behind his back and the other hand inserted in his coat front.[71] After he took command of the Army of the Potomac, he restored order and the confidence of the soldiers, and the men began to trust their commander. By early 1862, the men of the Army of the Potomac possessed "a certain cockiness, even, a feeling that [they] knew of no other soldiers who were quite as good."[72]

At a council of war on March 13, McClellan adopted a new plan that would transport his army to the peninsula formed by the York and James rivers in Virginia. The Army of the Potomac would use Fort Monroe, located at the tip of the peninsula, as its base of operations.[73] The Yankee troops would proceed up the peninsula toward Richmond, hoping to catch the Southerners off guard and possibly seize the capital city before Gen. Joseph Johnston's Confederate Army could react.[74] It was also during this time, March 14, that the army was reorganized and the New Jersey Brigade became the First Brigade, First Division, I Corps under Brig. Gen. Irvin McDowell.

As the Army of the Potomac prepared to launch its campaign to take Richmond, the soldiers of the army knew that McClellan cared for them and were confident he would lead them to victory. On March 14, 1862, McClellan issued an address to the army and announced, "I will bring you now face to face with the rebels. . . . I am to watch over you as a parent over his children; and you know that your General loves you from the depths of his heart."[75] One man serving in a New Jersey regiment restated part of McClellan's March 14 address in a letter home to his friend: "He says he will bring us face to face with the enemy and is satisfied that we will strike the death blow to the rebellion."[76] Another soldier wrote of the commanding general, "We put every fathe in our Gallant leader Gen. McClellan and Victory is ours wherever he leades."[77]

The first Union troops left Alexandria for Fort Monroe on March 17, but the New Jersey Brigade remained in its camp at Fort Worth. One officer explained, "Our camp was the centre of attraction all day & visitors thronged in from all the neighboring Brigades."[78] The flags that were captured on the expedition to Manassas were displayed in camp for all to see.

Lieutenant Howell took some time after returning to camp to record his thoughts on the upcoming campaign. "Our expedition is a large one," he wrote. "I think that there has been a determination to drive the enemy from the Virginia shore altogether. There are nearly 100 steamers in Alexandria to take our expedition down the river. To drive the enemy from the river will be at the expense of hundreds of lives."[79] He expected that the New Jersey Brigade would soon board transports for Fort Monroe and he and his men would soon be in battle.

As it became apparent to Howell that he would be among the troops transported to the Virginia shores to meet the enemy, he began to contemplate his own mortality. He did not make any mention in his letters home of possibly being wounded or killed until the middle of March. According to historian Earl Hess, "It was inevitable that, either during combat or between battles, the soldier would have to think about and come to grips with the real possibility of losing his life."[80] Howell sensed that a large battle loomed in the future and wrote, "I hope that I will not have the luck to be shot."[81] He frequently reassured his family that he would not "be foolhardy, and run into danger heedlessly."[82]

In dealing with his own mortality, Tom turned to his faith, as did many Civil War soldiers. "I shall put my whole trust in God," he confided to his mother, "for I will need his help pretty soon if I never did before[,] which of course is not the case[,] for everyone needs the help of God. I hope that amidst the many dangers that will surround me I may be protected from them all and also may have the prayers of those at home. . . . I wish you would pray for the safety of Arch Taylor, Bob Dunham and myself."[83] When he left home for the army, he took with him a number of religious tracts to hand out to the troops and later told his mother, "All those *tracts,* papers, and Testaments have been taken by the men."[84] Tracts were the most common form of religious literature given to the soldiers, and it seemed that as the prospect of a large battle loomed, the troops tended to have a greater interest in religion.[85]

Howell had good reason to be concerned about his own morality in March 1862. He had to worry about not only the upcoming move into enemy territory but also the possibility of being wounded or killed by bullets from his own troops. On March 21 he led a fatigue party to cut wood for the camp. While gathering wood, his men came under fire from the Fourth New Jersey, which had set up targets on the hill where his men were. "I beat a hasty retreat," Howell explained, "and ordered the fatigue party back into camp."[86] The next day, he was in command of Company H and was in the middle of drilling the men when he felt a bullet "whisp" past him. "It came from a soldier shooting down below the hill," he told his mother. "I wish you could hear a ball go through the air, one is not apt to forget the sound in a hurry[;] it reminds me of a child crying."[87]

Over the next two weeks, the regiment continued to drill and took part in three grand reviews, on March 19, March 25, and March 27. On March 19 McClellan reviewed Brig. Gen. William B. Franklin's division, of which the New Jersey Brigade was a part. This was the first time Tom saw McClellan, and he was impressed. "I saw the *man* and was very much pleased with his appearance," explained the young lieutenant to his mother. "He is not handsome, nor is he very homely, but half and half."[88] McClellan complimented the New Jersey Brigade, saying it "could compete with any this side of the Potomac."[89] During the review of March 25, also attended by McClellan, Lieutenant Howell commanded Company I and described the event as a great affair. The review of March 27 was similar to the others, except that British representative to the United States, Lord Richard Bickerton Pemell Lyons, was among those in the audience.

As March ended and April began, the men of the New Jersey Brigade still awaited orders to board transports and join the expedition to Fort Monroe, but events in Washington threatened to end any chance of that movement. As McClellan prepared to move his army to the Virginia Peninsula, President Lincoln required that the general leave behind an adequate force to defend the capital. McClellan informed Secretary of War Edwin Stanton that a force of 73,500 would be left to protect Washington, but Stanton realized by early April that the force guarding the capital was not 73,500, as McClellan had pledged, but in fact numbered only 26,761.[90] Now aware that the force left to defend the capital was inadequate, Lincoln and Stanton decided to detach McDowell's I Corps from McClellan's command on April 5 and keep it to protect Washington.

Meanwhile, Tom Howell and the rest of the New Jersey men continued to drill and prepare for whatever part they were to play in this campaign. On March 29 Howell again commanded Company H and took the men out for target practice. He was impressed with the sound made by the bullets as they "went ringing past at the double quick time."[91] On April 2 the men were given some indication that a move could come soon when Bob Dunham went to Washington to inquire about getting new rifles for the regiment. Anticipating another long march, Tom took the opportunity to purchase a new pair of boots. He explained that his old pair was too small and he switched them with someone for a pair of shoes during the march to Centreville. The new pair he bought was so large that "they cannot hurt me."[92] On April 3 he received the revolver, a .22-caliber Smith & Wesson Model 1, that he had requested his mother send him the month before. He told his mother that he now had everything he wanted as he and the rest of the men prepared to march back to Manassas the next day.

While McClellan planned to take Richmond by advancing up the Virginia Peninsula, Federal troops enjoyed remarkable success in the western theater in the first few months of 1862. In February, forces under the command of Ulysses S. Grant captured Fort Henry and Fort Donelson in western Tennessee. On February 23 another Union force captured Nashville, which was the first Confederate state capital to fall.[93] By early April, with most of Tennessee under Union control, Grant's troops moved toward Pittsburg Landing on the Tennessee River, where they were attacked by a Confederate force under Gen. Albert Sidney Johnston. The two armies clashed at Shiloh on April 6–7, 1862. The Union Army won the battle, which resulted in more than twenty thousand casualties between both armies, and the Confederates withdrew to Corinth, Mississippi. The high losses suffered by both armies at Shiloh would become commonplace in battles during the next three years of fighting.[94]

On April 5, 1862, the New Jersey Brigade was ordered to march to Manassas. Tom wrote that the weather was the worst he had experienced since he had joined the army, plus his new boots were giving him problems. He complained that they were too warm, and in a letter he posted from Colvin's Station, on the Orange and Alexandria Railroad, to his mother on April 11, 1862, he asked her to send him a strong pair of walking shoes. He also described the snow, hail, rain, and cold conditions he and his men were enduring on their march to Manassas, but he was quick to tell her that he was well so as to not worry her even more. He painted his mother a picture of the miserable conditions endured at the camp of the regiment, which he called a "mud hole," since it was situated in a low-lying field, and explained that the enlisted men often gathered around the fires in the pouring rain, shaking with the cold. He also explained that he lived the same way as his men and that his morale had reached "about two hundred below" on April 9 after sleeping that night with wet feet, but now his spirits were up, and he was used to "hard fare and the rough life of a soldier."[95]

The New Jersey Brigade never reached Manassas. Howell explained that on Friday, April 11, he was ordered to take thirty men to unload rail cars. While he was there, he overheard General Franklin, standing only thirty feet from him, tell a staff member that the New Jersey Brigade would move at 4:00 p.m. to Bristoe Station, about nine miles to the east.[96] Howell quickly went back to camp, ordered his things collected, and rejoined his detail at the railroad.[97] Just as he expected, the brigade was ordered to march at 4:00, reaching Bristoe Station around 10:30. The young lieutenant did not get much sleep that night, as he sat with the men of his company around the campfire, listening to them share their stories.

The next morning the Third New Jersey received orders to march to Fairfax Court House, but Howell did not join them. In order to speed up the march, the men of the regiment were ordered to leave their knapsacks behind. One man from each company and an officer, Tom Howell, were left behind to guard the knapsacks and transport them to Alexandria via railroad.[98] By April 15, 1862, the entire brigade was back in Alexandria, where the men awaited transport to join the rest of McClellan's army on the Virginia Peninsula.

### Civil War Letters of Thomas James Howell:
### January 12–April 15, 1862

[Original]

Camp Worth
Jan 12 1862

Dearest Mother
It was very hard for me to leave you, but I think it will be best for me in the end. You do not know how I like this kind of life; if nothing that I have undertaken before this will make a man of me, I know that this rough life will. I am writing these few lines after tea, at which we had oysters, etc giant bread, milk, sugar and very nice tea. You can see, that we do not suffer; I do not know what we shall have for breakfast or dinner tomorrow. After spending nearly the whole morning in Wash-

ington, I left for camp where I arrived safe and sound. Please tell all the sweet ones at Uncle Thomas's,[99] that I had no trouble in getting *passes.*[100] There is tremendous cheering going on in the camp of the 4th N. J. Vol. While I am writing the band is preparing to serenade me, they are doing it now; it is at the request of Lieut. Col. Brown.[101] I have not much more time to write, as I am going to turn out with the company. I am acting 1st Lieut. the captain being absent recruiting. I shall write tomorrow (Thursday) to Annie, Josh, Frank or Charley.[102]

Give my best love to all and keep plenty yourself; remember me to all enquiring friends.

Your most affectionate son
Tom

[Transcribed Copy]

[Camp Fort Worth]
Feb. 11th 1862

Dear Annie,
You cannot tell how I enjoy camp life. But before I begin please say or let Ma know somehow (though I suppose she will see this letter of course) that she need not be afraid of my breaking those resolutions which I made about drinking and smoking. I was very much pleased by the way in which Colonel Taylor[103] received me. He didn't expect me so soon but he will like me all the more for being prompt. Bob Dunham[104] will not put me on guard duty til I have let him know that I am prepared, which I think is very kind. It is a fine thing to be in a camp, that is if you want to get up early. This morning I was up at six to roll call and when at nine there was an undress parade when the orders of the day were read and also my appointment. The companies are out drilling in the bayonet exercise. There is something I want to tell you concerning the music. We have a good band and a fine drum and fife corps. The drumming is very fine. Please tell Uncle Thomas that he must prepare himself for more mud, that is to tramp through, than he ever saw in his life. Why the men can hardly keep step there is so much mud. All the regiments around have been cheering tremendously on account of the news received from the south.[105] But our regiment, not a man was heard cheering in it. They know better. Bob desires to be remembered to all. Give my love to all inquiring friends. Ask Miss Annie Carpenter[106] to remember me to Miss Lizzie Rogers.[107] Convey my very best love to Uncle Thomas' family and to Ma, Charlie, and Jos and Frank.[108] I shall write to Sam today or tomorrow.

Your most affectionate brother
Tom

[Transcribed Copy]

Camp [Fort Worth]
Feb. 16th 1862
Col George W. Taylor,

commander of New Jersey volunteer infantry.

Dear Jos,
Friday afternoon I went through the Fort Worth formerly called Fort Taylor with Lt. Spencer.[109] He is about one of the most amusing men I ever met. It is just behind our tents so we walked in and went all over except in the powder magazines, I saw the Whitworth arms[,] very fine ones. It is on the top of a hill and commands the country for miles around. The scene that is presented is certainly a fine one. There are hills all around and on everyone there are two or three brigades, cavalry[,]artillery and infantry, no end of them. It is a beautiful sight to see a brigade drilling and of course more so when it is done well. It has been snowing like all the world. I had a fuss with Lt. Col. Brown but he is a nobody. You will please see that those four photographs are sent to me as soon as possible.

As I said in my letter to Charlie I shall try to exercise my drill in drawing a plan of Fort Worth.[110] Taylor[111] and myself board at Mrs. Suthers'[112] where we have excellent fare. A valentine was sent to me. It had a very pretty piece of poetry on it I should like to know very much who sent it, I tell you. Remember me to all the young ladies. Give my love to Uncle Thomas and family and an abundance of love to Ma and Annie, and Charlie and Jos and Frank. I have written to them all. I have not had a letter up to the time of writing this.

Your most affectionate brother
Tom

[Original]
3d Regiment N.J. Volunteer Inf'ty
Col. George W. Taylor, Commanding.
Camp, Fort Worth
Feb 19th 1862

Dear Ma,
I never want to see Frank enter the Army. Camp life, generally speaking, I think *makes beasts* out of the men, instead of *making men*. I am pretty certain that is the case in our regiment; a good many of the officers are included, I will not mention their names, you may be certain your son *Thomas* is not among that crowd. I have not sworn neither have I smoked nor had strong drink in my mouth since I have been here. You speak about that wrapper, I should like to have it very much[;] it will be nice to put on for a change. Confound this mud I say; it is very deep at present. It is thought that we will move South pretty soon. Please tell Annie that I like Arch Taylor very much, he is sick at present, so I have command of the company. Yesterday I put them through two hours on the bayonet exercise. I can tell you that I live well here, have all I want and am comfortable generally. I was pleased upon receiving your letters and Annie's, I hope you will write often. Tell Josh and Charlie that I should like to hear from them. I have written to Sam[113] once, but I shall write either to Minnie[114] or Sam pretty soon

again. I forgot to say that we had a fire in camp the other night; a tent caught on fire, and such shouting—well it is a rare sound to hear in our camp. Tell Annie that I will write to her this week also that Arch Taylor speaks about her now and then. I find that a watch is absolutely necessary, every officer should have one; if you could see Uncle Thomas about it and get me a small silver one I will be much obliged to you, though I dislike to see you go to the expense. Pay-day comes at the end of this month,[115] and I will be able to send the greater part of it to you; my board is fifteen dollars a month, that is my meals, and excellent are they. Tell Josh, if you please, to remember me to Martin Gray,[116] I believe Sam's name is Gray.[117] The Potts[118] and all the rest. It is rather late and I am sleepy, so I shall have to stop, you will oblige me very much by not showing this letter, outside our family, it is not written well enough. Give my best love to Annie, Charlie, Josh, Frank and plenty to yourself my dear mother, remember me and give my love to all.

Your most affectionate Son.
Tom
2nd Lieut. Commanding Co. I
3rd N.J. Inf. Col. Taylor
Gen. Kearney's Brig.
Gen. Franklin's Div.

[Original]
3d Regiment N.J. Volunteer Inf'ty
Col. George Taylor, Commanding
Camp Worth
Feb 21st 1862

Dear Annie,
Your letter arrived safely and I was glad to get it I can tell you. You speak about my going to church at Alexandria; I did not go on Sunday; the road was too bad for walking, I told Bob Dunham that if he would lend me his horse I would go into town. I have come to the conclusion that going to Alexandria will only be a chance for spending money, and that foolishly, and therefore I think I shall stay away. What do you think to our moving South; one division on our right has commenced. It is thought that we will be off by next week. I have received Josh's letters and Ma's letter, and will answer very soon again no more time at present to write. I have sent my picture to Sam.

Your most affectionate brother
Tom
2nd Lieut. Commanding Co. I
3rd N.J. Inf.

P.S. Give my love to Ma, Charley, Josh, Frank, *Annie*, yourself and Uncle Thomas' family,
Tom

[Original]
3d Regiment N.J. Volunteer Inf'ty,
Col. George W. Taylor, Commanding.
Camp, Fort Worth, February 26th 1862

My dear Mother,
In your letter of the twenty-third, you speak about Sunday, well you should see how some of the officers keep that day; they swear and read novels all day. Some of those little books, papers and tracts I have given away, the men are glad to get them. About that box; I was glad to get the good things, that were in it. The pickles are good, but they leaked, which did no harm; the wrapper will be of service; the small stockings I have given away. Such blowing as we had yesterday, Bob Dunham went into Washington on Monday afternoon to get new tents for the soldiers. I had almost forgotten to say that I received that parcel from Capt. Knight.[119] Your photograph I have placed with the others. I hope that Aunt Sarah[120] will send me not only a few good things, but a whole box; you cannot imagine with what a feeling I opened that box of yours; it encourages a person, at least it happened so in my case. The storm on Monday blew down two thirds of the officers tents with their cook tents behind, consequently Having no place to get their meals they came to the *Sutler's*. I do not know whether I have told you about my board which is fifteen dollars a month. I haven't time to tell you what we get, but it is excellent fare. You ask whether I am comfortable—I am very comfortably fixed, though I might be more so at home. That tie you sent me is certainly a very nice one, and I am very much obliged to you for sending it. All those things from home by the box, will be useful. You ask about Arch Taylor, well he is very well now, he is a very nice fellow; the Captain being away we have two tents, with raging fires, you know the wood costs the Government nothing, and accordingly we use a great deal of wood. We have nice tables in our tents. I hope some one will thank Charley Clark's Sisters[121] for me, and also letting them know, they may make more. It is a good idea to have linen about when you cut your finger, already I have found it useful. The reason why I have not written to Uncle Thomas is that I have been expecting him every day; I wish you could with him come down to camp. Every afternoon a contraband woman comes into camp with very nice apples. In my letter to Jos I have given an account of my experience in the Guard House as Officer of the Guard. After a while I wish you please make up another box, and get contributions from Uncle Thomas'. Remember me, to all my friends, also to our *worthy Parson* & wife.

*And give my love to all my relations.*

Your most affectionate Son.
Tom
2nd Lieut. Co I 3rd N.J. Inf
Col. Taylor

P.S. Give my love to Annie, Charley, Jos, Frank, and yourself.
Tom.

[Original]
3d Regiment N.J. Volunteer Inf'ty
Col. George W. Taylor, Commanding
Camp Fort Worth, Feb. 28th 1862

My dear Mother,
I can only write a few words we have received our marching orders. We are to be ready, so far as to leave on few minutes notice, only four wagons are allowed to each regiment, officers are allowed only a carpet-bag, which I have not, though I can get one. We will leave everything behind in the shape of tents &c. I will write again and answer all letters.

Give my love to all,
Your most affectionate Son
Tom.

[Original]
Camp Fort Worth,
March 5th 1862.

My dear Mother,
Your letter of the 2nd had arrived, and I, in a bad place, sit down to answer it, the bad place of which I speak is the guard house. I was Officer of the Guard yesterday, but go off this morning at nine o' clock. As Officer of the Guard, I have nothing to do but walk or sit about the Guard House, that is I have no hard work to perform. I can go to my meals and stay about half an hour; but under the pretence of visiting the guards, I can leave the guard-house at any time in the day. I read the papers and write letters, in fact that is about all I can do. It is against the regulations to go to sleep whilst on guard but at night—after "Grand Rounds" I get to sleep with a blazing fire in front of me. We can not take off our swords, but have to sleep with them on; neither can we take off our clothes, nothing but our caps. I have to make out a report which is very easy; but the best part of it is in marching back to our tents the whole drum and fife corps marches toward from the Guard House every morning; marches to with the rear guard and from with the old guard. It is pretty tough, but that is to be expected, I did not come to play soldier far from it: before this letter reaches you I may be moving with the regiment. Officers are allowed only twenty pounds of baggage; I shall have to get a carpet bag, I have bought one already, and take what is necessary only. I think I shall send my trunk to Alexandria or over to Head Quarters, I am prepared almost for any advance, having exchanged my republican sword, for a cavalry saber.

All I want is a revolver, and I am bound to have one too; I think it is very important for an officer to have something besides his sword. There have been great times in Alexandria, quite a large number of the most influential people have been arrested; some of our officers proposed that the 3rd N.J. Inf be sent there under the command of Col. Taylor. I know for my part I would give them rats;[122] well, after turning your back towards them they would run a bayonet into you; that town should have been burnt down long before this; I would like to burn it myself, now. I have not spoken about that *subject* in your letter in any of mine, I do not think it is safe. I like you to give me good counsel, it is very acceptable. We have not moved yet though we are ready.

We are expecting to move every hour[;] do not have any drills; had none yesterday (Tuesday). I should think Edward would do very well as a servant especially since he has on better clothes. Bob has a very nice boy named Jesse; he was a slave; the woman who washed his clothes was also a slave. Arch. Taylor is a fine fellow, as I have said in one of my last letters, he and I are just like brothers; I wish you could see him. I have a slight cold, but it is not much, I use the Troches and Gum-Arabic,[123] by the way all the gum-arabic is gone, if you could send me some, and some lozenges I would be much obliged to you. I have not had time to read Annie's letter, I will answer it soon, also Josh's. I wish Charlie would write. I have [not] written to any of Uncle James' family, neither have I had a letter from Minnie or Sarah. I shall write to Uncle Thomas to day. I can tell you Ma that when the army moves it will be a great thing. I have been acting 1st Lieutenant all the time, Arch will be Captain I expect soon. I believe I will have to cease.

Give my love to all—Annie, Charlie, Josh, Frank. Many kisses.

Your most affectionate Son
Tom
2nd Lieut. Co I 3rd N.J.

[Transcribed Copy]

Camp Fort Worth
March 6th 1862

My dear sister,
Your letter dated March 2nd 1861 came yesterday while I was officer of the guard. I wonder what you were thinking about when you wrote 1861. I do hope that Charlie will get a position on a Philadelphia paper of some sort. You speak of Miss Mary Harbert[124] having told you that our regiment was under marching orders. It is a fact but Col. Taylor thinks that we will not be off before Saturday or Monday. Company I, that is my company, is a good company. I expect in battle you will have a good account of us. Uncle Thomas has written and says he might get down here. I hope he will come. Please tell him that the sutler's wagon goes to and from Alexandria every day[;] also the roads are improving rapidly. He will have no difficulty I think in reaching here. You will also tell him that I must have a revolver. Jos had better see about it. Arch Taylor has three and a knife in his boot besides his sword. The other day when [C]ompany I was out on picket a squadron of them

came across the body of a man who had been buried but also had been dug out again. The man had his head, his hands, and his feet cut off. I think it probable that he was murdered. He was dressed in citizen's clothes. I will not say anything about Bob Dunham. You must be very careful. I do not want this letter read by anyone outside of our own family. I should like to come home for two or three days. I think I could tell you and the rest a very great deal of which you would be very much surprised. Please ask Ma to send me about a dollar's worth of stamps as I have very little money to carry me to pay day which will not be for a month to come. I shall send my trunk to Alexandria. In it are two white blankets and other things that I cannot take. All last night the troops were moving. We are ready to move at a moment's notice. We are expecting our tents of which we are to have over 400, that is a man carries one part and another man carries another part. They are only large enough for two men. That box has not arrived[,] the one from the young ladies. Remember me to them and all my friends, Dr Garrison[125] and the like. I have nothing to say about Mary[126] and that vulgar fellow, Higgins.[127] Give my love to all.

Your most loving brother
Tom

I have not heard from Minnie or Sam yet. I will send a large and better lock of my hair soon. It is not quite long enough.

[Transcribed Copy]

Camp Fort Worth
March 8th 1862

Dear Annie,
Jos spoke in his last letter about my letters not being full of interesting facts. Now to tell the truth there has been nothing very great transpiring here. I am glad you remembered about the *Arabian Nights* [italics added]. The book should have been sent home long ago but I neglected to do it. We have been under marching orders for two days. Do not expect to wait much longer. Two rooms have been prepared for the purpose of packing away the officers' baggage. I shall take out of my trunk what I want and then send the rest to St George's Hall.[128] Where that is I do not know. It may be in Alexandria. On Saturday Company I went out on the parade ground for drill. Arch commanded the first platoon, I the second. It was a pretty heavy drill. We know nothing about our movements as yet though we are ready. All prepared for a sudden move. Two days rations on hand. We drill morning and afternoon. Battalion, brigade and company drills. There is one thing I fear[,] that is that I may have to stay in camp in case of an advance to keep guard. Something that I am not very anxious to have happen. Please tell Jos that I have not been able to draw a plan of Ft. Worth yet. I have received Ma's letter of the 27th and Jos' of the 28th. I will answer as soon as I am able. Yesterday, Sunday, I am sorry to say that the soldiers of two or three companies were engaged in a friendly fight with snow-

balls. Arch is a very fine fellow. I like him the more I am with him. I think I will have to close for the present. I will write soon. Also I shall write to Uncle Thomas and to Uncle Ben.[129] Remember me to all my young lady friends. I have not received that box from Miss Summers.[130] I am very well and do not expect to get sick. You need not let anyone outside of the family see this letter on account of the writing.

Your most affectionate brother,
Tom

I will send that wagonload of my hair of which you spoke in your letter.

[Original]

Fairfax Court-House
March Wed. 11th 1862

My dear Mother,
I have after a long and tiresome march undertaken to write you a letter informing you of my movements. Your letter with Annie's and the *Stamps* inclosed came to hand yesterday. I will make some remarks on Annie's, to answer her questions. About showing my letters, all I want is that when I say things that ought not to be mentioned out, I hope care will be taken to keep them in the family. I was not able to take my wrapper with me. I have one blue blanket and my India Rubber,[131] left those two white ones on my trunk and I believe they are in Alexandria. The 4th N.J. Inf is in a field to our right and of course I do not see Dr. Harbert,[132] Henry Taylor[133] is in Gen. Hooker's division down the Potomac river.

I do not think Arch Taylor will be made Captain soon, neither will I have a bar on my straps yet. Annie speaks of picket duty, all the officers have to go out. I think I am liked by my men generally. I wish Frank would write to me about his progress at school. Now then to turn to the movements of the 3rd N.J. Inf; we staid at Fairfax Station[134] on Saturday night; on Sunday morning we advanced to Sangster's Station,[135] and rested there about two hours; we then with skirmishers out ahead, advanced again up the hills having a squadron of cavalry also in advance, just then one of the skirmishers came back and told Gen Kearney[136] that the enemy were only a little way ahead, where upon the cavalry were ordered to charge them, immediately they, headed by a handsome young 1st Lieutenant did charge the enemy, and scattered them to the four winds, but with the loss of their Lieutenant; about half an hour before, that officer passed me on his fine horse; the way in which he was shot was this, at the head of his command he gave the word to draw sabre, and then said "who dares to be a coward." [W]ith the order gallop he was in the midst of storm; they attempted to form a square but broke and fled as he came down on them; they had nearly two hundred men, we had thirteen cavalry, we took fourteen men and one officer (a 2nd Lieutenant) named Stewart more than our whole cavalry for it was a most brilliant affair, well we chased them away; it was my sight of a fight.[137] The enemy should have cut our cavalry to pieces but they would not do it. I will have to stop though I could write eight or nine pages about our march to *Manassas*.[138]

The 3rd NJ. Inf was the first regiment there. Col. Taylor pushed us on till we were almost tired to death but we were paid for it; he raised the *American flag* on a large fort at Manassas Junction. I will write to Annie or Jos and give an account of our march from Sangsters Station [to] Manassas.

Much love to Charley Annie, Jos, Frank, all of Uncle Thomas' Family, and yourself. He can send me a revolver by directing it to me in the care of Mr. William J. Taylor[139] Sutler 3rd N.J. Inf.

Tom

[Transcribed Copy]
Fairfax Courthouse [VA]
March 15th 1862

Dear Brother,
I will commence where I left off in Ma's letter. That little fight was quite exciting, being the first I was ever in. It was all General Kearney's and Col Taylor's work though. The order was to advance to Fairfax Station but the General ordered Col Taylor to go on to Sangster's Station, which instruction the Col was only too glad to carry out. By the way on Friday morning of last week, I guess it was the fifth of March, We left Burk[e's] Station,[140] that is Company I and one or two others[,] to go out on Picket. Company I was stationed on a hill along the railroad hardly a mile from Fairfax Station. We were the advanced pickets[,] more being outside of us, the enemy being about a quarter of a mile from where we were. Arch Taylor saw them and when he took out a squad of men to picket to the right of our position. The next morning Saturday, I guess it was about eight, I went up the railroad with four of my men to see what was to be seen. The men had their muskets ready for the enemy or anybody else. We walked along a short distance and I told them to keep quiet for I did not know but that I might meet some of the enemy or that they might hear the noise and come upon us unawares. Although I had made up my mind that if we were attacked I would show my men and also the enemy what I was and what I was made of and that they had Howell blood to contend with. Well we kept on til we reached Fairfax Station, six houses, a railroad station, a store. Having stationed a man on the platform we disbursed to see what we could find. On returning to the platform we found that we had quite a number of things, among them two bags of corn. I was going to empty it in a brook but on second thought I took it with me to feed the horses of the regiment.

Saturday March 15th.
Last night, Friday, our brigade marched from Fairfax Courthouse to the Camp Fort Worth over 15 miles, and arrived at Camp at about 2 in the morning. Well it was like getting back home again but our leaving

Fairfax broke up my letter, I not having time to finish it. At one o'clock we leave for the south to join General Burnside's army.[141] It is raining and possibly we will not leave. But I shall send this letter anyhow. We have been almost marched to death the last five days. But we were payed by being the first regiment in Manassas. We have seven of their flags, almost every soldier has a sword or a dirk.[142]

Your most affectionate brother
Tom

[Transcribed Copy]
[Camp Fort Worth]
[March 15th 1862]

My dear mother,
I did not say in my letter to Jos that Uncle had been to Fairfax and that I had seen him. When we left camp we little thought that our regiment would be ordered back to this camp but it is the case nevertheless. Before this letter reaches you our regiment, brigade and division may be on its way down the river to attack the enemy on the Virginia shore at some point not known and then you will hear of some tremendous fighting! The 69th N.Y.[143] is also going. But then again we may not get off for two or three days. I suppose we are going to get on the rear of the enemy which if done will be the cause [of] or will bring on some of the greatest battles this country ever witnessed. I shall put my whole trust in God for I will need his help pretty soon if I never did before[,] which of course is not the case[,] for everyone needs the help of God. I hope that amidst the many dangers that will surround me I may be protected from them all and also may have the prayers of those at home. I think that there has been a determination to drive the enemy from the Virginia shore altogether. There are nearly 100 steamers in Alexandria to take our expedition down the river. To drive the enemy from the river will be at the expense of hundreds of lives. I have exchanged my dark blue overcoat for Mr Taylor's, he's the sutler Arch's brother,[144] a sky blue one. I did exchange with one of the privates but took mine back. I was sorry not being able to carry Jos' letter out for our march was a very interesting one on account of its length. I thought it was about 800 miles. Well, it was hard to advance to Manassas and then fall back to our camp three miles from Alexandria. The afternoon of the day we reached Manassas we received our orders from General Franklin[145] to fall back to Fairfax. When we reached Centreville[146] we had an order from General McClellan[147] to push on and overtake the enemy who as they retreated burned bridges after them but the order came too late. I am glad to hear that Charlie has a position in Philadelphia.[148] Ma you must excuse me for not writing more than I have the last week or so but I have been so busy marching etc that I have had but little time to write. Our expedition is a large one. From 50 to 60,000 troops maybe more maybe less but they are coming in all the time. As for my health I am very well except for a slight cold that is now almost

gone. Our regiment will follow Col Taylor's wheresoever he takes it into his head to lead us. I wish you would remember me to all my friends and give my love to all my relations. I do not know when we will be payed off, soon I hope.

Your most affectionate son
Tom

P.S. I shall send my trunk home soon as I do not need it, as we are going to have some severe fighting soon I think. I wish you would please pray for the safety of Arch Taylor, Bob Dunham and myself.

[Transcribed Copy]

Camp Fort Worth
March 19th 1862

My dear sister,
It is thought that we may leave this morning. If we do I will write a few words and send them home to let you all know where I am going. Arch and I are all right on the provision question from Mr. W. J. Taylor the sutler. He will take plenty of the good things of life with him so you see we wont starve, that is certain. I can hardly believe that we have been to Manassas but it seems as though we had never left camp. We are having beautiful weather, just the right kind for March. All our ammunition and provisions are on board the steamers. Colonel Taylor and in fact all the Colonels of our divisions were down in Alexandria yesterday morning to examine the steamers in which we are to embark. If the enemy stay where they are now and we attack them[,] I am pretty certain that blood will flow. I hope that I will not have the luck to be shot. It is not my style. But I think that those at war should have the prayers of those at home. I was officer of the guard yesterday and it was certainly a beautiful yesterday. My being officer of the guard kept me from brigade drill[,] something I do not like much on account of the trouble and fatigue. But I will have enough of that before I am out of the service. Have you heard anything from Miss Lizzie Rogers? In as few words as possible, have you heard of her from Annie Carpenter in the last few days? I wish you would remember me to Miss Mary Harbert, the two Miss Dunhams[149] and all the rest. I do not think of anything else at present except that you will get Annie Carpenter to remember me to Miss Lizzie and also to Aunt Sarah. Give my love to all, Ma, Charlie, Jos and Frank.

Your most affectionate brother,
Tom

P.S. I am very well now, growing some, I think. I should like to see my sweet sister once more. T.

[Transcribed Copy]

Camp Fort Worth
March 21st 1862

Dear Jos,

Having finished Annie's letter I think I can manage to write to you about matters and things in our regiment therefore I hope I have not exhausted myself on dear Annie's epistle. There has been a court marshal in here for the last two or three days. The Major[150] was presiding and three or four were tried and one was sentenced to stand on a barrel for twenty days. That is, he would attend all the drills but all the time that he was not so occupied he was obliged to take his lofty stand. Besides he has a string around his neck to which was attached a board on which was written the word "dirty" because he was the most unclean person in Company C. Captain Buckley.[151] Then there is another who has to wear a ball and chain on his leg from nine A.M. to one P.M. each day and every afternoon he has to have hard labor as his portion. This morning I saw to the putting on of his chain. Dr. Cox,[152] our surgeon, is in arrest for treason which comes from the fact the Dr. went with a flag of truce into the enemy lines after the battle of Bull Run[,] and while in the enemy's camp he met a friend and told this friend that when he wrote home to give his, Cox', love to his relations. Well, Dr. Cox's friend wrote the letter and told the relations that the Dr. had been in their camp and had sent his love to them. This old letter was found at Manassas.[153] So the Dr. is arrested and tried for treason but I think he will be released in a few days.[154] There is a guard over his tent which is sealed. The Dr. had a rumpus, you know, and I think that maybe Collett has been playing the opossum on Dr. Cox. It is now nearly half past twelve o'clock and I cannot go to sleep until after grand rounds which happens any time after twelve. As soon as Capt. Buckley goes on the rounds I am going to throw myself down in my blankets and go to sleep. I cannot take off my sword but sleep with it on. I shall try and sleep til morning at any rate. I do not suppose Charlie can write having his time so much taken up. I am very well.

Give my love to all. Remember me to all the young ladies.

Your affectionate brother
Tom

P.S. I send you this song by our chaplain who is not worth a darn. I would not hear him preach for a considerable sum of money. He is not liked by the men at all. His name is Darrow.[155] I wish that he had stayed where he came from. Remember me to Mart and tell him he has not answered my letter yet. Also remember me to Will and Bob Potts,[156] also to Mrs Gray.[157]

[Original]

Camp Fort Worth,
Mar. 22nd [18]62

My dear Mother,
After having some sleep, I find that I am much refreshed in "mind, body, soul and estate." It is about half past nine, Saturday night, and

"The Rough Life of a Soldier" 49

after the toils of the day, I am rather tired; please to tell Jos that if he wishes to exercise his voice, he had better take command of a company, and put that company through the bayonet exercise for two hours; that is what I did this morning, the Captain of Co. H[158] being Officer of the Day, and his 1st Lieut.[159] being off duty, the company has no 2nd Lieut. I was yet asked by Bob Dunham to take charge of said company. Upon returning from drill I received Annie's letter with your little note enclosed, which I will answer, also yours of the 12th and 20th of Mar. There is one thing certain, I shall not, as you say, be foolhardy, and run into danger heedlessly, but when duty calls, I shall not think of danger; now this morning while drilling company H, I had just ordered "rest," where *"whisp"* went a bullet past me; it came from a soldier shooting down below the hill; I wish you could hear a ball go through the air, one is not apt to forget the sound in a hurry[;] it reminds me of a child crying. Yesterday afternoon (Friday) I was out about a mile with a fatigue party cutting wood for the camp, I merely looking on, seeing that the men kept at their work; well it so happened that Gen. Kearney ordered the Brigade out for target firing, and the 4th regiment came over where my men were stationed, and putting up targets commenced firing into the hills on which the men were at work, three of the men came very near being shot, so I beat a hasty retreat and ordered the fatigue party back into camp. I suppose you know that our Division was reviewed by Gen. McClellan on Wednesday afternoon. I saw the *man* and was very much pleased with his appearance, he is not handsome, nor is he very homely, but half and half. As he came up towards Col. Taylor he bowed gracefully to him[,] at which the Col. Raised his cap; and one of the staff said "that is Col. Taylor." Col. Taylor was the only Col. to whom Gen. McClellan spoke on Wednesday. It was really a beautiful sight. Gen. McClellan said to Franklin, that our Brigade could compete with any this side of the Potomac, I think before this letter reaches you our Division will have left, we are going along very well, have no cold, eat a great deal, and taking all things into consideration, I think I will do. I shall answer Annies letter immediately; I have not had a letter from Jos for three or four days, and none from Charley since I have been in the service. I am glad to hear that Frank is getting along so well at school. Give my love to Annie, Charley, Jos, Frank. I shall write again soon.

Your most affectionate son
Tom

[Transcribed Copy]
Camp Fort Worth
March 24th 1862

Dear Annie,
Before the mail closes I will have time to answer your letter and say something more. To begin with, Sutler Taylor is about one of the best men living. It is only because of my being a friend of Arch's and Arch's

doing that I was permitted to take my meals at the sutler's. I eat just as much as I please for only $15.00 a month, which is only about 53 [cents] a day. I like the sutler very much. His wife has been down here several times. I was pleased with her. By the way, Arch wrote to his sister, Charlotte,[160] and told her I would exchange my picture for hers. I have not received hers yet nor do I expect to get it. If we had known that we would leave Manassas so soon we might have brought away many valuable things but you see our departure was sudden and unexpected. That certainly was a funny mistake of Jos about all the colonels of our division being drowned. On Saturday[,] 15 thousand men of our division went down the river in steam boats.[161] I suppose their destination was Fortress Monroe.[162] The whole Army of the Potomac with the exception of General Banks army will go the same way.[163] We may not go today but if we do I will write immediately. General McClellan is also going with the army. In all our heavy marching, from this camp to Manassas and back I did not give out and fall behind the regiment once. Many of the men did. Well I think I will do [well] in the marching and I hope I will get along in the fighting, though I tell you, I felt like falling out of line and resting by the roadside. Then I thought that the officers should set the men a good example, that if I gave out the men would think that they had an equal right so I kept on and did not think of fatigue but only when we would stop for the night. Wouldn't I sleep! Here I am now, safe and sound, my feet alright and I ready for another long march. Wish you would give my love to Aunt Sarah Stratton the next time you see her. Also tell Aunt Rebecca[164] not to get jealous on account of the progress of Frank. It is really something disgusting and very much like Aunt. I am very much pleased with Frank's success and I hope that he will keep ahead of James Carpenter.[165] Yesterday afternoon, Sunday, there was a funeral. It was of an artillery soldier. Yesterday morning while walking across to the company parade I noticed one of General Kearney's aides on his horse at the lower edge of the parade. It was at reveille. As soon as the drums had ceased to beat he rode off. It turned out that General Kearney sent his aides to all the regiments to see if all the officers turned out at reveille and it was found that in the 1st Regiment only four officers came out with their companies. In the 2nd Regiment some of the officers did not appear so the general sent for the Colonels and gave them thunder. Lt. Barnard[166] was the aide sent to our regiment. He returned and reported; "All right!" Reveille was changed from half past six to six. General Kearney wanted to see how the men and officers got up in the morning[,] whereupon the General sent his aide over to Colonel Taylor who told him that General Kearney sent his compliments and was glad to find that the good order and military discipline was still kept up. So you see we are the 3rd New Jersey yet first in everything. I am very well. Give my love to inquiring friends. Give my love to Ma, Charley, Jos and Frank and a certain very sweet sister. Ask Jos what he thinks of my handwriting.

Your most affectionate brother

Tom

[Transcribed Copy]

March 26th 1862

Dear Annie,

Your letter arrived yesterday noon. I received it as soon as I came in from brigade drill though I did not find time to read it until late this afternoon. And tonight being at a table by a warm fire in the guard house I am officer of the guard, again. But before I go on I will tell you that I volunteered because I have a wholesome dread of commanding the guard when we move. I have been caught that way before. Therefore I am not anxious for it to happen soon again. Well, I thought that this would be a good time to answer your letter. I did think that letter writing was entirely stopped but I am very glad that such is not the case. My trunk is safe at home you say. It is better to have it there than in Alexandria. I kept the key not knowing how to send it home. As for that wrapper it is packed up in one of Arch's boxes or in my box. I am sorry that I brought it with me and if I can I will send it home for it will be far more useful there than here. As for that valentine I wish you to take good care of it. I wonder if it is not from Miss Lizzie. I hardly think it is. You will let me know if you find out. I am pleased that Uncle has bought me a revolver. If he directs it to the care of Wm. Taylor, Alexandria, Va 3rd N.J. Infantry I will get it soon. About Bob having sent a letter. He told me the other morning that he had written a long letter at which I was very much surprised of course. You mentioned having heard a fine sermon from Dr. Newton.[167] I should like to be home once more and hear him myself. I suppose you saw a report of the fine review on Tuesday afternoon by General McDowell.[168] It was certainly a great affair. There were between 30 and 40 thousand men on the grounds. The 3rd N.J. regiment looked better than any regiment on the field and General Kearney complimented Lt. Col. Brown on the fine appearance and marching of our regiment. Well the 3rd did march right up to the mark. There seemed to be no end to the artillery, cavalry and infantry. In the morning at ten A.M. we went out to brigade drill and when we were going through a certain movement General Kearney who was right near our front ranks said, "Very fine, very fine. Elegant. Elegant." So you see we get all the praise. You must remember that we deserve it! Our division will not leave til the last. General McClellan is going with us so we will not get off for some little time yet. My collars I use but the cuffs I have given away because I cannot use them and they would only be in the way. I have not been in Alexandria since the day I passed through to join my regiment. I am very well in mind, body and estate. I do not know the exact time of pay day although I have heard that it is next week. Col. Taylor and Bob have been to Manassas and beyond alone on horseback. I remember now and tell you that I had command of the company on Tuesday afternoon at the review. General McClellan and wife[169] were there besides many other distinguished officers. Bare it in mind that I do not call General

McClellan's wife an officer. Give my love to all inquiring friends, young ladies. I do not know whether I can get Jos letter off tonight. I am writing to him. Give my love to Ma, Charlie, Jos and Frank.

Your most affectionate brother
Tom

[Original]

Camp Fort Worth
March 28th

Dear Ma,
I received your letter yesterday (Thursday) noon, but could not answer till this morning, the mail leaves at eight, so I cannot write much. We had another large Review yesterday, our, Franklin's Division and Gen King's.[170] The troops marched like stone walls, Gen. McClellan, Gen. Franklin, Lord Lyons,[171] Gen. King and many others were there. They are going to give us enough Reviews anyhow. I am glad that Charley has something to do now, when you see him give my love to him, I shall write to day or tomorrow to him.

I am very well. We are having beautiful weather now. Remember me to all; Give my love to Charley, Annie, Jos and Frank.

Your most loving and affectionate Son
Tom.
2nd Lieut Co I 3rd N.J. Inf.

[Transcribed Copy]

Camp Fort Worth
March 29th 1862

Dear Annie,
On returning from brigade drill yesterday afternoon, your letter was given to me but I have not had time to answer it until tonight. It is nearly ten but I was determined to write to you no matter how tired I might be. I had command of Co. H yesterday morning. I think I carried them through pretty well considering all things. In the afternoon we went out about a mile to fire at a target. Each fired ten rounds. I was with a corporal about thirty feet from the target and of course I heard the bullets as they went ringing past at double quick time I can tell you. All today it has been snowing and raining. I was up with my fatigue party when it commenced. After a while I ordered them in. When we were marching off the field yesterday, brigade drill, we were marching by divisions front, that is two companies in a line; well as [we] were marching by General Kearney he remarked to General Birney,[172] "That third is a very fine regiment, a very fine regiment." We get all the praise of course. While I think of it I will mention that General McClellan left for Alexandria this afternoon, Saturday, with his whole staff, guards and baggage. I think that Minnie, now that she is staying in our part of the country[,] could write to me also Jos. Allow me to tell you,

Annie, letters are very acceptable. Tomorrow morning, Sunday, there will be a skirmish drill from 7 til 9. I think that we are going pretty soon. This afternoon at the request of Bob Dunham I ordered the men to cut wood for the field officers, Taylor, Brown and Dunham so two men from company A, and one Corporal from Co. I went to work. Well pretty soon Vickers[173] went down to the wood pile and ordered the men back to their tents, that is his men. So having found out what had happened I immediately went to the colonel and informed him of it. He told me to tell Capt. Vickers that he wanted to see him. So Vickers went to the Colonel's and pretty soon back went the men. So much for walking over the orders of a fatigue party for I can order those men to do anything I want. Nor has Vickers or any other officer the right to interfere. I have taken the names of the two men and have the whole transaction in my head for I think Vickers will get rats[174] from the colonel. Bob advised me to be ready in case I am called on. There is a company of Indians with an Indian band too.[175] They arrived this afternoon. I have not been to Alexandria yet nor do I intend to see myself there if I can help it. I believe I have exhausted my news now and therefore I will stop. I write you to remember me to Miss Mary Harbert also all the other young ladies. Give love to Aunt Rebecca, in fact to all relations. I wish Ma could send me another box of good things etc. Give my love to Ma, Charlie, Jos and Frank.

Your most loving brother
Tom

P.S. The stock of the 3rd is very high now I would like you to know. Colonel Taylor is the senior colonel in General McDowell's army [corps]. A great thing, you know. My health is extensive, in other words it's good. I hope to give a good account of myself when it comes to fighting. I do not believe that I will get that box from Miss Annie Summers.

    Arch Taylor is a fine boy. I send Col. Taylor's picture. Arch is going to give me his. He gave me the Colonel's. He is a very heavy fellow. I am much obliged for the postage stamps.

[Original]

Camp Fort Worth
Mon. Mar 31st

Dear Ma,
Your letter came yesterday (Sunday) noon, and I will say what I have [to] say which is not much. One Saturday while out with my fatigue party it commenced to snow very hard, it seemed very odd, so after standing it as long as possible I ordered them in. All Sunday it rained late in the afternoon and till about ten in the evening there were thunder storms all around. We will be paid off on Wednesday I think and by Saturday or Monday we will I believe be on the Potomac. McDowells Army Corps has commenced to embark to day, and it will not be long before we follow.[176] We have our orders how everything is

to be carried on on shipboard. There is an Artillery regiment down below Fort Worth, they are there to defend it, well a company of New York Indians with a band arrived there[;] they are to form apart of the regiment of Artillery[.] I am very well in *"mind"* body, soul and estate. As far as I know it is very well here, at present no news of any kind. Yesterday morning (Sunday) an order came from Gen. Kearney to drill skirmish drill for two hours, from seven until nine o'clock, fortunately it rained and saved me from a unpleasant drill, not that the drill itself is unpleasant, but the state of the ground was very. It is Monday morning and I have not received my revolver, if Mr. Markley[177] is in Washington I will get [it] I suppose. I shall try to get the wrapper and send it home. Give my love to Aunts Sarah and Anna Carpenter, also to Minnie, remember me to Dr. Garrison and wife. Give my love to Annie, Charley, Jos, Frank,

Your most affectionate son
Tom.
2nd Lieut, Co. I, 3rd N.J. Vol. Inf
I shall answer Jos letter Some time to day

[Transcribed Copy]
Camp Fort Worth
Wednesday, April 2nd 1862

Dear Jos,
Last night I wrote to Charlie and I suppose it will get to him at about the same time this will. See that he gets it if he is not at home. Uncle Thomas' letter came yesterday noon in which he speaks about things in general. He says he sent the revolver by Mr. Markley[,] who will get Mr. Alison[178] to convey it to me. If he does not I will remember it. I will say that Mr. Alison through Mr. Taylor, the sutler, will pay us, the officers, off today. The major will pay the troops tomorrow. Mr. Taylor is an intimate friend of the major's and the major allows Mr. Taylor to pay the officers off first for it is easing the major, he coming in a hurry and wants to pay off as soon as possible. We will be paid by Taylor today. Mr. Taylor said that next month he would pay the regiment off himself but it will take over 36,000 dollars. He can do it with ease. I tell you that these sutlers or at least a good many are making a great deal of money though Mr. Taylor told me of some sutlers who were going to ruin. Then again he spoke of a certain division sutler who was making over a thousand dollars a day, a rather large amount, I would like you to notice! That last term is very much used now by the officers. I was officer of the guard yesterday thereby escaping drill morning and afternoon. Skirmish drill is the only drill at present. On Monday we went out in the morning for regimental skirmish drill so when we reached our drill ground we sent out one half of the regiment on skirmishes and reserves. Arch Taylor commanded the first platoon, the skirmishers. I the second, the reserves. Well the skirmishers would advance and fire their cartridges and then retreat and rally on the left group and rally by

*"The Rough Life of a Soldier"*

fours and rally by section and rally by platoon and rally on the reserves at the left. I immediately order fixed bayonets, break off, a four files from right and left to the rear making as it were a square or the incomplete side of a square, I then charged bayonets. Meanwhile the skirmishers take the double quick[,] in fact run as fast as they can. They break off to the right and left so as to uncover the front of the reserves. I then give a volley while the skirmishers form in behind the reserve. Then we deploy again and so on. After a while we rally on the batallion and then the other half goes out. This drill is very exciting when they can fire as fast as the enemy. I think that Dr. Cox will get off soon, as soon as he can, and he will give Major Collett something not very pleasant I can tell you![179] I suppose Gert[180] is rushing around pretty generally or is she more of a lady now? If you want to you may remember me to her though don't put yourself to any trouble. I don't think that I told you that that young lady who was in on McDowell's staff last Wednesday at the great revue last week, she was secretary Chase's daughter and a swell looking young lady she is too.[181] You will please tell Will Potts that I have been so busy lately that I have not had time to write to any outside my own family but I will try to answer his letter either today or tomorrow. Please tell Aunt Rebecca that nothing would please me more than to get a letter from Sue or Annie[182] and you will not forget to give my love to Aunt Sue[183] and tell James that he might write too, for I get letters from Charlie de Haven[184] and Richard Stickney.[185] Arch Taylor used to study three hours a day on short hand. He says that the phonographic prayer book and testament are not to be had, that it is the old editions for love nor money. The way he obtained his was by stealing it from his teacher so he told me. Everything goes on as usual here in camp. I am well and would like to be home for two days but as I cannot do that will write. Tell Sue that I would answer her letters regularly if she were to write. Remember me to all my friends. Give my love to Ma, Annie, Charlie and Frank.

I am your most affectionate brother
Tom

[Transcribed Copy]
Camp Fort Worth.
Wednesday April 2nd 1862

Dear Annie,
After written to Jos and Charlie I think it time to answer your letters[,] which business I find very pleasant. I can tell you, although I do not believe there is much to say, we will see, there may be more than I think. There has been a great deal of amusement lately on account of a little boy who was in the drum corps.[186] He is no larger than George Browning,[187] in fact a very small boy is he. Well, he is a very good drummer and as the drum major said he is an ornament to the Corps. It is amusing to see him march. He has to take such long steps. At reveille and retreat he creates quite a sensation, everyone stopping to gaze at

him. This boy will make a better drummer as he grows up. I don't believe there is a finer drum corps in our whole division. I wish you could hear it once. I don't think you would forget it soon. When the drum and fife corps, being at the head of the regiment which marched to the music, I tell you there is no describing the feeling one has. I don't wonder that General Kearney praises our regiment as he does. It is a fine sight to see our regiment march by company front. You speak of General McClellan's wife. I did not see her though she was there. Your letter with Ma's enclosed came at noon. I was very much pleased to get it or rather them. General McClellan has gone to Fortress Monroe where from what I hear he will be with the army. Bob went to Washington this afternoon to see about getting the rifles for our regiment.[188] Minnie owes me a letter and I wish you would get her to send it. Charlotte's brother Arch was in the skirmish but the Colonel's son, Arch, is not with the regiment. There was no drill today so I had the whole day to myself. Will Taylor's wife[189] was in camp all this afternoon. I did not see her for I was trying to get some sleep. Mr. Taylor paid off the officers. My expenses have been very heavy and I can only send home between 30 and 40 dollars. I shall not keep one cent of it myself. As soon as you get this letter answer it so that I may know whether you have received the money. I shall send in this 10 dollars. If I can I will send Ma's letter tomorrow before the mail closes at 8 in the morning. I will try to give her some account of what I have had to spend. Remember me to all and give my love to Ma and Jos and Charlie and Frank.

Your most loving bro
Tom

I wish you would give me some kind of description of Gert Browning, not that I like that young lady very much

[Original]

Camp Fort Worth,
Wed. Apr 2nd 1'62

My dear Ma,
As I said in Annie's letter I was pleased at receiving your letter, inclosed *with* Annies. I shall make search for that *wrapper*, because it was packed away in a box of Arch Taylor's, and I think the box was sent to Alexandria the day after we left camp for Manassas. If I find it I will send it home, I know that it is perfectly safe; the regiment is paid off tomorrow (Thursday). Lieut Spencer of Co. C[,] whose position I now hold, had a servant[,] a soldier of the company, well every officer has to pay 24 dollars and twenty-six cents a month to his servants, who gets besides this his regular pay, between having to pay for two months, I have my board at the Sutlers, also I had to get boots, one new pair were so small and hurt my feet so much, that the morning after I arrived at Centreville, I was obliged to give them away for a pair of shoes, now I have just bought another pair of boots, but they are so large, that they

cannot hurt me. Then for washing, and for many little things that add up [to] make a large amount. I will not have to pay for servant next month at all and if I had only known more, I would not have had to pay a cent, I will be able to send home thirty-five dollars, next month or for March and April I will let you have nearly the whole amount of my pay. Mr. Taylor did not bring my revolver to day, I suppose he will tomorrow. All those *tracts*, papers, and Testaments have been taken by the men. The weather now is very cold and damp. I am very well, and hope you will write on getting this letter with the two *five dollar* bills.

You will please give my love to all Minnie, Annie, Charley, Jos, and Frank[,] Uncle Thomas' and Edwards[190] families Aunt Sarah, in fact all my relations.

Your most affectionate son
Tom.
2nd Lieut, Co. I 3rd N.J. Inf.
Fort Worth near Alexandria

[Original]

Camp Fort Worth,
Fri. Apr 4th 1862

My dear Ma,
It is about one o'clock at night, and I am up yet. Well the truth of the matter is, that we are going to march tomorrow back to Manassas, I suppose that we will go in the cars. The order came this morning, so we are not going to Fortress Monroe as first order said. This letter reaches you on Monday morning, we will be in Manassas by the time and twenty miles beyond; I have the revolver, and am very much obliged to Uncle for it. You will please direct the letters to follow the regiment. I have everything I want, am very well.

Give my love to Annie, Charley, Jos and Frank.

Your most affectionate son
Tom
2nd lt. Co. I, 3rd N.J. Inf

[Original]

Camp Colvins Station
Fri Apr 11th 1'62

Dear Ma,
We have been so much occupied that I have had no time to write to you. The last few days have been the worst, that I have passed through since being in the Army; on account of the weather; it was nothing but snow, hail and rain until Thursday morning—early. We are stationed now at Colvin's Station, sometimes called Catlett's,[191] on the "Orange and Alexandria Rail Road." This Station is only four miles from the town of Warrington or Warrenton.[192] Our camp is in a large field, which I call a mud hole; it is rather low a [sic] of course when it rains;

we get plenty of water. Everything is mud outside of the little tents of the soldiers; they have logs of wood, small branches of pine trees and straw for their beds, so you see they get along very well. Arch and I have an officers tent, and with a fire in front at night we get along very well. There is one thing certain on Monday, Tuesday and Wednesday my spirits went down double quick, it was so cold that after coming in to the tent we would just pull off our boots, then roll ourselves in the blankets and stay that [way] all the morning, after noon and night. I did pity the poor men who would gather around the fire in their overcoats, with the rain pouring down upon them, and shaking with the cold; but it was the same way with your *soldier Son*; I am not afraid to live as my men, that is, in the provision line, I can live in hard crackers and a cup of coffee or bread and ham or a corn cake and coffee, the corn cake I get at any of the farm houses about. The whole Brigade is encamped in the field; Over to the right beyond the railroad, there are fields containing, some of them over three hundred acres; again there is a field of four hundred acres, which lot of ground is covered with the most beautiful green, it is grain, about a half of a foot above ground; you can picture to yourself such a sight. Those are large fields too. The country around about where we are is generally flat, but as we get towards Warrington, it is more hill country than any thing else. I have been around the country here, and I guess the people are mostly rebels, I never go without my revolver. I will not write anything, in the letter about our leaving from Camp Fort Worth to our present camp, but will put it, the account, in my letter to Annie. I shall try and make my epistles as interesting as possible. There is one thing you can do for me more my dear Ma, that is to get to me a small box, and send me about four pairs of those blue stockings, and pair of strong walking shoes just like Jos'. He knows what I want; the shoes must be a little longer than his, also the soles must be wide. I can't get along with the boots, they are too warm altogether. They have cost me now more than I can afford. If you could send me some more of *that writing paper*, also some envelopes, we can not get those things in this part of the country; in fact there is nothing to be had. Beautiful land, exceedingly fine grain land, *but it is there*, and that is all. I have been to half of a dozen places, and have asked for this and that but the only answer I can get is *"it is all gone."* I have seen quite enough of the *Sacred soil* of Va. Such a class of people, they are not fit to live. I think that we will march to Warrington by Sunday or Monday though we may move tomorrow, Saturday. You will please have all letters directed as before, but be sure and put upon them the words *"Follow the Regiment."* Please send the box, and direct it to the *care* of *Thomas Harris, Postmaster of the* 3rd N.J. Inf.[193] It will go by *Adams Express* to *Capt. Bush*[194] the *Agent* at Alexandria, where *Harris* will get it. I am sorry to put you to so much trouble and expense. I thought I would have been able to have sent more of my pay home but I could not, I only retained fifteen dollars to furnish myself with provisions, which is not over large when it has to do until the 1st of May, the next pay day. I will be paid for two months by the first of May[;] two thirds of my pay I will send home for certain. It could not be expected that a young officer would know how to spend money the first month he had been in the service, at least that is my opinion and I have found it to be the case though I will own that one can spend more than another, now Arch Taylor not having any use for his money at home spends every cent of it on himself he is not at all mean, but he likes to spend money any how. I like to spend or *waste* money you may call it as much as anyone but then I know I have a Mother, Sister and little or rather a young brother to help support, so without being *mean*, for I hate that, I can *use* and *send* home. Annies letter came on Tuesday, it was dated Saturday Apr 6th[;] I shall answer it this afternoon. I am here *reclining* on our bed; Arch sound asleep at my left side; I have my boots off and also my coat, in other words taking it easy; my spirits which on Wednesday were about two hundred below, are now higher than a five story house. I will own that I suffered some on Tuesday and Wednesday, also the night sleeping with wet feet, but I am very well, and used now to hard fare and the rough life of a soldier generally[.] I will like to have a few white hankerchiefs; for as we go South, when the young ladies appear I want to appear more than so, so. I have not had the time to write to Uncle Thomas yet, you will have to explain it to him, I should like to hear from Charley, more from Jos and from you dear Ma. It is quite cold at night, but pretty warm in the day time. I am very well[;] all I want now, is to have more sun. I like to have warm nights and days, while I am a soldier, I can take cold weather at home in the winter.

Saturday Apr 12th
Yesterday noon as I was writing the letter an orderly came and told me that I was to report immediately to the Officer of the day (Capt. Vicars), so I had to stop. Well with thirty men I was ordered to the Station House only about a quarter of a mile down the rail road to unload the cars. While there, I heard Gen Franklin say to one of his *Staff* that the New Jersey Brigade would move at four o'clock. Gens Franklin and McDowell were standing only about thirty feet off to my left; on hearing the news I can tell you that I left my fatigue party, and went back to camp double quick, ordered my things collected together, then I went back to the Station House. Four came, the drums beat, and the regiment fell in, and marched down the railroad on their way back to Bristoe Station,[195] eight or nine miles from Colvins or Catletts Station. As soon as the fatigue party had finished their work, we fell in with our guards, who brought up the rear of the regiment [W]ell we marched back to Bristoe Station[,] reached it at half past ten (last night) and encamped. I sit in front of my camp fire hearing my men tell their stories, and did not go to bed until half past two exactly; I slept only about two hours and a half for reveille beat at half past four or a quarter to five this morning[;] that is a soldiers life. It is now nearly eleven o'clock on this (Saturday) morning, and a beautiful day it is. I am seated on several knapsacks by the railroad waiting for the cars to come along. The Third Regiment had orders to march back to Fairfax Court House, they left their knapsacks here at the Station with a guard of one man from each

company and an officer. I obtained permission of Col. Taylor to ride in the cars all the way to Alexandria, and go right on board of the transports. We will be off by one, and get in Alexana. By four this afternoon.

You need not send that box until I let you know, I shall write to Annie and Jos. Yesterday I received all the letters. Several were dated Monday Apr 5th or Tuesday and I only received them yesterday noon, so a regular correspondence, which I should like above all things. Give my love to all Uncle Thomas family and everybody generally. I received Annie Carpenters letter which I shall answer; also Uncle's.

Give my love to Annie, Charlie, Jos and Frank

Your most loving son,
Tom

[Original]

Camp at Alexandria
Tuesday Apr 15th '62

Dear Ma,
We are now encamped at Alexandria or out at the end of one of its streets. I expect the Colonel will give me permission to [go] into town this morning; for I have to get a pair of shoes and several other things which will be useful on a voyage.[196] I arrived in Alexa. on Sunday night, upon the cars. We will probably get off tomorrow or next day. It is breakfast time and as I owe Annie and Jos letters I will give you a short letter and send long ones to them. Give my love to Annie, Charlie, Jos and Frank, also, many kisses to yourself and Annie.

Your loving son
Tom
2nd Lieut. Co. I, 3rd NJ Inf.

## NOTES

1. The purpose of the visits to Virginia by Thomas Preston Carpenter is unknown. According to a pass he received on June 10, 1861, he was given permission to cross the Alexandria Bridge and enter Union lines, but the extent of that visit is not known. Thomas P. Carpenter, Pass to Cross Alexandria Bridge, June 10, 1861. CW-2, Civil War Records, Box 6, GCHS.

2. Ezra J. Warner, *Generals in Blue: Lives of the Union Commanders* (Baton Rouge: Louisiana State University Press, 1992), 493–94.

3. George W. Taylor to Gov. Charles S. Olden, January 30, 1862. Record Group–Department of Defense, Adjutant General's Office, Civil War, 1861–1865, Regimental Records 1861–1865, 3rd Regiment, Box 6, Folder 30, New Jersey State Archives, Trenton, New Jersey.

4. Louis Henry Carpenter to Mother, February 13, 1862. Carpenter Family Papers (#0115), HSP.

5. Louis Henry Carpenter to Annie Carpenter, February 17, 1862. Carpenter Family Papers (#0115), HSP.

6. Carpenter and Carpenter, *Samuel Carpenter and His Descendants*, 127.

7. Ibid., 127–28.

8. Warner, *Generals in Blue*, 240.

9. William J. Jackson, *New Jerseyans in the Civil War: For Union and Liberty* (New Brunswick, NJ: Rutgers University Press, 2000), 63.

10. Joshua L. Howell to Annie Howell, August 5, 1862. Transcribed copy, author's collection.

11. The prayer book is located in H-41, Howell Family Collection, GCHS.

12. Camille Baquet, *History of the First Brigade, New Jersey Volunteers* (Trenton: State of New Jersey, 1910), 5–6. The Fourth New Jersey would join the New Jersey Brigade in August 1861.

13. Ibid., 7.

14. U.S. War Department, *The War of the Rebellion: A Compilation of the Official Records of the Union and Confederate Armies*, 128 vols. (Washington, DC: U.S. Government Printing Office, 1880–1901), series I, vol. 2: 315 (hereafter cited as *O.R.*) The New Jersey Brigade joined Runyon's division on July 12, 1861.

15. *O.R.* I, 5: 122.

16. Joseph G. Bilby and William C. Goble, *"Remember You Are Jerseymen!": A Military History of New Jersey's Troops in the Civil War* (Hightstown, NJ: Longstreet House, 1998), 66.

17. Warner, *Generals in Blue*, 258–59.

18. *O.R.* I, 5: 16.

19. Archibald S. Taylor to Joshua Howell, December 2, 1862. Thomas Howell Pension Records, National Archives.

20. Tom Howell to Joshua Howell, February 16, 1862. Transcribed copy, author's collection.

21. Robert B. Roberts, *Encyclopedia of Historic Forts: The Military, Pioneer, and Trading Posts of the United States* (New York: Macmillan, 1988), 801–802.

22. No remains of the fort exist today. It was destroyed for development in 1970. Benjamin Franklin Cooling III and Walton H. Owen II, *Mr. Lincoln's Forts: A Guide to the Civil War Defenses of Washington* (Shippensburg, PA: White Mane Publishing, 1988), 70.

23. Benjamin H. Wiley, "A History of the 3 Reg't N.J. V. from the Formation up to the Battle of Gaines Mill Virginia June 27th 1862." Benjamin H. Wiley Papers, Burlington County Historical Society, Burlington, New Jersey.

24. Letter Book, Third New Jersey Infantry Regiment. Record Group 94, National Archives, Washington, DC.

25. *West Jersey Press*, February 19, 1862. His appointment also was reported in the *Philadelphia Inquirer* on February 14, 1862.

26. Tom Howell to Mother, February 19, 1862. H-41, Howell Family Collection, GCHS.

27. McPherson, *For Cause and Comrades*, 53.

28. Tom Howell to Joshua Howell, April 2, 1862. Transcribed copy, author's collection.

29. Tom Howell to Annie Howell, April 19, 1862. Transcribed copy, author's collection. By the end of the month, though, he seemed to have gotten over whatever upset him and he told his siblings to remember him to Gert.

30. Tom Howell to Mother, April 11, 1862. H-41, Howell Family Collection, GCHS.

31. Tom Howell to Mother, February 19, 1862. H-41, Howell Family Collection, GCHS.

32. Tom Howell to Mother, May 26, 1862. H-41, Howell Family Collection, GCHS; emphasis in original.

33. Daniel P. Buckley to Mother, June 24, 1862. D. Penrose Buckley Papers (#1775), HSP.

34. U.S. War Department, *An Act Establishing Rules and Articles for the Government of the Armies of the United States* (Albany, NY: Websters and Skinners, 1812), 13.

35. Tom Howell to Mother, June 22, 1862. H-41, Howell Family Collection, GCHS.

36. Lorien Foote, *The Gentlemen and the Roughs: Violence, Honor, and Manhood in the Union Army* (New York: New York University Press, 2013), 19–20.

37. Tom Howell to Annie Howell, February 11, 1862. Transcribed copy, author's collection.
38. Tom Howell to Mother, February 19, 1862. H-41, Howell Family Collection, GCHS; emphasis in original. Tom also makes mention to his mother on two other occasions, May 26, 1862, and June 7, 1862, about his intent on "keeping his promise" to her by not drinking or smoking.
39. Foote, *Gentlemen and the Roughs*, 55; Rotundo, *American Manhood*, 39.
40. Joseph Bilby, "An Officer and a Gentleman . . . sort of," *Military Images* 13 (Jan./Feb. 1992): 24–25.
41. Tom Howell to Mother, June 22, 1862. H-41, Howell Family Collection, GCHS.
42. Daniel P. Buckley to Mother, June 24, 1862. D. Penrose Buckley Papers (#1775), HSP.
43. Foote, *Gentlemen and the Roughs*, 30–31.
44. Tom Howell to Joshua Howell, June 20, 1862. Transcribed copy, author's collection.
45. "Taylor, Archibald S.," Memorial of Officers, Record Group–Department of Defense, Adjutant General's Office, Civil War, 1861–1865, Regimental Records 1861–1865, 3rd Regiment, Box 6, New Jersey State Archives, Trenton, New Jersey.
46. Col. George W. Taylor to Gov. Charles S. Olden, June 5, 1861. Record Group–Department of Defense, Adjutant General's Office, Civil War, 1861–1865, Regimental Records 1861–1865, 3rd Regiment, Box 6, Folder 30, New Jersey State Archives, Trenton, New Jersey.
47. On April 15, 1862, Captain Leonard H. Regur (1820–1915) wrote General Kearny stating, "On the tenth of March I was taken with Erysipelus and have sinse that time have been confined to the house[. M]y health is slowly improving and I hope soon to be able to join my Regiment." Erysipelas, which the captain suffered from, is a skin disease that causes lesions on the face, arms, or legs. The captain never returned for duty in the field and resigned his position on July 11, 1862. Leonard Regur Pension File, National Archives, Washington, DC.
48. Col. George W. Taylor to Gov. Charles S. Olden, May 31, 1861. Record Group–Department of Defense, Adjutant General's Office, Civil War, 1861–1865, Regimental Records 1861–1865, 3rd Regiment, Box 6, Folder 30, New Jersey State Archives, Trenton, New Jersey.
49. Robert Dunham to Captain Yard, January 23, 1862, and Robert Dunham to Hon. Charles S. Olden, May 30, 1861. Record Group–Department of Defense, Adjutant General's Office, Civil War, 1861–1865, Regimental Records 1861–1865, 3rd Regiment, Box 6, Folder 30, New Jersey State Archives, Trenton, New Jersey.
50. Col. George W. Taylor to Gov. Charles S. Olden, May 31, 1861. Record Group–Department of Defense, Adjutant General's Office, Civil War, 1861–1865, Regimental Records 1861–1865, 3rd Regiment, Box 6, Folder 30, New Jersey State Archives, Trenton, New Jersey.
51. Tom Howell to Mother, June 16, 1862. H-41, Howell Family Collection, GCHS.
52. Philadelphia City Directory, 1861, 1179.
53. Louis Loeb to Mother and Kate, October 15, 1861. Loeb Pension Records, National Archives, Washington, D.C.
54. Loeb sent his mother twenty-five dollars on April 26 and June 12, 1862. Copies of the checks are in his pension records. National Archives, Washington, D.C.
55. Tom Howell to Mother, March 5, 1862. H-41, Howell Family Collection, GCHS; Tom Howell to Annie Howell, March 6, 1862. Transcribed copy, author's collection.
56. Russel H. Beatie, *Army of the Potomac: McClellan's First Campaign, March 1862–May 1862* (New York: Savas Beatie, 2007), 69.
57. O.R. I, 5: 542.
58. Tom Howell to Joshua Howell, March 15, 1862. Transcribed copy, author's collection.
59. Isaac Clark to Lizzie, March 24, 1862. File #18, Box 7, Civil War Letters Collection, GCHS. In his report of the week's action, Colonel Taylor mentioned that he took

"some five companies, or parts thereof" in his march to Sangster's Station. O.R. I, 5: 542.
60. Beatie, *Army of the Potomac*, 72–73.
61. Tom Howell to Mother, March 11, 1862. H-41, Howell Family Collection, GCHS.
62. "Secesh" was regional slang for "secessionist."
63. Isaac Clark to Lizzie, March 24, 1862. File #18, Box 7, Civil War Letters Collection, GCHS.
64. Daniel P. Buckley to Mother, March 17, 1862. D. Penrose Buckley Papers (#1775), HSP.
65. O.R. I, 5: 543.
66. Tom Howell to Mother, March 11, 1862. H-41, Howell Family Collection, GCHS.
67. Tom Howell to Annie Howell, March 24, 1862. Transcribed copy, author's collection.
68. O.R. I, 5: 55.
69. Brian K. Burton, *Extraordinary Circumstances: The Seven Days Battles* (Bloomington: Indiana University Press, 2001), 2–3.
70. Stephen W. Sears, *To the Gates of Richmond: The Peninsula Campaign* (New York: Ticknor and Fields, 1992), 3.
71. Bruce Catton, *Mr. Lincoln's Army* (Garden City, NY: Doubleday, 1951), 60.
72. Ibid., 15.
73. David G. Martin, *The Peninsula Campaign, March–July 1862* (Conshohocken, PA: Combined Books, 1992), 57.
74. Ibid, 55.
75. As quoted in Stephen W. Sears, *George B. McClellan: The Young Napoleon* (New York: Ticknor and Fields, 1988), 166.
76. Isaac Clark to Lizzie, March 24, 1862, File #18, Box 7, Civil War Letters Collection, GCHS.
77. John R. Pedrick to Mother, June 16, 1862, File #155, Box 7, Civil War Letters Collection, GCHS.
78. Daniel P. Buckley to Mother, March 17, 1862. D. Penrose Buckley Papers (#1775), HSP. The flags were later sent to Governor Olden in New Jersey.
79. Tom Howell to Mother, March 15, 1862. H-41, Howell Family Collection, GCHS.
80. Hess, *Union Soldier in Battle*, 138.
81. Tom Howell to Annie Howell, March 19, 1862. Transcribed copy, author's collection.
82. Tom Howell to Mother, March 22, 1862. H-41, Howell Family Collection, GCHS.
83. Tom Howell to Mother, March 15, 1862. H-41, Howell Family Collection. GCHS.
84. Tom Howell to Mother, April 2, 1862. H-41, Howell Family Collection. GCHS.
85. Wiley, *Life of Billy Yank*, 272–74.
86. Tom Howell to Mother, March 22, 1862. H-41, Howell Family Collection, GCHS.
87. Ibid.
88. Ibid.; emphasis in original.
89. Ibid.
90. Sears, *To the Gates of Richmond*, 34. McClellan apparently counted some troops twice, included troops in the Shenandoah Valley, and even added to his number troops that were still in Pennsylvania.
91. Tom Howell to Annie Howell, March 29, 1862. Transcribed copy, author's collection.
92. Tom Howell to Mother, April 2, 1862. H-41, Howell Family Collection, GCHS.
93. McPherson, *Battle Cry of Freedom*, 402–403.
94. Ibid., 413.
95. Tom Howell to Mother, April 11, 1862. H-41, Howell Family Collection, GCHS.
96. On the night of April 10, McClellan sent Franklin word that his division was to move at once and join the army on the peninsula. O.R. I, 11(3): 87–88.
97. Tom Howell to Mother, April 12, 1862, H-41, Howell Family Collection, GCHS.
98. Ibid.

99. Thomas Preston Carpenter (1804–1876) was the brother of Tom Howell's mother. He served as an associate justice of the supreme court of New Jersey from 1845 to 1852. At the time of the Civil War, he was a lawyer in Camden. Carpenter and Carpenter, *Samuel Carpenter and His Descendants*, 90–91.

100. Unless otherwise indicated, all emphasis appears in the original letters.

101. Henry W. Brown (1816–1892) was the lieutenant colonel of the Third New Jersey. Brown was born in Boston with the name Henry W. Barnes. He served in the Fourth U.S. Artillery from 1839 to 1844. When the Civil War began, he was living in Philadelphia with his wife, Rebecca, and working as a clerk. Bilby, "Officer and a Gentleman," 24–25.

102. These are four of Howell's nine siblings: Anna, or Annie (1848–1913); Joshua (1842–1893); Francis, or Frank (1849–1872); and Charles, or Charley (1837–1891). Four of his siblings died before Tom Howell joined the army in 1862.

103. George W. Taylor (1808–1862) was the colonel of the Third New Jersey. Taylor was from Clinton, New Jersey. Before the Civil War, he was employed in the mining and manufacturing of iron ore. Warner, *Generals in Blue* , 493–94.

104. Robert T. Dunham (1840–1885) lived on Sixth Street in Camden, just a few blocks from Tom Howell. Dunham and Howell were friends before the Civil War. Dunham was a law student when the Civil War began and was a nephew of Col. George W. Taylor. He was commissioned as First Lieutenant of Co. I, Third New Jersey, and then became adjutant. Camden City Directory, 1863, 43; Col. George W. Taylor to Gov. Charles S. Olden, May 31, 1861. Record Group–Department of Defense, Adjutant General's Office, Civil War, 1861–1865, Regimental Records 1861–1865, 3rd Regiment, Box 6, Folder 30, New Jersey State Archives, Trenton, New Jersey; William S. Stryker, *Record of Officers and Men of New Jersey in the Civil War, 1861–1865* (Trenton, NJ: John L. Murphy, Steam Book and Job Printer, 1876), 175.

105. Howell may be alluding to General Grant's campaign against Fort Henry, which fell on February 6. Grant later captured Fort Donelson on February 16. On February 17 the success of Grant's troops at Fort Donelson was shared with the Third New Jersey in General Order No. 23, in which Colonel Taylor stated, "Let us hope that the New Jersey Brigade will soon be called upon to share the Glory of our Western Compatriots in arms by replacing the old flag on the ramparts of Richmond." Regimental Order Book, Third New Jersey Infantry, National Archives. Washington, D.C.

106. Anna Stratton Carpenter (1843–1869) was Tom's Howell's cousin. Anna was the second child of Thomas Preston and Rebecca Carpenter. Carpenter and Carpenter, *Samuel Carpenter and His Descendants*, 91.

107. Attempts to identify this person have been unsuccessful.

108. "Jos" is the spelling Tom often used for his brother Joshua's name as well as for his uncle Joshua Blackwood Howell. Tom sometimes spelled his brother Charley's name "Charlie."

109. Howell is referring to Lewis C. Spencer (1835–1896). Spencer was the original second lieutenant of Company I. The twenty-six-year-old Spencer was promoted to first lieutenant of Company C on January 30, 1862. He lived in Warren, New Jersey, when the war began. Stryker, *Record of Officers and Men*, 175; 1860 United States Federal Census.

110. Tom mentions on March 9 that he did not draw it, but a drawing of the fort can be found in D. Penrose Buckley Papers (#1775), HSP.

111. Archibald S. Taylor (1842–1863) was the first lieutenant of Company I, Third New Jersey. Taylor was a nephew of Col. George W. Taylor. He became first lieutenant on June 6, 1861. Stryker, *Record of Officers and Men*, 175; 1860 United States Federal Census.

112. Attempts to identify this person have been unsuccessful.

113. Samuel Bedell Howell (1834–1903) was Tom Howell's oldest brother. He was a doctor and a graduate of the University of Pennsylvania in 1858. At the beginning of the Civil War, he lived in Minersville, Pennsylvania. Howell, *Book of John Howell and His Descendants*, 2: 591; *Catalogue of the Trustees, Officers, and Students, of the University of*

*Pennsylvania. Session 1858–59* (Philadelphia: Collins, 1859), 41; 1860 United States Federal Census.

114. Maria (Minnie) Howell was the wife of Samuel Howell. They were married in April 1859. She was twenty-six years old in 1862. Howell, *Book of John Howell and His Descendants*, 591; 1860 United States Federal Census.

115. According to the *Revised Regulations for the Army of the United States, 1861*, a second lieutenant's total monthly pay was $105.50. U.S. War Department, *Revised Regulations for the Army of the United States, 1861* (Philadelphia: J.G.L. Brown, Printer, 1861), 525.

116. Martin Gray was a nineteen-year-old law student from Camden. He lived with his parents, Philip and Sarah Gray, and his three siblings at 709 Market Street. 1860 United States Federal Census; Camden City Directory, 1863–1864, 55.

117. Samuel Gray was the brother of Martin Gray. The twenty-four-year-old Samuel was a lawyer. 1860 United States Federal Census; Camden City Directory, 1863–1864, 55.

118. The Potts family lived at 529 Cooper Street in Camden, just a few blocks away from Tom Howell. Camden City Directory, 1863–1864, 102.

119. Capt. Franklin L. Knight (1838–1895) of Company D, Third New Jersey. Knight lived at 31 North Third Street in Camden. Stryker, *Record of Officers and Men*, 160; Camden City Directory, 1863–1864, 75.

120. Sarah Jane Stratton lived at 1405 Locust Street in Philadelphia. She was forty years old. Philadelphia City Directory, 1862, 647; 1860 United States Federal Census.

121. Charles P. Clark was born around 1840. He was a lawyer and lived at 30 South Third Street in Camden. His two sisters were Annie and Sarah. In 1862 Annie would have been around twenty-three years old and Sarah would have been around nineteen. Camden City Directory, 1863–1864, 32; 1870 United States Federal Census.

122. Howell used the word "rats" a number of times in his letters. It seems to be the word he used instead of the word "hell." He most likely would not write the word "hell" because he promised his mother that he would not swear.

123. Troches were lozenges; gum arabic was used for coughs.

124. Mary Virginia Harbert (1847–1905) lived at 421 Cooper Street in Camden with her parents, Samuel and Georgianna, and two siblings. Camden City Directory, 1863–1864, 59; 1860 United States Federal Census.

125. Joseph F. Garrison, M.D., D.D. (1823–1892) was the rector of St. Paul's Episcopal Church in Camden from 1855 to 1884. This was the church that Tom Howell's family attended. Prowell, *History of Camden County*, 336.

126. Howell is likely referring to Mary Harbert.

127. Howell is likely referring to John D. Higgins, who lived at 328 Market Street in Camden, just a few houses from the Howell family. Higgins was thirty-two years old and was a teacher in a private school. There is no evidence to explain why Tom referred to him as a "vulgar fellow." Camden City Directory, 1863–1864, 63; 1860 United States Federal Census.

128. St. George's Hall was a building on the grounds of the Virginia Theological Seminary. The building was constructed in 1856 and used as a dormitory. The seminary was located near Fort Worth, which was the camp of the Third New Jersey during the winter of 1861–1862. Charles E. Goode and Peter Leach, *Archaeological Evaluation for the Proposed Chapel of the Ages at the Virginia Theological Seminary Alexandria, Virginia* (Alexandria, VA: John Milner Associates, 2013), viii. https://www.alexandriava.gov/uploadedFiles/historic/info/archaeology/ARSiteReportVaTheoSeminaryChapel.pdf (accessed July 24, 2015).

129. Dr. Benjamin Paschall Howell (1808–1881) was a brother of Tom Howell's father. At the time of the Civil War he lived in Woodbury, New Jersey. Howell, *Book of John Howell and His Descendants*, 2: 460–63.

130. Howell is possibly referring to Anna C. Summers (1845–1908) of Philadelphia. 1850 United States Federal Census.

131. The army began issuing rubber blankets to infantry in November 1861. They were used as rain covers or as ground cloths when the men had to sleep in the field.

132. Samuel C. Harbert (1817–1888) was the regimental quartermaster of the Fourth New Jersey. Before the Civil War, he was a manufacturer of agricultural machinery. He was from Camden and was the father of Mary Harbert. It is unclear why Howell refers to Harbert as "Dr.," as he knew Harbert before the war and definitely would have known Harbert's occupation. It is possible he meant to put the "Dr." in front of Henry Taylor, who follows the reference to Harbert in the letter. Taylor was assistant surgeon of the Eighth New Jersey. Stryker, *Record of Officers and Men*, 183; Camden City Directory, 1863–1864, 59; 1860 United States Federal Census.

133. Henry Genet Taylor (1837–1916), usually listed as H. Genet Taylor, was the assistant surgeon of the Eighth New Jersey, which was attached to the Third Brigade, Hooker's division. Taylor graduated from the University of Pennsylvania with a medical degree in 1860 and lived at 312 Market Street in Camden, just two houses from the Howells. *Catalogue of the Trustees, Officers, and Students of the University of Pennsylvania. Session 1860–61* (Philadelphia: Collins, 1861), 44; Camden City Directory, 1863–1864, 126.

134. Fairfax Station was a railroad station on the Orange and Alexandria Railroad and was located two and a half miles south of Fairfax Court House.

135. Sangster's Station was a railroad station on the Orange and Alexandria Railroad and was about three miles east of Bull Run (Manassas).

136. Philip Kearny (1815–1862) was born in New York City. He lost his left arm in the Battle of Churubusco in 1847 during the Mexican-American War. When the Civil War began, he was offered command of the First New Jersey Brigade and given the rank of brigadier general. Warner, *Generals in Blue*, 258–59.

137. This is covered in the reports of General Philip Kearny and the colonels of the brigade in *O. R.* I, 5: 537–45. Col. George Taylor states in his report that he had with his command sixteen men and one corporal under 1st Lt. Henry B. Hidden from the First New York Cavalry. Hidden's charge produced thirteen prisoners, which were from the First Maryland.

138. Manassas is twenty-five miles west of Washington, D.C., and was the site of the first major battle of the Civil War in July 1861, which ended in a Confederate victory. Manassas Junction is important because the Orange and Alexandria Railroad and the Manassas Gap Railroad met there.

139. William Johnston Taylor (1815–1881) was the brother of Col. George W. Taylor.

140. Burke's Station was a railroad station on the Orange and Alexandria Railroad.

141. Brig. Gen. Ambrose E. Burnside led the Union invasion of North Carolina in January 1862. On March 13, 1862, he attacked New Berne, North Carolina. How Howell got the information that his brigade was being sent to join Burnside in North Carolina is unknown. It is possible that Tom's uncle Joshua Blackwood Howell told him. A soldier in his uncle's unit, the Eighty-fifth Pennsylvania, wrote on March 15, 1862, "It is the talk that we are ordered to help Burnside out of a scrape." Ronn Palm et al., *The Bloody 85th: The Letters of Milton McJunkin, a Western Pennsylvanian Soldier in the Civil War* (Daleville, VA: Schroeder Publications, 2000), 23. Tom may have assumed that his unit would be sent as well. There is nothing in the *Official Records* to substantiate this.

142. A dirk is a type of dagger.

143. The Sixty-ninth New York was a regiment in the Irish Brigade. They were in the Second Brigade, First Division, II Corps. Sears, *To the Gates of Richmond*, 359.

144. Howell is mistaken here. William J. Taylor was not Arch's brother, although Arch did have a brother named William J. Taylor (1836–1903). Possibly Arch's brother helped out the sutler, which may explain the confusion, but it is clear from other letters that he is not the sutler. In other letters, Howell mentions that the sutler's wife came to visit, but Arch's brother was not married at this time.

145. William B. Franklin (1823–1903) was born in York, Pennsylvania, and graduated from West Point in 1843. He fought in the Mexican-American War and won a brevet

for gallantry at Buena Vista. Prior to the Civil War, he was in charge of the construction of the Capitol dome. When the Civil War began, he became a brigadier general and was the commander of the First Division, I Corps in early 1862. Warner, *Generals in Blue*, 159–60.

146. Centreville is about five miles north of Manassas Junction. The town had a population of two hundred people in 1862. The town was strategically important to both sides because of its proximity to the railroad lines near Manassas and because it was a little more than twenty miles from Washington, DC.

147. George Brinton McClellan (1826–1885) was born in Philadelphia. He attended West Point and graduated second in the class of 1846. McClellan fought in the Mexican-American War and worked as an engineer for a railroad company prior to the Civil War. Once the war began, he received a commission as a major general and became commander of the Army of the Potomac shortly after the Union defeat at Manassas (Bull Run) in the summer of 1861. Sears, *George B. McClellan* , 1–27, 51, 68–95.

148. Charley, who was six years older than Tom, obtained a job as the music and entertainment director of the Institute of Pennsylvania Hospital in Philadelphia. Dr. Thomas Kirkbride gave Charley the position, which required him to live at the facility. Charley would visit his mother in Camden on his days off but never again lived with her. "Richard Washington Howell," unpublished paper, Howell Family Collection, GCHS.

149. Howell may be referring to Robert (Bob) Dunham's two sisters, Ann and Jane. Ann was twenty-four years old and Jane was nineteen in 1862. 1850 United States Federal Census.

150. Maj. Mark Wilkes Collett (1826–1863) was from Patterson, New Jersey. He mustered in as major in June 1861 when the Third New Jersey was formed. Stryker, *Record of Officers and Men*, 150.

151. Daniel Penrose Buckley (1836–1862), known as "Pen," was from Philadelphia. Before the war, he graduated from the University of Pennsylvania and was a lawyer in Philadelphia. In May 1861 Buckley was given a commission as first lieutenant of Co. C, Third New Jersey, and was promoted to captain of the company on January 30, 1862. Philadelphia City Directory, 1861, 115; *Catalogue of the Trustees, Officers, and Students, of the University of Pennsylvania. Session 1858–59* (Philadelphia: Collins, 1859), 43; Stryker, *Record of Officers and Men*, 157.

152. Lorenzo Lewis Coxe (1838–1866) was the surgeon of the Third New Jersey. He was from Philadelphia and graduated from the Homeopathic Medical College of Pennsylvania in 1858. Stryker, *Record of Officers and Men*, 150; 1850 United States Federal Census; *Eleventh Annual Announcement of the Homeopathic Medical College of Pennsylvania. Session 1858–1859* (Philadelphia: King & Baird, 1858), 14.

153. This is not exactly what happened. According to E. Burd Grubb in Baquet's *History of the First Brigade* , Coxe was taken prisoner by the Confederates in October 1861 but was released a day later. While a captive, however, he was taken to Manassas and was questioned by Confederate commander Joseph E. Johnston. After being released Coxe met with Colonel Taylor, and nothing more was spoken of the incident until the Third New Jersey advanced to Manassas in March 1862. While at Manassas, members from the regiment entered General Johnston's tent and examined some of his papers. Among the papers was a report of a conversation between one of Johnston's staff and Dr. Coxe. "This report stated that Dr. Cox[e] had given Gen. Johnston all the information regarding the troops at and around Alexandria." Baquet, *History of the First Brigade* , 336–40.

154. The papers discovered at Manassas were forwarded to Washington, and Dr. Coxe was arrested and sent to the Old Capitol Prison in Washington.

155. George R. Darrow (1820–1906) lived in Trenton, New Jersey, when the Civil War began and became chaplain of the Third New Jersey when the regiment formed in June 1861. He resigned on January 3, 1863. 1860 United States Federal Census; Stryker, *Record of Officers and Men*, 150.

156. William J. Potts and Robert B. Potts were the sons of Robert and Sarah Potts of Camden. The Potts lived at 529 Cooper Street. In 1862 William was nineteen years old and Robert was eighteen. Camden City Directory, 1863–1864, 102; 1860 United States Federal Census.

157. Sarah W. Gray was the wife of Philip J. Gray of Camden. The Grays lived at 709 Market Street, just a few blocks from the Howell family. Sarah was the mother of Martin Gray. 1860 United States Federal Census; Camden City Directory, 1863–1864, 55.

158. William E. Bryan (1822–1893) was from Northampton, New Jersey. He enlisted as the captain of Company H on June 1, 1861, and became major of the regiment in June 1863. 1860 United States Federal Census; Stryker, *Record of Officers and Men*, 172.

159. William Spence was from North Bergen, New Jersey. The thirty-four-year-old Spence enlisted as first lieutenant of Company H on June 1, 1861. Stryker, *Record of Officers and Men*, 172; 1850 United States Federal Census.

160. Charlotte Taylor (1845–1893) lived in Clinton, New Jersey, with her parents, Lewis H. and Jane C. Taylor. 1860 United States Federal Census.

161. Howell is mistaken here. No one from his division left. It seems that the only troops to leave on March 22 were from Fitz John Porter's division. O.R. I, 11: 6.

162. Fort Monroe is located at the tip of the Virginia Peninsula. Construction of the fort began in 1823 and was completed in 1834. The fort, which was the largest permanent seacoast fortification constructed before the Civil War, was designed to protect the entrance into Hampton Roads. Maj. Gen. George McClellan used the fort as a staging area for his Peninsula Campaign. Richard P. Weinert Jr. and Col. Robert Arthur, *Defender of the Chesapeake: The Story of Fort Monroe* (Shippensburg, PA: White Mane Publishing, 1989), 30–40, 124–33.

163. Maj. Gen. Nathaniel P. Banks (1816–1894) was sent to the Shenandoah Valley to fight the Confederate force under Maj. Gen. Thomas J. "Stonewall" Jackson. Jackson was campaigning in the Shenandoah Valley attempting to keep the entire Federal Army from concentrating on Richmond.

164. Rebecca Hopkins Carpenter (1813–1896) was the wife of Thomas Preston Carpenter. Carpenter and Carpenter, *Samuel Carpenter and His Descendants*, 90.

165. James Hopkins Carpenter (1849–1909) was the youngest child of Thomas Preston and Rebecca Carpenter. Ibid., 91.

166. William C. Barnard (1841–1862) lived with his mother, Margaret, at 413 Bridge Avenue in Camden, New Jersey. In 1859 he entered the United States Military Academy at West Point, but he resigned on September 25, 1861. He received a commission as second lieutenant of Co. G, Third New Jersey, on December 16, 1861, and then became a member of General Kearny's staff. Camden City Directory, 1863–1864, 18; *Official Register of the Officers and Cadets of the U.S. Military Academy, West Point, New York, June 1861*, 15; Stryker, *Record of Officers and Men*, 169.

167. Rev. Richard Newton, D. D. (1813–1887), lived in Philadelphia at 251 S. Thirteenth Street with his wife, Lydia. Newton was the minister at St. Paul's Episcopal Church in Philadelphia, which was located on Third Street below Walnut. The Howell family frequently attended service at this church. Newton was also the recording secretary of the Pennsylvania Bible Society. Obituary, *Philadelphia Inquirer*, May 26, 1887; Philadelphia City Directory, 1861, 740.

168. Irvin McDowell (1818–1885) was a graduate of the West Point class of 1838. He served as an aide-de-camp to Gen. J. E. Wool in the Mexican-American War. On May 14, 1861, he was appointed as a brigadier general and was the commander of the Union Army during its defeat at the Battle of Manassas (Bull Run) in July 1861. In March 1862 he was made commander of the I Corps of the Army of the Potomac. Warner, *Generals in Blue*, 297–99.

169. Mary Ellen Marcy McClellan (1836–1915) was born in Philadelphia and was the daughter of Maj. Randolph Marcy. She met George McClellan in 1854 but was not interested in him, since she was in love with A. P. Hill. Her father would not give his blessing for the marriage between his daughter and Hill. In 1859 she reconnected with

"The Rough Life of a Soldier" 69

McClellan and accepted his proposal. The two were married in May 1860. Sears, *George B. McClellan*, 41–42, 61–63.

170. Brig. Gen. Rufus King (1814–1876) became a brigadier general on May 17, 1861. On March 8, 1862, he was given command of a division in McDowell's I Corps. Warner, *Generals in Blue*, 269–70.

171. Richard Bickerton Pemell Lyons (1817–1887) was the British Minister to the United States from 1858 to 1865.

172. David Bell Birney (1825–1864) was colonel of the Twenty-third Pennsylvania. On February 17, 1862, he was promoted to brigadier general. He took command of a brigade in Hamilton's division in the III Corps. Warner, *Generals in Blue*, 34–35.

173. David Vickers Jr. (1840–1908) was the captain of Co. A, Third New Jersey. Before the Civil War, Vickers lived at 534 Cooper Street in Camden. He was promoted to major in 1863. Camden City Directory, 1863–1864, 131; Stryker, *Record of Officers and Men*, 152.

174. Howell most likely wanted to say that the colonel would give Vickers hell, but the pious Howell would not swear.

175. It is not clear what Howell is referring to here. He may be referencing a group of twelve Iroquois soldiers that were members of Co. K, Fifty-seventh Pennsylvania. The regiment was in the First Brigade, Third Division, III Corps. Laurence M. Hauptman, *Between Two Fires: American Indians in the Civil War* (New York: Free Press, 1995), 72.

176. Howell's meaning here is unclear. His regiment was part of McDowell's corps, but none of McDowell's men were sent "on the Potomac" at the end of March.

177. Albert W. Markly (1825–1875) was a merchant who lived on Cooper Street in Camden with his wife, Josephine. Camden City Directory, 1863–1864, 85.

178. Thomas S. Allison (1810–1871) was the secretary of state of New Jersey from 1851 to 1861. When the Civil War began, he became a major and was made paymaster of New Jersey's Military Pay Department. *Trenton Times*, August 1, 1904.

179. Dr. Coxe was released from the Old Capitol Prison after a few months. According to Grubb, Coxe returned to the regiment for only a few days. He was not received well by the officers and men, due to his questionable loyalty to the Union cause, and he resigned on May 2, 1862. He took a position as a surgeon on one of the Pacific Mail steamers. While serving on the steamer he contracted a disease and died in November 1866. Grubb believed that Coxe was wrongly accused and blamed this false accusation for cutting short Coxe's "brilliant career." Grubb stated, "He [Coxe] told me himself, that in the interview in General Johnston's tent he had purposely given him all the false information that he could think of, and that he had purposely stated Montgomery's troops to be twice their actual strength." Baquet, *History of the First Brigade*, 339. Grubb's cousin, Capt. Daniel P. Buckley, wrote home on April 14, 1862: "Ned [Grubb] and I have long doubted his [Coxe's] loyalty but never imagined that he would be guilty of any such dastardly treason." D. Penrose Buckley Papers (#1775), HSP.

180. Gertrude Taylor Browning (1846–1906) was the daughter of Abraham and Elizabeth Browning. She lived with her parents and three siblings at 415 Cooper Street in Camden. In 1862 she was a student at St. Mary's Hall, a private Catholic school in Camden. Camden City Directory, 1863–1864, 26; 1860 United States Federal Census; *St. Mary's Hall: Register* (Philadelphia: King & Baird, 1862), 9.

181. Howell is speaking of Chase's twenty-one-year-old daughter, Katherine "Kate" Chase (1840–1899). For more on Kate Chase, see John Oller's *American Queen: The Rise and Fall of Kate Chase Sprague, Civil War "Belle of the North" and Gilded Age Woman of Scandal* (Boston: Da Capo Press, 2014).

182. Susan Mary Carpenter (1840–1914) and Anna Stratton Carpenter (1843–1869) were the two oldest children of Thomas Preston and Rebecca Carpenter. Carpenter and Carpenter, *Samuel Carpenter and His Descendants*, 91.

183. Howell may be referring to Susan Barton Hopkins (1788–1869), who was the mother of Rebecca Carpenter, the wife of Thomas Preston Carpenter. Ibid., 94.

184. Howell is likely referring to Charles DeHaven (1850–1887), who lived on Broad Street in Camden. He was the son of Charles and Mary DeHaven. Camden City Directory, 1863–1864, 40.

185. Richard W. Stickney was thirteen years old and lived on Broadway in Camden. He was the son of James W. H. Stickney, who was the captain of Co. F, Third New Jersey. Camden City Directory, 1863–1864, 122.

186. Howell may be referring to Peter Cassady, who was the drummer of Co. I, Third New Jersey. Cassady was from Morris Township, New Jersey, and was fourteen years old in 1862. Stryker, *Record of Officers and Men*, 176; 1850 United States Federal Census.

187. George Browning (1850–1906) was Gertrude Browning's brother. 1860 United States Federal Census.

188. The Third New Jersey was originally armed with flintlock smoothbore muskets altered to percussion in 1861. By the end of 1862 many of the men in the regiment were armed with Springfield rifles.

189. Twenty-eight-year-old Jane Taitt Taylor was the wife and cousin of the sutler William J. Taylor.

190. Edward Carpenter (1813–1889) was the youngest brother of Mary Tonkin Carpenter Howell, Tom Howell's mother. Edward lived in Philadelphia with his wife, Anna, and their six younger children when the Civil War began. Their two oldest sons, Louis Henry Carpenter and James Edward Carpenter, joined the Union Army. Carpenter and Carpenter, *Samuel Carpenter and His Descendants*, 100–101.

191. Colvin's Station, or Catlett's Station, was a station on the Orange and Alexandria Railroad. The village developed in 1852 after the arrival of the railroad. In 1853 it was named after the Colvin family, but the name was later changed to Catlett's Station. The village included a station, depot, store, and several dwellings. Catlett Historical District–National Register of Historic Places Registration Form, http://www.dhr.virginia.gov/registers/Counties/Fauquier/030-5162_Catlett_HD_2008_NR_final.pdf (accessed June 7, 2015).

192. The latter, Warrenton, is the correct name of the Virginia town. While at Catlett's Station, Howell says they are four miles from Warrenton, but he is mistaken. They may be four miles from Warrenton Station on the Orange and Alexandria Railroad, but they are roughly nine miles from the town of Warrenton, the Fauquier County seat. In 1860 it had a population of 604 people. From Town of Warrenton, Virginia, website, http://www.warrentonva.gov/General/History.aspx (accessed June 7, 2015).

193. Howell is referring to Thomas S. Harris (1841–1902), who was a private in Co. I, Third New Jersey. In 1861 the chaplain of each regiment served as the postmaster. By 1862 the commanding officer of each regiment chose a reliable noncommissioned officer or private to act as postmaster. From Benson J. Lossing, *Pictorial History of the Civil War in the United States of America* (Hartford: T. Belknap, 1868), 224–25.

194. It is unclear who Howell is referring to here.

195. Bristoe Station is a station on the Orange and Alexandria Railroad. It is located between Manassas Junction and Catlett's Station.

196. It seemed that many of the men wanted to make a few purchases before the voyage to the Peninsula. Capt. Daniel P. Buckley mentioned in a letter dated April 14, 1862, that he had permission to go into town because he needed some smoking tobacco and a new pair of shoes, since his pair cut his feet very badly due to constant wetting and drying. D. Penrose Buckley Papers (#1775), HSP.

*Part II*

# "Hot Work Soon Enough"

On April 17, 1862, the New Jersey Brigade boarded five transports and started down the Potomac River toward Virginia. The First New Jersey would make its voyage to Virginia on board the *Hero*, the Second New Jersey and General Kearny on the *Elm City*, the Third New Jersey on the *John A. Warner*, and the Fourth New Jersey on the *Kent* and the *Arrowsmith*. The *John A. Warner* (fig. 2.1) was a 527-ton side-wheel steamer. The ship was owned by the Delaware River Steamboat Company and was one of 113 steamships that were chartered by the government to transport Major General McClellan's army to the peninsula.[1]

According to an officer from the regiment, the soldiers welcomed the change of locale because it broke up the monotony of camp life. While on the ships, the troops enjoyed "chess, cards, tobacco and other small articles condusive [sic] to general comfort. Time passed so pleasantly that we agree in wishing that our voyage was to last for a week or two longer."[2] However, some of the men became sick, overcome with diarrhea, but Tom Howell remained well. Like other soldiers on the transports, he enjoyed the views afforded by the ship as it sailed down the river. He noted the multitude of ships on the river and was excited when the *John A. Warner* steamed past George Washington's home. "As we passed Mount Vernon our band played, and the troops tolled the bell on the John A. Warner," the young lieutenant wrote to his mother. "The house is the same that one sees in pictures. I saw his [George Washington's] tomb through the trees."[3]

On April 19 the ships carrying the New Jersey Brigade reached the Chesapeake Bay, and the men prepared to land near the Confederate positions outside Yorktown. McClellan's army had been outside the city of Yorktown since April 5, when the "Young Napoleon," believing the rebels defending Yorktown possessed a substantial force, made the decision to lay siege to the city.

The transports carrying the New Jersey Brigade steamed into the Poquoson River on April 20 with the men expecting to see battle soon. Tom was aware that he had now arrived near the seat of war, and he wrote to his brother Joshua that the New Jersey troops were to land near the

***Figure 2.1*** **Photograph of the *John A. Warner*. *Source*: Courtesy of the Historical Society of Frankford.**

Confederate batteries at Gloucester Point, opposite Yorktown, and that a severe fight was likely. He told his brother that he hoped the Third New Jersey would lead the storming party and that he envisioned himself in the upcoming fight: "Imagine me with a sword in one hand and a revolver in the other up to my middle in water, going ashore. It will be exceedingly interesting, will it not?"[4] It is apparent that the young lieutenant still had a romantic view of war, but that image would soon be extinguished once he became a witness to the harsh realities of war.

As Howell mentioned, Franklin's division was to be used against the Confederate defenses at Gloucester Point. McClellan intended to land the division three and a half miles south of Gloucester Point and have the Union troops take the Confederate position by surprise, but problems arose in coordinating this plan with the navy and the attack was delayed.[5] For three days the troops remained on their transports on the Poquoson River with the men hoping to participate in the action around Yorktown. Captain Buckley described sitting on the ships under the Virginia sun, where the hands and faces of the soldiers assumed "their summer radiance which will take several seasons of civilization to restore their pristine whiteness."[6]

On April 23, 1862, the brigade disembarked at Ship Point. The men made camp in a cornfield and speculated where they would be sent next. It was still believed they would most likely assault the Confederate defenses at Gloucester Point. As the prospect of battle loomed near, Tom took the opportunity to write home and let his mother know that he was alive and well but expected to have "hot work soon enough."[7] The tone of his letters to his mother, and even his sister Annie, is interesting. He always seemed to make a point of reassuring them that his health was well and that he would not act recklessly and put himself in harm's way.

After a week, the brigade remained at Ship Point and the men were growing bored and frustrated. Howell believed they would remain in their present location "for the rest of their lives."[8] Captain Buckley wrote to his father that the brigade was "living in that half horse half alligator style, going on shore in clear weather and returning to the John A. Warner when it rains."[9] He said it was "less like war than anything," adding that Colonel Taylor "amuses himself [by] catching fish in a large drag net."[10] Although it appeared to be a leisurely experience for the troops, it offered a stark contrast to what was taking place just a few miles away; they were constantly reminded that action was not far from them, since the continual bombardment of Yorktown could be heard in the distance.

As the Army of the Potomac prepared to assault the Confederate positions at Yorktown on the Virginia Peninsula, Union forces in the western theater continued to build on the successes they had experienced earlier in the year. In late April, ships under the command of Flag Officer David Farragut silenced the batteries defending New Orleans, and on April 29, Union troops led by Maj. Gen. Benjamin Butler occupied the city, the largest in the South.[11] In Mississippi on May 25, Confederate general P.G.T. Beauregard evacuated the strategic city of Corinth, which was the most important junction on the Memphis and Charleston Railroad and believed to be the key to controlling the Mississippi Valley. Between February and May 1862, Union forces conquered fifty thousand square miles of territory, captured New Orleans, and put thirty thousand enemy soldiers out of action.[12]

On May 1 the men of the New Jersey Brigade received the news that they were getting a new commander; Philip Kearny had received a promotion to command a division in front of Yorktown.[13] Command of the New Jersey Brigade, which remained in Franklin's division, now fell to Colonel Taylor. The new commanding officer of the regiment became Lieutenant Colonel Brown; Bob Dunham became the assistant adjutant general with the rank of captain; and Lt. Edward Burd Grubb joined Taylor's staff as an aide. "I am very sorry that Col. Taylor has left our regiment," Tom proclaimed in a letter home. "I do not believe that we could have a better commander. Still I rather like the promotion of course."[14] Captain Buckley did not have the same confidence as Howell in the leadership ability of Colonel Taylor. Buckley wrote his mother on

May 16, 1862, that Taylor "knows no more of military matters than a bull & we have not the slightest confidence in him, except to his *personal* bravery."[15] In another letter the captain elaborated on this subject:

> Kearny was assigned to Hamilton's Division and has left us permanently. It is a serious loss to our Brigade as few men can so entirely command the confidence and love of his command. As to his [Taylor's] capacity[,] time will show but I for one of a good many take leave to doubt it. There are several applicants for it [colonel of the regiment] in the Brigade none of whom, Brown included, would please us much. We would prefer a Regular officer but they must be very scarce now. If Brown is promoted Collett of course will be made Lt. Col. [T]hat makes another scramble for majority there being no less than three captains in the Regt ready to cut throats over it. Adjt Dunham of course follows the fortunes of his uncle in the capacity of Asst. Adjt. Genl. for which he is as competent as Erin's [Buckley's sister] cat. It is unfortunate that the change should occur just as we anticipate some serious work.[16]

The Senate confirmed Colonel Taylor's promotion to brigadier general on May 9, 1862.

By the beginning of May, McClellan had abandoned his plan to have Franklin assault Gloucester Point, so the rest of Franklin's division disembarked at Ship Point on May 3. The commanding general now intended to use Franklin's division to support the III Corps in the planned attack on Yorktown.[17] During the night of May 3, Tom Howell received permission to take it easy and sleep on board the *John A. Warner*, even though it seemed bugs had overrun the ship.[18] While he tried to sleep, the booming of the cannons around Yorktown could be heard all night, with a sound so loud that it shook the windows and doors of the transport. The Confederate bombardment of the Union lines that night was intended to cover the withdrawal of Johnston's army from Yorktown.

Early the next morning, May 4, orders came for Franklin's division to move. McClellan discovered that the Confederates had abandoned their positions at Yorktown and Gloucester Point and were retreating up the peninsula. By the afternoon, the commanding general came up with a new plan for Franklin's division. Franklin's men would re-embark and move up the York River, landing at West Point, the terminus of the Richmond and York River Railroad and the place where the Pamunkey and Mattapony rivers joined the York River.[19] This movement would cut off the retreating Confederates, but it was essential that Franklin move his division quickly if he hoped to get to West Point before the Confederates.[20]

Unfortunately, as mentioned earlier, Franklin's entire division was on land and it would take a while to load the troops and artillery onto the transports. According to Tom Howell, the men of Franklin's division were on their transports by 10:30 p.m., and the ships anchored for the night after sailing through the mouth of the York River.[21]

Early the next morning, May 5, the transports reached Yorktown and Franklin went ashore to meet with McClellan.[22] While the men of the division sat on their transports, some officers received permission to go two at a time for an hour to investigate the Confederate defenses of the city, but Howell was not one of them. Captain Buckley was allowed to visit the Confederate defenses, and he recorded a detailed description of the rebel positions:

> The rebels have actually vamosed leaving by far the strongest position that we have yet seen. . . . It is now surrounded with a wall of earthworks two miles in length and bristling with siege guns. Its natural position is one of strength, situate on a high bluff commanding the river. Gloucester Point on the east bank of the river here 1½ mile wide, lies opposite. This too is covered with earthworks mounting 100 lb. rifled guns.[23]

The Confederates left behind seventy-seven pieces of artillery as they abandoned Yorktown and Gloucester Point, but those guns were described as being smoothbore cannons, not rifled guns as the captain suggested.[24] The captain proclaimed his satisfaction with McClellan's plan and explained, "The evacuation of so strong a position without a fight is another of the greatest tribute[s] to McClellan's strategy. There must be something very rotten in secesh or they would not give up the result of so many months hard labor without a fight."[25]

Although McClellan intended to use Franklin's division to cut off the retreating Confederate army, he did not order Franklin to move his division from Yorktown until 9:40 p.m. on May 5.[26] This is because parts of the main body of McClellan's army clashed with the rear guard of the Confederate army at Williamsburg on the morning of May 5, and McClellan held Franklin in reserve until he was certain that the rebels were being driven from the town.[27] After Franklin received his 9:40 p.m. order from McClellan to "push your movement as rapidly as possible," the division suffered further delays and did not leave Yorktown until early morning on May 6, because the navy was reluctant to navigate the York River in the darkness.[28]

Franklin's division arrived at Eltham's Landing, three miles from West Point, around 3:00 p.m. on May 6, forty-eight hours too late to cut off the Confederates.[29] The three brigades of the division went ashore that night on an open plateau and were under the cover of the Union gunboats. By mid-morning on May 7, Franklin's men moved forward into the woods, conducting a reconnaissance of the terrain, and ran into the rear guard of Gen. Joseph E. Johnston's Confederate Army as it was falling back toward Richmond. A skirmish ensued between the two forces near Eltham's Landing. The Third New Jersey, along with the Fourth New Jersey, was placed behind Brig. Gen. John Newton's brigade, which battled rebel soldiers from Brig. Gen. John Bell Hood's Texas Bri-

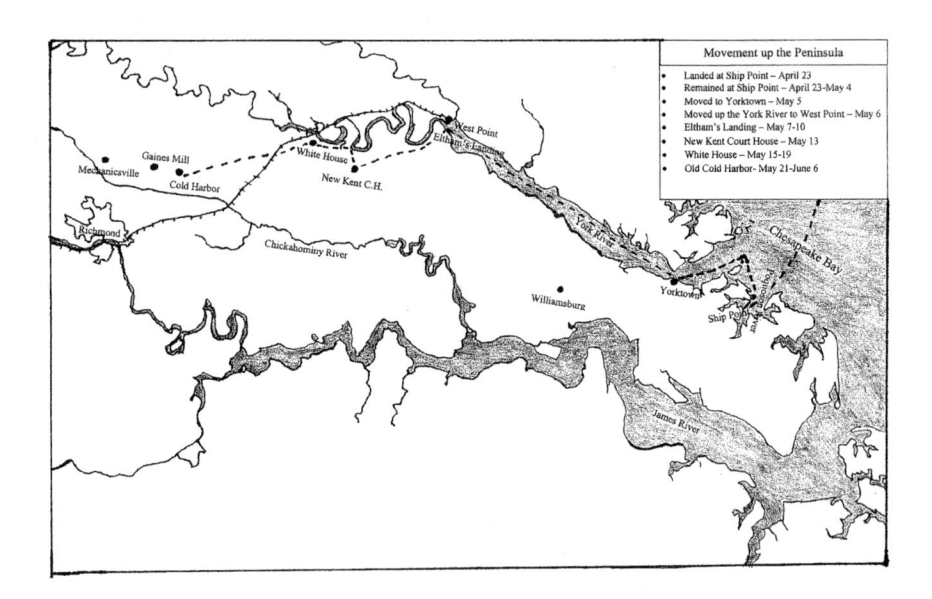

***Figure 2.2*** **Map of the movement of the New Jersey Brigade up the peninsula (The dashed line indicates the movement of the brigade).** *Source*: **Courtesy of the author.**

gade. The Jerseymen were held in reserve throughout the battle and did not see action, but Tom Howell got a taste of combat as the shells from the Union gunboats screamed overhead, and he listened as the fighting raged in the woods to his front. The young lieutenant explained, "Our troops behaved very well, charged the enemy several times and drove them through the woods some distance; they were the Texan Rangers and fought with great spirit." "Half a dozen times I thought we would make a rush to support the brigade of skirmishers in the woods but didn't."[30]

By the middle of the afternoon, the battle was over and the New Jersey Brigade moved into the woods to relieve troops that had participated in the fighting. The Third New Jersey replaced the Fifth Maine from Brig. Gen. Henry W. Slocum's brigade, which was positioned along the road where the action took place. The Jerseymen took refuge behind a fence, and Howell was able to assess the scene of destruction wrought by the battle: "The trees and fence rails were cut in every direction with balls and shells. . . . One ball from one of the gunboats cut in half and went in to the ground, bursting, made a place large enough to put a government wagon in."[31]

The brigade remained in its position along the road throughout the night, and every man slept with his weapon in case the Confederates launched another attack. At daybreak the troops were sent forward about a mile and a half and halted at a farm. The farmhouse was deserted and the men took opportunity to loot it of its possessions, even though McClellan had issued orders about respecting the property of Southerners and against pillaging.[32] With no indication of remorse, Howell told his brother that he took "some candles, a tumbler, a ball of twine, a bottle of cologne, several other things. In fact I went over things pretty thoroughly. My men and those of other companies followed me and that is the way we do unto those who are in the rebel army."[33] Captain Buckley mentioned that he made off with a four-year-old mule, which now had "the honor to transport my blankets."[34] It seems that Yankee soldiers respected the possessions of those Southerners who remained in their homes, but as historian Stephen W. Sears asserts, "If the owners abandoned their property and fled to the Confederate lines . . . the men took it as a sign of their hopelessly secessionist spirit, in which case their property did not deserve respect."[35] After relieving the home of its valuables, the troops marched back to their position near Eltham's Landing later that afternoon.

In the letters he wrote to his family, Tom did not specifically speak of "crushing the rebellion" or call the Confederates "traitors." At the same time, though, he did not use any kind words in describing the enemy. In one letter written shortly after the clash with the Confederate troops at Eltham's Landing, he described how one Union soldier was caught in a swamp by a few Confederates and asked the men for a quarter. Instead, the Southern troops shot the man dead on the spot. Howell was outraged and wrote, "I would like to know what should be done with such an enemy, I say we ought to shoot them like dogs."[36] Shortly after this incident, he noted that he was "anxious for a dash at those rebels" so that justice could be brought to an enemy who appeared to be acting without honor.[37]

By May 10, the main body of McClellan's army had linked up with Franklin's command. On that day the Third New Jersey and Fourth New Jersey marched three miles to a large plantation on the Pamunkey River named Romancoke, which had been bequeathed to Robert E. Lee Jr. by George Washington Parke Custis, the father-in-law of Gen. Robert E. Lee. The plantation was over four thousand acres and Howell estimated that two hundred slaves lived on the property.[38] The other two regiments from the New Jersey Brigade did not accompany them, because General Franklin sent those men to New Kent Court House the day before to assist Brig. Gen. George Stoneman's cavalry.[39] Tom was apparently appalled when he saw the condition of the slaves on the Romancoke Plantation. He told his brother, "I have heard more from these slaves on this place than I ever supposed. The master is very wealthy and yet he could only afford to give to one old slave one pair of pantaloons in three years. And I do not believe that there is one piece of the original cloth left in them."[40] It seems that his parents' contempt for the institution of slavery rubbed off on Tom, who was dismayed by how poorly the slaves lived yet how well the master survived.

The two New Jersey regiments remained at the plantation for the rest of May 10 and took to the road again the next day. Although the troops covered a distance of only four miles during the day's march, Howell was exhausted, complaining that the journey was warm and dusty.[41] The troops of the Third and Fourth New Jersey were still nine miles from New Kent Court House, but Lieutenant Howell still believed they would be in Richmond before the end of the week.

The men remained idle throughout the day of May 12. However, late in the evening, orders arrived for them to march early the next morning to New Kent Court House. The soldiers broke camp at 4:00 a.m. on May 13, but after a short march they were halted and forced to wait as the rest of the division passed. During this delay Howell was standing near the road and witnessed some excitement. He later recounted to his mother what he saw:

> I saw a large party of horsemen coming down one of the side roads, some one said there comes Gen. McClellan[;] sure enough, he did come, and as he turned into our road, such cheers that our regiment and the 8th NY gave him, well I never saw a man so much pleased as himself, he showed it in his face, he took his cap off and went down the road amid the most tremendous cheering I ever heard I think; he passed so near me that I could have touched his horse with my hand; You should have seen me waving my cap. He had his whole Staff with him, and his body guard, a regiment of cavalry, regulars, and his Infantry.[42]

After General McClellan passed, the New Jersey regiments continued their march, arriving at New Kent early that afternoon and rejoining with the other two regiments of the brigade. The troops then continued on to Cumberland Landing, where they made camp that evening. Howell mentioned that the march that day was "the worst I have experienced or passed through yet, it seemed as if all the dust in Virginia was called on our road, and all the heat of the Sun right on us."[43] His spirits were raised that evening, however, when he received a package from home, which included some stockings that Annie had made for him; a new pair of shoes, since he did not like the pair he bought before the campaign started; a carpet bag; some cake; and paper.[44] The arrival of this package made him long for home, and he wrote his mother, "I should like to be home this Summer but I expect we shall have to continue *our excursion* through most of the Southern States yet."[45]

As McClellan's army made its slow, methodical march up the peninsula, the New Jersey Brigade, and the rest of Franklin's division, remained at Cumberland Landing until May 15. They continued their march along a muddy road that followed the Pamunkey River to White

House Landing, and the men made camp a few hundred yards from the York River Railroad bridge, which connected West Point to Richmond.[46] White House was the plantation of Gen. Robert E. Lee's son William H. F. "Rooney" Lee and the place where George Washington had courted his future wife, Martha Custis.[47] General McClellan arrived at White House on May 16 and decided to use it as his base for the next stage of his campaign against the Confederate capital.[48]

Tom Howell and the rest of the New Jersey Brigade stayed at White House until May 19, and he took this opportunity to write his family and reflect on the upcoming movement toward Richmond. He was excited that the army was nearing the Confederate capital, which he believed was being evacuated by the rebels, and he expected only small fights with the Confederates, but nothing extensive. He also used this time at White House to think about home. He told his mother that he "should like to spend *one more quiet Sunday* at home" and hoped to be home soon, but that he was "anxious to finish or help finish this little affair in the South."[49] This was the second letter he wrote that week in which he expressed his desire to be home.

Captain Buckley, who had been sick most of the previous week with a bilious attack, used this time at White House to speculate who would become the next colonel of the Third New Jersey. Buckley, Howell, and others in the regiment disliked Lieutenant Colonel Brown and hoped he would not get the job. The captain believed the choice for colonel lay between Lt. Col. Robert McAllister of the First New Jersey, who Buckley called "a regular old granny," and Lt. Col. William B. Hatch of the Fourth New Jersey.[50]

General McClellan reorganized his army during his stay at White House, creating two new corps, the V Corps and VI Corps, to be commanded by two of his friends. Franklin was given command of the VI Corps, and command of his former division now fell to Brig. Gen. Henry W. Slocum. Brig. Gen. Fitz John Porter would command the V Corps.[51]

On May 19, McClellan led the V and VI Corps on a five-mile march to Tunstall's Station, a stop along the Richmond and York River Railroad. The next day the troops covered another seven miles and continued their march toward the Chickahominy River on the morning of May 21. Lieutenant Colonel McAllister explained McClellan's intention in a letter to his wife. "We are making a flanking movement on their left," he told her, "and will no doubt take them where they least expect it."[52] McClellan planned to keep Porter's and Franklin's corps, along with Brig. Gen. Edwin Sumner's II Corps, on the north side of the Chickahominy to link up with McDowell's I Corps, which he expected to march from northern Virginia and arrive just north of Richmond.

On May 17, McDowell was instructed by the Federal High Command in Washington to march overland to the Pamunkey River and link up with McClellan, who had been notified that he should soon expect the I

Corps to appear on his right flank.[53] But McDowell postponed his march because Brig. Gen. James Shields's division was delayed in joining the I Corps, although McDowell still expected to link with McClellan by the end of May. However, the I Corps never made it to the peninsula. On May 24 President Lincoln countermanded McDowell's movement so that the I Corps could deal with the new threat posed by Confederate Maj. Gen. Thomas "Stonewall" Jackson in the Shenandoah Valley after Jackson routed Maj. Gen. Nathaniel Banks's force at Front Royal and pursued the Yankees down the valley.[54] McClellan was outraged by the president's recall of McDowell but continued his plan for putting Richmond under siege.[55]

During the march of May 21, Howell described the excessive heat and the toll the day's journey had taken on the men. The events of this day also led to furthering the feud between Lieutenant Colonel Brown and Howell. On that day the young lieutenant was serving as officer of the guard and had a difficult time keeping the men together. Brown was angry about Howell's performance and later reported his dissatisfaction to Capt. William E. Bryan of Company H. The captain told Howell of his conversation with Brown, which sent the lieutenant into a fury. He explained the situation to his mother in a letter the next night:

> Capt. Bryan came to me and said that Col. Brown had been giving him the mischief, on account of my not being able to keep the guards together, well that made me angry, he also said that if the officer of the guard couldn't *keep* the *guard* together, the officer of the day would have to take it.... I plainly told the Capt. that if Col. Brown was not able to keep the regiment together, he must not expect the officer of the guard to keep his guard in good order.... You must know that when I get angry, and I have not been really angry since I entered the army, I generally make a mire of *some sort, kind* and *class*. I have a great deal of Howell blood as well as of the Carpenter in me, and I will have my rights no matter what Col. Brown or any other man says to the contrary.[56]

Howell was not going to have his honor diminished by Brown or anyone else, for honor guided the manhood of a significant number of Northern men.[57] He believed that "this is a great deal of talk for a little boy of any size, standing and experience, but as I said before, I am a Howell."[58] Nothing more came of this incident, but the acrimony between the two men continued. The New Jersey Brigade and the rest of Franklin's corps made camp that evening at Old Cold Harbor.

Franklin's corps remained near Cold Harbor for the next two weeks as McClellan prepared for his final assault on the Confederate capital. The New Jersey Brigade spent this time on picket duty along the Chickahominy while the soldiers used the opportunity to check out the rebel pickets. Howell pointed out that he and his men could clearly make out the uniforms of the Southerners and that the two parties were so close that they were undoubtedly within rifle range of the Confederates, but no shots were exchanged.

Tom Howell wondered during the last week of May if the Confederates would even attempt to defend Richmond. "It is hard to believe that the rebels will stay and fight after having retreated so far," he confided to his brother. "My opinion is that they will not, though we may have skirmishes."[59] The young lieutenant was confident that McClellan would be able to take the rebel capital without much of a fight and expected to "see funny sights and have gay times" along the way.[60] He assured his family, however, that if the Confederates decided to fight, he would not be rash and put himself in harm's way, but they could also be certain he would not "be backward," since a man would never shirk his duties.

Tom reported to his brother that he believed he had gained the support of the soldiers in his regiment. He was always worried about what others thought of him, so he made it a point to lead by example, treat the men with respect, and conduct himself as a gentleman. "I am very strict when strictness is needed. But when I am off duty I am the quiet gentleman," he explained to Joshua. "In fact I always treat them as men should be treated. I am always gentle and manly in my contact toward them."[61] He believed he had proven to the soldiers of the regiment that even though he was only seventeen years old, he was worthy of his commission. Unfortunately, there is no way to confirm this through letters and diaries from the soldiers he commanded. None of the men under Howell's command recorded their opinions of the young lieutenant, so we can only speculate on whether his assessment was accurate.

With the Yankee army sitting just a few miles from Richmond, Lieutenant Howell took the opportunity to voice his disapproval of the army's policy of issuing whiskey to the troops. Each soldier was given a gill of the liquor each day to ward off the effects of exposure, and as a "Christian Gentleman" Howell believed that alcohol was a bad thing that would prove to be the "ruin of a great number."[62] He again reassured his mother that he still remained true to his promise that he would refrain from the consumption of hard liquor while in the army, although he admitted that he had some beer, but he did not elaborate on whether this was a one-time occurrence or how much beer he had consumed. He told her that he intended to continue to be strong, even though other soldiers sometimes pressured him to take a drink or smoke a cigar. He believed that these vices were to be avoided by an honorable gentleman.

On May 28, 1862, Tom wrote his sister Annie to inform her that he had been told that a Camden newspaper had reported he had been killed.[63] He assured her he was still "alive and kicking" and hoped to remain that way for many years. His thoughts again returned to home, and he said he would like to be there to spend the Fourth of July with his family. "Be sure that I shall try my best to get home," he told her. "The principle fighting should be over by that time."[64]

Captain Buckley was looking forward to the upcoming struggle for the Confederate capital. He was confident that the Union Army would win, the rebellion would come to a close, and he could return to a regular life. His fear, though, was that the rebels would continue their Fabian policy and that he and the rest of the army would be sent "for a tramp in the cotton states."[65] Buckley also mentioned that the Yankee army suffered severely at this time with sickness. "Our Regt will hardly muster 700 effective men now," he informed his mother, but the ground chosen as the camp of the Third New Jersey near Cold Harbor was well drained and had a good water supply, so the health of the regiment slightly improved.[66] By the end of May 1862 one-fifth of McClellan's army suffered from "Chickahominy fever," a typho-malarial fever. The men were physically unfit to fight, because Union campsites had become breeding grounds for diseases as human waste contaminated the water supply. At that time disease-causing microorganisms were unknown, so bathers, animals, cooks, defecators, drinkers, and launderers all shared the camp's water source.[67]

The Third New Jersey was sent on picket duty along the Chickahominy River on the morning of May 30, 1862. As the men relieved troops from the Twenty-seventh New York from Col. Joseph Bartlett's brigade of Slocum's division, the same division as the New Jersey Brigade, Confederate artillery from the other side of the river opened fire. The Union soldiers took shelter behind the woods near the river and waited for the shelling to cease. Captain Buckley explained in a letter that this was the first of many experiences "of antagonistic shell[ing]" and that it "caused a considerable ducking of heads among the nervous."[68] Later that afternoon the skies opened up with a violent thunderstorm and dumped a tremendous amount of rain on the area throughout the night. The Chickahominy River rose several feet and overflowed its banks, turning the whole meadow into a "swamp varying from 6 inches to 3 feet deep."[69] The regiment was relieved early the next morning and waded through waist-high water on its way back to camp, suffering only one casualty on picket that day: Pvt. Landric Leeson, of Company C, who accidentally shot himself in the foot and had to have the second toe on his left foot amputated.[70]

On May 31, 1862, Confederate general Joseph Johnston's army struck the blue-clad men south of the Chickahominy in what has become known as the Battle of Fair Oaks or Seven Pines.[71] By committing twenty-two of his twenty-nine infantry brigades to the battle, Johnston hoped to crush the two army corps, III and IV Corps, that McClellan had separated from the rest of his army. With the flooding of the Chickahominy, many of the bridges the Yankees had built spanning the river were destroyed, further isolating the two Union corps. Johnston's troops, however, were plagued by bad roads and lack of coordination from their commanders and failed to destroy the Yankee command.[72] During the course of the fighting on

May 31, Johnston was seriously wounded and Confederate president Jefferson Davis named Robert E. Lee as the new commander of the troops outside Richmond. The next morning the Confederates renewed the attack, but as they were unable to make headway against the Union position, they withdrew back to their lines by early afternoon. Neither side made any gains from the battle, which resulted in more than six thousand Confederate and five thousand Union casualties.

Although Tom Howell and the rest of the men of the VI Corps were not involved in the battle, they were able to hear the fighting since they were positioned just north of the Chickahominy River. Howell wrote his mother:

> It was very exciting; we stood with a large number of officers, upon a hill, about two hundred yards from camp, watching the shells bursting over the trees, and such a continued roll of musketry I never did hear. . . . Ma you should hear the heavy firing of musketry, and then think that a great number of those balls will "*take positions*" in the limbs and other parts of the body of our troops, and also in those of the Rebels, pleasant thoughts."[73]

He mentioned that the VI Corps was under orders during the battle to cross the Chickahominy to support the troops south of the river, but, as mentioned earlier, the torrent of the river destroyed many of the bridges spanning it. Buckley noted, "The creek is too much swollen for an immediate move as the artillery can't cross but . . . when we do move may God be with us."[74]

After the Battle of Fair Oaks, the Northern soldiers realized they were not going to take the Confederate capital without a fight. "Everything points to a severe struggle for Richmond and before long McClellan is encouraging the army with Napoleonic orders calling for high deeds of valor," Captain Buckley wrote to his father. "We are very confident of success. May we never be shaken in that belief."[75] Tom Howell shared these same sentiments. In a letter written just a few days after the battle, he told his mother that he was now certain there was going to be a tremendous battle to take Richmond. He predicted that if the Yankee troops crossed the river and advanced on the rebel capital, the fields south of the Chickahominy would be covered with the bodies of dead Union soldiers. "Many a poor fellow full of life now, will bite the dust then," Howell wrote. "I hope I may escape, there is no telling how ever what will take place, still I hope I may *be prepared* for any thing that *may* take place."[76] As the possibility of a major battle loomed, he again took time to consider his own mortality. "If a man gets hurt," he thought, "he has the consolation to think that he was wounded, probably until death, while fighting for his *country*."[77]

Tom's uncle Col. Joshua Blackwood Howell, of the Eighty-fifth Pennsylvania, was involved in the fighting around Fair Oaks, and the family was unaware if he had emerged from the battle unscathed.[78] In the week following the action, Tom tried to allay the fears of the family by telling them that the colonel was not on the list of casualties, yet he was not certain whether his uncle was unhurt or not. "I hope that nothing has happened to Uncle Jos," he wrote a cousin, "because I have made up my mind that if he has been hurt or captured the enemy shall have little mercy from me!"[79] In just a few months Tom Howell had grown to loathe the South "and everything belonging to it and will be glad to see the north once more. If I return from this war safe and sound I shall never travel in the south again."[80]

On June 4, while the New Jersey Brigade waited along the banks of the Chickahominy River for orders to advance forward with the rest of the army toward Richmond, Lieutenant Howell was chosen for the first time as "officer of the day" for the Third New Jersey. As officer of the day, one's duties included maintaining good order and cleanliness of the camp, ordering patrols and rounds made by the officer of the guard, visiting the hospital and reporting on its condition, and making rounds at least once during the night between midnight and reveille visiting the guards.[81] Howell explained that the duty was "not so bad after all, a man can order the whole regiment to work or *do any thing else* that he thinks proper."[82] Being given this responsibility for the first time demonstrates that Howell's superiors had confidence in the young lieutenant's abilities as a leader.

The New Jersey Brigade broke camp on June 6, 1862, and marched about two and a half miles to Mechanicsville, Virginia, where they relieved troops from Col. Joseph J. Bartlett's brigade, and remained at this location for almost two weeks. The New Jersey men, now just four miles from Richmond, encamped at a farm owned by a man named Curtis. While picketing the area around Mechanicsville, Howell noted that the Union soldiers had climbed to the tops of the trees and could see plenty of rebel soldiers and the spires of churches in the Confederate capital. However, he still feared that the Southern troops might abandon Richmond and that McClellan's army would have to follow them, exposing the Northern soldiers to the hot summer sun of Virginia. "I am not going to have myself burnt up with a Sun the like of which has never been felt or seen in Camden," Tom told his mother.[83]

Shortly after arriving at Mechanicsville, Union troops received word that Gen. Henry Halleck's army had forced the Confederates to abandon Corinth, Mississippi, on May 30, 1862. Celebrations ensued throughout the camps of McClellan's army. Tom informed his mother that one of the men in his company wanted to go down to the river to inform the rebels of the news, but the young lieutenant would not allow it, fearing the Southerners might open fire and harm the Yankee soldier. "I have a number of young soldiers in the company," Howell said, "the loss of whom would be a heavy blow."[84] Tom had grown to care for his men and did not want to see any harm come to them, although he did lose one man in his company during the stay at Mechanicsville, as Pvt. Henry Berga succumbed to disease on June 7, 1862.[85]

With many men of the regiment still suffering from the effects of "Chickahominy fever" and the prospect of possibly being wounded in the upcoming struggle to take Richmond, Lieutenant Howell began to think about the competency of the doctors in his regiment. He mentioned that Dr. John V. Mattison, the surgeon of the Third New Jersey, was ill and in the hospital, so the surgeon's duties now fell to the assistant surgeon, Edward Welling. Howell was unsure of Welling's ability. "It is a sad thing when men are taken sick, go to the hospital and then are not well taken care of," he explained to his mother, so he asked her to ask Charley, Tom's older brother, about Welling's competency.[86] Tom believed Charley would be able to give some assessment of Welling's abilities, since Charley and Welling attended the College of New Jersey (Princeton University) at the same time, although Charley Howell was one year behind Welling.[87] Tom mentioned that if he got sick he would go to Lewis Oakley, surgeon of the Fourth New Jersey, or Dr. Henry C. Clark, assistant surgeon of the Second New Jersey, for care, but assured his mother that at this time he was in good health.

On June 15, the New Jersey Brigade marched to a farmyard located about one and a half miles west of Mechanicsville and prepared for an attack by the Confederates. According to Howell, artillery covered the road while the Union troops positioned themselves on a hill overlooking a meadow in front of the river. "We could have commenced shelling them before they even had time to cross and then if they had pushed forward from the woods into the broad field they would have been cut to pieces by grape and shell," the young lieutenant said. "They would have caught rats from us and would not have been able to return the compliment."[88] The Confederates did not attack, however, and the New Jersey men were spared a heavy fight. All of this came about because rebel cavalry crossed the Chickahominy River and attacked Union wagon trains. Between June 12 and June 15, twelve hundred Confederate cavalrymen, led by Brig. Gen. J. E. B. Stuart, rode around McClellan's army and informed General Lee that McClellan's line north of the Chickahominy was vulnerable.

Even though much of the Union Army remained in the same positions around Richmond in the middle of June that they had been in at the end of May, Tom Howell was still extremely confident in the abilities of General McClellan. He believed the general was playing his old game and would take Richmond with little fighting, which was the same technique used at Yorktown. "[H]ere at Richmond," Lieutenant Howell told his mother, "I believe he [McClellan] intends not only to approach [the Confederate works around Richmond] but surround them and capture very near their whole force."[89] Tom believed there was no doubt this strategy would end the war, and if the rebel capital fell, he planned to resign his commission and return home, because he was "anxious for this miserable war to be *closed up.*"[90]

As the Union Army sat just a few miles from Richmond poised to take the rebel capital and possibly end the war, McClellan kept a close watch on the movement of the enemy's troops by utilizing the army's Balloon Corps. The American Civil War saw the introduction of balloons filled with hot air or gas, and the use of these balloons for observation purposes reached its peak during the Peninsula Campaign. Heading up this newly formed Balloon Corps was Thaddeus S. C. Lowe, who had become interested in aeronautics during the 1850s and convinced President Lincoln in 1861 to create an Aeronautical Corps that could survey battlefields and the positions of enemy troops.[91]

Lowe had two balloons in operation within McClellan's lines around Richmond. The balloon *Washington* was near Mechanicsville and the *Intrepid* was close to Dr. William Gaines's farm near Cold Harbor.[92] Tom mentioned Lowe in a letter on May 27, 1862, but did not go into any detail about the balloons, although he must have seen one or both of Lowe's balloons, since the New Jersey Brigade was near Cold Harbor for two weeks and Mechanicsville for almost another two weeks. Howell's friend Captain Buckley got an up-close-and-personal look at the *Washington*, which was only two miles from the camp of the Jersey troops near Mechanicsville. The captain accompanied his cousin E. Burd Grubb to the balloon, and Grubb, who had gone up in the balloon earlier in the day, told the balloon operators that Buckley had been sent by General Taylor to corroborate what Grubb had seen on his earlier ascension. Buckley later wrote to his father that when he and Grubb ascended into the sky he did not experience any dizziness as he had expected. He mentioned that the view from eight hundred feet above the earth was grand and that Richmond could be seen "in full sight tho not close enough to distinguish streets.... Such a sight must be seen to be appreciated. The sensation was decidedly novel and not easily to be forgotten."[93]

On June 19, 1862, the corps under Franklin's command was ordered to move south of the Chickahominy to Fair Oaks. Tom Howell described it as a grueling march that took its toll on his men: "It was a very fatiguing march all the way from Mechanicsville and by a round about way at that. At one time I had not fifteen men in the ranks, most having fallen out."[94] After arriving at Fair Oaks, Howell took notice of the devastation caused by the battle three weeks earlier and saw the numerous graves that covered the battlefield. He was impressed with the sight of trees cut in two by the firepower of both armies and noted that one tree had eighteen bullet marks in its trunk. As for the graves on the battlefield, he observed that the bodies of both "the enemy as well as those of our men are put in [trenches] promiscuously."[95] The battlefield emitted a strong smell for weeks after the battle as the rain washed away the earth from the graves and exposed the decaying bodies.[96]

With the arrival of Franklin's VI Corps at Fair Oaks, four of McClellan's five army corps (the II, III, IV, and VI) were south of the Chickahominy River, with only Porter's V Corps remaining north of the river. On June 21 half of the men of the Third New Jersey were ordered, along with men from the other regiments in the brigade, to build a corduroy road so that heavy artillery could be brought to the front for a possible siege of Richmond. Howell had command of the detail, whose work was supervised by the U.S. Army Engineers.[97] Some of the men chopped down trees while others used shovels to form a road. The split logs were placed on the road and covered with eight inches of dirt. Howell believed this road would "last fifty years."[98] These corduroy roads, along with the eight additional bridges built by the engineers across the Chickahominy River, would link together the two wings of McClellan's army as it straddled the Chickahominy.

While he was at Fair Oaks, Tom Howell grew frustrated with army life, as did many soldiers, and he believed that "a man no matter whether he be an officer or private is not benefitted by entering the army."[99] He was considering resigning his commission if he was "spared through the coming battle," but he hoped that McClellan's army would succeed in defeating the Confederates outside of Richmond and end the war.[100] Tom urged his sister to keep his plan a secret. He informed her that he would not resign before the battle, because some would interpret it as a sign of fear or cowardice, and that would injure his reputation and honor. He mentioned in a letter home to Joshua that he was fed up with Lieutenant Colonel Brown, especially his excessive drinking, as well as problems caused by 1st Lt. Archibald Taylor. Although Arch had grown to become Howell's closest friend in the army, Tom believed Arch was attempting to increase the tensions between Brown and Howell, but he assured his brother, "I shall be very careful and keep my eyes wide open and my ears."[101] Tom explained to Joshua in the letter that their uncle Thomas Preston Carpenter was attempting to use his political influence to prevent Brown from becoming colonel, and Tom thought Arch had something to do with informing Brown of this. Howell told his brother that he would keep on "friendly terms" with Taylor but that he knew Arch was a "selfish ungenerous fellow."[102]

By June 24, McClellan had devised a plan that would push his entire line south of the Chickahominy forward to Old Tavern, the high ground at the intersection of the Nine Mile Road and the road to New Bridge, which would force the Confederates into their works around Richmond and enable the general to bring up his heavy artillery and shell the city into submission. The commanding general explained, "If we gained that, the game is up for Secesh—I will then have them in the hollow of my hand."[103] Tom Howell, now sporting a "remarkable goatee," wrote in his letters that the Union troops occupying the three-mile-long line of fortifications facing Richmond were constantly under arms during the last week of June 1862, as everyone expected the commencement of a battle at any time. He informed his siblings that if the Confederates attacked, they would "get the mischief," since the Union works were, in his opinion, "strong and extensive," but the Confederates did not advance.[104]

On June 25, 1862, McClellan ordered the III Corps divisions of Brig. Gen. Joseph Hooker and Brig. Gen. Philip Kearny, along with one brigade each from the II and IV Corps, to attack the Confederates at Oak Grove, in what would become the first of the Seven Days' Battles. Possession of Oak Grove would enable McClellan to use the II and III Corps to attack Old Tavern in the flank on either June 26 or June 27.[105] The battle proved to be indecisive, however, as the Union forces were able to advance their picket lines by only six hundred yards at the cost of 626 casualties.[106]

In a letter to his mother on June 25, Tom Howell mentioned that Kearny's advance had brought on a sharp fight and that his regiment was under marching orders to go to the front. In the postscript to this letter, Tom proclaimed, "We are going out to the front immediately," but he was not engaged in the fighting at Oak Grove.[107] In a letter to his brother the next day, Howell explained that the brigade had marched two hundred fifty yards down the Richmond and York River Railroad to act as a reserve for Brig. Gen. Israel B. Richardson's II Corps brigade.[108]

As McClellan attempted to advance his lines south of the Chickahominy River, Confederate general Robert E. Lee made plans to attack the isolated Union V Corps positioned north of the Chickahominy. Lee's bold plan would alleviate the pressure on the Confederate capital and could possibly destroy an entire Union corps. Lee decided to leave two divisions, numbering some 28,900 men, under the command of two major generals, John B. Magruder and Benjamin Huger, to face the 76,000 bluecoats south of the Chickahominy River. The bulk of the rebel army, 55,800 men, under the commands of major generals Thomas "Stonewall" Jackson, Ambrose Powell Hill, Daniel Harvey Hill, James Longstreet, and a part of Brig. Gen. J. E. B. Stuart's cavalry brigade would attack the Union V Corps north of the Chickahominy under the command of Brig. Gen. Fitz John Porter.[109]

On June 26, 1862, in the second of the Seven Days' Battles, the Confederate forces attacked Porter's corps at Mechanicsville. The Third New Jersey, along with the rest of Franklin's VI Corps, remained in its position south of the Chickahominy River. One soldier of the regiment recounted, "We were in reserve that day. Firing was very heavy on our right, and we thought there was a general engagement along the whole line."[110] Lee failed to break Porter's defenses behind Beaver Dam Creek, and the Confederates suffered a loss of 1,475 men to only 361 Union casualties.[111]

After the battle on Porter's front ended, McClellan boasted, "We have completely gained the day—not lost a single foot of ground. McCall has done splendidly as well as Morell. Tell our men . . . they are put to their trumps & that with such men disaster is impossible."[112] Tom Howell, writing to his brother at 10:00 p.m., explained the elation in the Union camps after word was received of Porter's victory. "You have never heard such cheering in your life from way back in the rear out to the pickets and from the right to the left," he described.[113] Despite boasting about his victory and inflicting severe losses on the rebel forces, McClellan, believing he was severely outnumbered, ordered Porter to withdraw his corps eastwardly toward Cold Harbor and set up a defensive position behind the Boatswain's Swamp.

## Civil War Letters of Thomas James Howell: April 18—June 26, 1862

[Original]

On board of the John A. Warner[114]
Friday Morn. Apr. 18th, 1'62

Dear Ma,
Yesterday (Thurs.) morning, the Col received orders to be ready to march with the other regiments of the Brigade at half past nine o'clock. Nine came, with it a few taps of the drum; the hill, which five minutes before had been covered with tents, was now a hill spotted only with men and stacks of muskets. We waited in the hot sun a half an hour, a *heavy* roll from the drums, the Col's *forward,* and our regiment was under arms, and we were marching along the road, a mighty one, on our way to town; we were encamped only a half a mile outside of Alexandria. It was a very pretty sight as we marched through the town all the way down Washington Street, which is quite a wide one, the sidewalks were alive with people; a whole regiment of cavalry was drawn up on both sides of the street. We were rather tired by the time we reached the boat landing[,] not so much from walking as from the dust and heat [of the] sun; our coats were just covered with dust. Our regiment marched, immediately upon arriving, on board the John A. Warner where we are now, *and where we will stay until we march off.* We officers have the ladies cabin to bunk in; last night I slept on a bench, or rather a *cain* [he drew a picture of the ship here] bench, of some kind, I never saw the like before; excuse the steamboat I was attempting to make but did not succeed; it is something like an old boat, that passed down the river. We are a few miles below Alexandria and about a mile and a half above Fort Washington;[115] after staying here all night, we are at last under way, with a large brig behind. It is nearly one o'clock, Major Allison has been and now is on board paying off the men. I am in a hurry to finish this letter so then Col. Cook,[116] I believe his name is, may take it to Alexandria, when he goes back; he came with us that he might take home any money, the men may wish to send to their wives

and children. There is one thing I am very sorry to see, that is, the men are gradually beginning to forget those things left at home. I received all the letters; yours, Annie's[,] Jos'[,] and Marts.[117] There have been and are now over four hundred sick of that Summer complaint of which you know. I have not had it yet. I do not know exactly what it is from. I suppose it comes from a change of water and from a slaughter house which was on one side of our camp. It was enough to have made the whole regiment sick, and I suppose the greater part will be[;] a quarter of the officers have it. I have escaped everything as yet, and hope that I *may escape everything,* and at least come home with all bones safe, with some bars on my shoulder straps and with honor to myself, or having acquired it. I will give an account of our passing Fort Washington and Mount Vernon,[118] and the enemies forts &c. in my letter to Annie or Jos. The Maryland shore is one long broken line. Here it is about fifty, sixty or probably more in height[;] there it is twenty-five or thirty and so on. Often it is very low, and back on the banks are fields of the most beautiful green I ever saw[,] just like velvet. The river is filled with ships, steamships, steamboats, tugs, in fact all kinds of water craft going down the river with cavalry horses, wagons and troops on board.

Frank has not written for a long time; I always like to hear from him and from all. Remember me to all. Give my love to Aunt Sarah Uncle & Thomas's family, Uncle Ed's, also to Charley, Annie, Jos and Frank.

Much love and kisses to yourself. Please not to direct my letters as the last was. Simply [address it to "]Lt. T. J. Howell, Co. I, 3rd N.J. Inf. Col Taylor. To follow the regiment.["]

Your most affectionate son
Tom

[Transcribed Copy]
On board the John Warner
April 19th 1862

Ask Ma if she can send me a valise like the one we saw in Market St. the day I was with her, above 4th, I believe. If she can get it into the box, send it as soon as possible. Mine is not worth anything.

Dear Annie,
We are now fast leaving the Potomac River. We are four miles from land. The water is a beautiful green. Last evening, about 6 or 7 o'clock, the sky became as black as ink with lightning off to the west. Being some distance from the land I made up my mind that we would have a great time of a storm. We being on such a boat as the John Warner which is not accustomed to the sea. But we had nothing more than rain and after a while we came to a halt, four or five miles from the shore. Early this morning we were under way again. Now in Chesapeake Bay. No land in sight. Nothing to see but wild ducks, beautiful green water, cloudy sky. Before I forget it I will remark that the box Ma is going to send to me may be directed by way of Fortress Monroe, Adam[s]'s

Express. I should like at least six pairs of stockings, also those shoes, not to forget the other things. A boat leaves Baltimore every evening at 6 o'clock which reaches the Fortress at about six next morning. A boat leaves Fortress Monroe at 6 every evening and arrives at Baltimore at 6 next morning. So letters and boxes can reach us with very little difficulty. There is one thing I like, that is the Bay when I write is as smooth as the Delaware River but I suppose as we get down near Fortress Monroe there will be quite a roll and then seasickness. It is thought that we will reach our destination by evening today. We will land within 7 miles of General McClellan's camp. I do not exactly know how many miles from Yorktown.[119] We will not go to Fortress Monroe but will land in a creek south east of Yorktown. I believe it is ten or fifteen miles from the fortress. This boat carries us through the water finely though we have this brigantine in tow. She has four or five sails set, or had twenty minutes ago, I have not been out on deck for some time. We live well on board and have to pay 36c [cents] for it. We have everything we want and more too. This is the sixth trip of this boat down to Fortress Monroe. That is she has carried six loads to the Fortress and one back. There is no necessity of being sorry on account of my going to Yorktown. Capt Regur has not returned to his regiment yet and I don't suppose he ever will. His surgeon has given him up or had from last accounts.[120] I expect Arch Taylor will be Captain but as for my being 1st Lt. that is something I cannot remark upon. It would be a great thing indeed on account of being such a short time in the army. Yesterday I wrote to Ma, Uncle Bernard[121] and my young Sunday school scholar, William Mackay.[122] I sent Ben Howell[123] my photograph. If I have time before dinner I will write to Jos. I owe letter[s] to Mart, and Uncle Thomas and Annie Carpenter. Just tell Annie that I will answer as soon as I can. Wish you would ask Sue to write. While I think of it I will say that I want thin stockings for hot weather. It is very warm now. I am very well.

Remember me to all my young lady friends with the exception of Gert Browning. I don't want to be remembered to her. Give my love to all, to Ma, Charlie, Jos etc. much love to my dear sister Annie.

Tom

P.S. Give me an account of Frank's progress at school and anything of interest in Camden. Send letters to ["]Fort Monroe. 3rd N.J. Follow the regiment.["]

[Original]
On board the John A. Warner
Saturday Apr. 19th '62

Dear Ma,
After the fashion of Newspapers—Still later; it is just six in the afternoon; we have arrived in the Poquosin River, I could not begin to count the ships and steamboats that are now in the cove, and as far as the eye can see up the York River. While I am writing an officer of the Sixth

N.J. Inf. came on board, and told us some of the news, which is that three of the enemies forts were taken, and one was taken and retaken three times, also that one hundred and forty-one (141) killed and wounded were brought in from the scene of action.[124] I shall try and write as often as possible.

Your affectionate son
Tom
2nd lt. Co I 3rd N.J. Inf

Love to Annie, Charley, Jos and Frank
Please and not forget to send the box.
This is written in a hurry not having much light.
Tom.

I have not had time to write to Jos to day, I have sent my other letter to you, by Col. Cooke [H]e will mail it from Trenton also the letter to Annie; this will go by Mr. W. J. Taylor to Fortress Monroe, from there to Baltimore.
Tom.

[Transcribed Copy]
On board the John A. Warner
Sunday April 20th 1862

Dear Jos,
Though quite hungry I think I can write to you before dinner. It is now nearly 1 o'clock. I write my letters today for the reason that we are now waiting for orders. The officer of the day is up in the wheel house. He has been there all morning for the purpose of watching the Elm City, which boat has General Kearney and the staff on board. As soon as she gets under way we are to follow. She is about three quarters of a mile away from us. The orders are that if the general moves we are to follow whatever the risk may be[,] and you know the 3rd New Jersey is the regiment to obey such orders and Arch and I are the boys to go also with the regiment. It is thought that we are to land near the first battery. You know I hope we lead the storming party although I am not anxious to be hurt. But that is not to be thought of. This morning after reveille I went up on the hurricane deck to get some fresh air and some exercise. Although it was raining I walked up and down for over a half hour when I came down hungry and ready for our nice breakfast for which I pay as I said, 36c [cents]. I wrote to Mart Grey this morning. I don't like the idea of writing on Sunday but I may not have another chance for a long time. I expect we will very soon see nothing but warfare and war. I sat in the wheelhouse for several hours this morning watching the large fleet of vessels. I find that early tomorrow morning we leave so as to reach Gloucester Point[125] by daylight[;] then after that I will have to write another letter although I may not. Gloucester Point is near the enemy's batteries, very near. We will probably have a severe fight before night tomorrow. General Kearney sent word by Bob Dun-

ham[,] who was over on the Elm City[,] that we would land under fire. I have an elegant revolver, Smith and Wesson, patent.[126] Imagine me with a sword in one hand, a revolver in the other up to my middle in water, going ashore. It will be exceedingly interesting, will it not ? With the balls flying all around. The weather is stormy and cloudy, damp and cold. I believe I have told you all the news. Remember me to my friends. My love to Ma, Annie, Charlie and Frank. Direct mail to ["]Lieutenant T. Howell, Company I.["]

Your most affectionate brother
Tom

P.S. Do not forget that box containing those shoes.

[Original]
[Written at the top of the April 24th letter, below]
I send you a real confederate note[;][127] at least it was given to me by one on board the Warner. I bought it for seventy-five cents of[f] an oyster man from the shore. Please do send those things as soon as possible[.] [B]y some mistake four pairs of stockings were misplaced and [I] have but two pairs.
Tom

Camp at Ship Point
Thursday, April 24th 1862

Dear Ma,
Yesterday morning at half past nine, we got under way and steamed slowly up the York River. Before I go on I will describe the bay here. I may call it a *bay* on account of several rivers and creeks that flow into a large *basin*, which runs into the Chesapeake. I do not think the map gives one a good idea of the *water* here in this part of Virginia. Well as I was going to say, we went up the York River about half a mile, where as I said in my letter to you of yesterday there was a wharf formed of boats. We made fast and marched ashore forming what is called [a] column of companies. After waiting twenty minutes or more, we took up our line of march along the fields for a short distance, when upon coming to a narrow part of the road, formed by the tents of the *first Regular Cavalry*,[128] our regiment broke into platoons, which was the time to see a pretty sight, the Third marching to the lively music of the drum and fife corps. Our encampment is about three quarters of a mile from the boat in a corn field, I might as well call it a large plain, for there is no fence to be seen, just a broad surface, a wide surface, and I suppose a *deep*— —Last night Arch and I slept on a bed composed of straw and blankets, one India Rubber under and one above the other blanket; although it was a rather cool night, still we were quite warm and comfortable. This morning I was not very much pleased to hear the *Orderly Sergeant*[129] call out "Fall in Co. I," [T]he drums did not beat reveille on account of orders given by an officer of Gen. McClellan Staff, that there should be no music of an[y] kind, for in case of the long

roll it could not be distinguished. I did not get up, that is certain; our bed being in front of the stacks of arms, I, when the roll was called, turned over and ordered the Sergeant to dismiss the company. Upon getting up, I saw the McClellan Dragoons [130] drawn up into line, two or three batteries also, all ready to start, in about an hour they left and went up towards Yorktown. Our boat is thoroughly cleaned from her hurricane deck to her hold and from stem to stern. We will probably stay on shore to day. Our destination is known to be Gloucester Point opposite the Rebel batteries. The first Connecticut battery [131] is but a quarter of mile from the enemys works, and we are to support this battery; we will land under cover of the battery and our gunboats so you see we will be in for it pretty soon; why we can hear the booming of the guns, and the shots from the skirmishers. I expect we shall have hot work soon enough, and enough of it, that is certain. I will say before I forget it, that as we passed Mount Vernon our band played, and the troops tolled the bell on the John A. Warner. The house is the same that one sees in pictures. I saw his [George Washington's] tomb also through the trees. I shall write to Uncle Thomas and Annie Carpenter this afternoon if I have time. I believe I have told all the news. I shall write constantly and should like to get letters whenever you can write and send them. You will please direct my letters not to Washington but to Fortress Monroe via Baltimore.

Lt. T. J. Howell
Co. I, 3rd NJ Inf
Col. Taylor
Franklin Division
Fortress Monroe

Give my love to all also to Charley, Annie, Josh and Frank, much love from your affectionate son. Pay day is coming around again and if I live I hope to send you quite a neat sum.
Tom

[Transcribed Copy]
On board steamer John Warner
Saturday April 26th 1862

Dear Annie,
Having nothing else to do I send you another letter. The Captain of the Warner [132] was saying the other day that he would like to take the boat to Fortress Monroe. I do not know whether he will or not. I should like to go there very much indeed. I have not had a letter for three or four days. I expect to get some today. News is pretty scanty today. I have had no breakfast. I will have to stop. Being on the eve of a battle soon I think it is best to let you know how I get along. I am very well. Hope to see that box soon. I have one pair of stockings on my feet and one blue and one heavy pair in my trunk. I have lost one of the blue ones. Give my love to all.

Your most affec. brother
Tom

[Transcribed Copy]
Camp at Ship Point
Wednesday April 30th 1862

Dear Jos,
Ma's letter written on the 18th, Annie's on the 21st also yours came yesterday. It seems to me that they take an everlastingly long time to come. I look for a letter every day. We are about a mile from the place where we landed before. The boat is in the river, I suppose forty miles from the shore. We are encamped about 125 feet from the water. We have a delightful breeze from the bay. To tell the truth we are comfortable in every respect. We have a fine field for drill being encamped in one corner, being what I should call a surface entirely surrounded by trees. I was drilling the company at skirmishes yesterday. They were firing while advancing. Pretty soon I gave the command "double quick" and then they came to a ditch on the other side of the fence that surrounded the field. Just beyond the ditch were thick woods and my idea was to have them skirmish behind the trees. When they saw the water one or two called out "Lieutenant, we cant get over here!" though if I had repeated the order they would have gone across. The drill was one hour and a half in length. Skirmishing is a nice drill and no mistake. I would have laughed if they had gone in to the water. They ought to get used to such things. Every night you ought to hear the firing. First would come the report of the gun, immediately after the report of the shell. A pleasant sound. There has been no movement of any kind as yet. I expect that we will remain here for the rest of our lives. There is something else I want to speak of. I am not interested in hearing anything concerning Sam Caldwell.[133] I know that man. If you will take the trouble I suppose you may remember me to Gert. This afternoon I received letters from Will and Bob, I shall answer as soon as possible. It is very dull here at present. This evening it's raining. I hope the next letter I send you may be more interesting. I should like to have those shoes as soon as Ma can get that box ready. I must have from seven to ten pairs of stockings. I shall answer Annie's and Ma's letter tomorrow morning. Pay day will come in a few days I suppose. The pay rolls are all ready. Tell Sue and Annie that I should like to here from them. Give my love to Ma, Annie, Charlie and Frank.

Your loving brother
Tom

P.S. I should like another spoon, just the same kind as Ma gave me when I left home. I am very well and hope you are all well at home. I wish you would write as soon as you can. I have sent some confederate bank notes[134] from the people here. I wish them kept. They are worth something. I can say in after years that I got them when I was in the army at the time of the war.

[Transcribed Copy]
Camp at Ship Point
Thursday May 1st 1862

Dear Annie,
My letter to Jos yesterday was written in a hurry as one can see but I hope this will look better. In your letter written on the 21st you speak of going to Minersville. I wish you could go. I think you might get Sam to answer my epistle. He is certainly a poor correspondent. You may tell Sue that I may have not heard from her yet. I should like to get letters from them all. The firing in the direction of Yorktown is constant. I heard this morning that the enemy were retreating though pretending to defend their works.[135] I understand that we will be held in reserve until we attack. Though I suppose nobody knows anything about our movements. This morning we had just gone out to drill when it commenced to rain. So the drum beat the recall. Back we went. All the afternoon there has been heavy firing in the direction of Fortress Monroe. I expect Iron monsters[136] have had another fight. There is another thing I wish to tell you. All the stockings you make I wish you would put by for me. Even if I have a thin pair in the morning at night a thick pair is needed. It is quite cool at night here. There is nothing new at all and I don't suppose there will be for the next six months. We have a fine camping ground, on account of its being high ground. Somehow I must find something to say to put in Will and Bob Potts' letters. I shall also write to Ma this evening. You would be amused at my anxiety to get letters from home. I ask the post master every day at noon if he has brought letters. I send 3 ten cents to Bob Dunham's sister. You will give it to her with my best regards. And tell her that she understands about it. Remember me to all my friends. Give my love to Ma, Charlie, Jos and Frank. I am very well indeed.

Your most affectionate brother
Tom

P.S. I suppose Frank is getting along well at school. He might write letters. As soon as that box is ready I will be ready to receive it.

[Original]
Camp at Ship Point
Friday May 2nd 1862

Dear Ma,
Last night the heavy firing in front of Yorktown woke me, I guess it was about one or two; it was kept up all night, and also all the morning so far being now nearly ten. At present I have a young fellow with knapsack and gun marching up and down in front of my tent; he when the company fell in for dress parade did not move briskly and instead of falling in with his musket at his shoulder was cleaning his bayonet, again, when ordered by the 2nd Sergeant[137] to come to shoulder arms,

swore that he would not until he was ready[;] his case ought by rights have a court-martial, but I thought that marching him up and down until drill time, and making him drill too would be enough. I think that I might say something about my living, we had pretty good living on board of the Warner, now we have fish, eggs, ham, fresh meat, corn cakes, crackers, butter, sugar and coffee also tea quite a variety. We manage to get along I can tell you. As to that wrapper, I am very much afraid that it is lost, but if I hear anything about it, I will try and find out where its residence is, if I can get it, I [will] send it home, if not *why of course* it will not reach Camden.

I am sorry, for it was certainly a very nice one. Col. Taylor is appointed Brig. General of our Brigade, Bob is the Assistant Adjutant General with the rank of Captain. Lieut. Grubb[138] of Co. C is another of his Staff. Gen. Kearney has gone to take command of Hamilton's Division before Yorktown.[139] This morning I received your, Annies and Jos' letters dated 29th also that *tract.* I am very sorry that Col. Taylor has left our regiment, I do not believe that we could have a better commander. Still I rather like the promotion of course. Anything to raise New Jersey. I should like two toothbrushes if you could send them conveniently. I am very well. This morning the Sun came out and made it very warm for drill.

Remember me to Aunt Sarah and all my friends. I think that we shall move pretty soon. I have not received the box yet[;] I suppose it will reach here tomorrow or next day.

Give my love to Annie, Charley, Jos and Frank.

Your most affectionate son
Tom
2nd Lieut., Co. I, 3rd N.J. Inf.

[Transcribed Copy]
Camp at Ship Point
Saturday afternoon May 3rd 1862

Dear Jos,
Today about one I finished a letter to Will Potts. It will go tomorrow morning. I shall always try to answer letters sent from home although I am not able to write long answers. There is very little news flying about here at present. About one very heavy firing commenced and has been kept up without intermission. I should like very much to go out to the lines and would if I could. I may yet. I have a great mind to send in and get permission from General Taylor to go to Fortress Monroe and see the sights. Liet. Wilson[140] of Co. A. is going tomorrow morning. The steamers " Hero" and "Kent" have arrived in the river from the bay. They were stationed at anchor. They will land the troops they have on board by eight this evening. General Taylor's idea is I suppose to have the brigade all together which is a good idea. Colonel Taylor has not received the title of general yet, that is he is not a regularly appointed general yet though he will be without doubt. I shall write to Ma this

evening and send a copy of General Kearney's address to the first brigade. Bob is acting assistant Adjutant General with the rank of Captain. General Kearney's first aide is Lt. Grubb. He is from Burlington. His father is very wealthy. There will be three, four or six promotions in the regiment. I will speak of them in Ma's letter. I have not time at present. If I get home safely I will tell you things that will astonish you. I think the shoes will suit me. The last two days have been very warm, not withstanding which we have to drill morning and afternoon. Give my love to all around and about. Remember me to all the young ladies. Miss Mary Harbert (her father is well incidently)[,] Miss Gert Browning. In fact to all of them you may remember me. My love to Ma, Annie, Charlie and Frank.

Your loving brother
Tom

[Original]

Camp at Ship Point
Satur. Evening May 3rd '62
Dear Ma,
It is about half past nine having obtained permission of Col. Brown to sleep on board, I shall be able to take it easy. The reports of the guns coming from the direction of Yorktown are very heavy, one seemed to shake the boat. They are firing constantly, I should like to know whether we are returning the fire from the enemy. Lt. Spencer of Co. C. who was up towards our lines said that the enemy fired at our works at night [O]ur troops only work after dark. While writing a report came so loud that the windows and the door of the wash room shook a good deal, now you must know that the reports must be loud to make windows of a boat on water shake, but that is a fact. I expect that they will keep up the firing all night. I have been on shore but twice to day and if any letter or letters came I will get them tomorrow morning early. The whole *Brigade* has landed. I send you a copy of Gen. Kearney's address. I should like it kept.

I am very well, please remember me to all. Give my love to Annie, Charley, Jos and Frank.

Your most loving son
Tom
2nd Lt. Co. I. 3rd NJ. Inf.
Col. Brown
Gen. Taylor Bri.

[Written on side of May 3rd letter as if in answer to his mother's letter]
I wish that when you write to Uncle Ben Howell, you would tell him that I have received no answer to my letter. I should like to get a letter from them very much. I sent him my photograph too. If I thought that Uncle Jos' Regiment[141] was before Yorktown, of course it is, at least I think so[,] well if I thought that he was out there I would try and see him if possible.

Tom

[Copy of Gen. Kearny's "Address" sent with Tom's letter]
HeadQuarters 1st Brigade
Franklins Division
May 2nd '62

General Order No. 55

An order from the General-in-Chief assigns me to a Division, in the trenches before Yorktown. Citizen, and General like yourselves, I have left comfort and home, to fulfil duties in the field. Previously, shortly after our advance to Manassas, when offered a Division, I refused promotion sooner than separate myself from your fortunes. It might then have appeared a personal ambition, but under the present circumstances the command of troops under fire cannot be refused. I leave you under the command of your senior Col., one of the bravest of the brave, and most gallant of the gallant.

Officers in taking leave of you it is with feeling of great personal regard towards you all, any apparent asperities in service were but the machinery of discipline (II). On my departing Col. Taylor 3rd N.J. Vols. will assume command of this Brigade.

P. Kearny
Brig. General

[Original]
Steamer John A. Warner
Yorktown Mon. May 5th '62

Dear Ma,
We are on the move again, yesterday at one o'clock came the order from Col. Taylor to embark immediately, so we struck tents, but did not get on board until nearly half past six; the brigade embarked in the order of the number of the regiments that is the 1st 2nd 3rd and 4th; we would have been on board in an hour if there had been small boats enough.[142] Well about half past ten we were under way and steamed around the mouth of the York River where we came to anchor for the night, the "Elm City, Hero, Warner, Kent and Arrowsmith" upon which boats the Brigade is stationed, the 2nd on the Elm City; the 1st upon the Hero, the 4th upon the Kent and Arrowsmith and the 3rd upon the Warner[;]well, as I was endeavoring to remark, we were altogether. As our boat came alongside of the Elm City, which had started before us and was at anchor, we heard Bob's voice coming over the water saying that we were to get under way at three in the morning precisely; he gave the same order to the other boats as they came up. This morning we were under way at three according to orders, and by breakfast time were opposite Yorktown. No one can imagine the strength of this place, and of Gloucester Point opposite; there were five or six of our gunboats at anchor ahead of us. Before I go on I will say something about the evacuation[.] Friday morning early, I guess about

two, some of our outposts suspected that all was not right and they advanced some distance towards the lines of the enemy and Gen. McClellan also thought that something was wrong, so *he* went up in his balloon[;] he saw that the enemy had left, and down he came with a rush[;] in a few minutes orderlies were flying in every direction, soon the whole army was in motion. Two of my men were at Yorktown yesterday all morning and a part of the afternoon, one of them said that some of the prisoners said that the Rebels have been leaving Yorktown the last three weeks. We have had a tremendous force in front of the enemy, it has been kept so quiet (that is the movements of troops), that no one has really known the strength of our Army[;] why Loeb,[143] my servant, who was one of the two of my company, who having visited the lines, was *the important* man, said that he thought he had seen troops at the great review before Lord Lyons, but the soldiers that he had seen yesterday exceeded everything; the artillery the thought extended for four miles, and of the cavalry he supposed there were over twenty thousand, and no end to the Infantry. To turn to our Division it is in the River on board of the transports, waiting for further orders. Gen. Franklin has gone ashore to get his orders. Col. Taylor has been on shore all the morning exploring the country I suppose. He has his HeadQuarters upon the Elm City. The enemy certainly left Yorktown as they did Manassas, that is in a very great hurry, although if they had remained they would have defended a position of great strength, but they have gone and McClellan is after them. There are only about thirty or forty houses in the *Town*; it is not as large now as it was in the revolution, singular I think. They have left about twenty guns on the River front, and some on their works surrounding Yorktown; I understand they succeeded in removing most of their guns. The officers have permission to go ashore, two at a time, so I will have something more to say soon. I expect to get the box today, probably not as we have advanced. I am very well. It is raining some this morning, in fact not a very pleasant day to go on shore, still I do not care, but so I get to see Yorktown; possibly I might not if we were to move up the River, I understand our next move is to West Point[144] quite a long distance beyond here. Give my love to Annie, Charley, Jos and Frank.

Your most affectionate son
Tom
2nd Lieut. Co. I. 3rd N.J. Inf.
Col. Brown

[Original]

Camp Potopotank Va.
Thurs. Eve. May 8th 1862

Dear Ma,
I have made a mistake in my other letter, about being encamped at Ship Point, we are not quite there, but are opposite to the village of Potopotank,[145] a funny name. This morning as soon as we got back to camp I

saw the post master and thinking that if we were suddenly to move I would not have a chance to write to you for some time, I took a sheet of paper from my note book and wrote you those few words; but as I find that the post master does not leave until tomorrow morning I will write while I have daylight, it being nearly seven, I will have to hurry. An account of our voyage up the York River after leaving Yorktown I will write in a letter to Annie this evening. Yesterday (Wednes) morning just after guard mounting, I was officer of his company, the answer he received was to have every man in camp to fall in with my guards and immediately join the regiment; well I went through the camp and soon had every man sick and well under arms; we then marched out and had hardly gone half way when our regiment on the double quick advanced, so we had to follow; after joining, the regiment remained at rest for about half an hour. It was exciting to hear the cheering of our men, after sending in a volley or when battery "D"[146] would send its shells right into the woods among them. Why the gunboats away out in the River sent shells into the woods. I was amused at the singing of the large shells through the air. Well we had to stand and listen while the fighting was going on. The Goslin Zouaves[147] were cut up a good deal, Co. B had twenty left or only that number reported at one [once]; they were relieved then.[148] There was treachery on the part of the enemy, one of the Goslin Zouaves was caught in a swamp and two negros and three white Rebels attacked him, he called for quarter, but the black Rebels called y'all the d—n Northerners, and they shot the Zouave dead on the spot, I would like to know what should be done with such an enemy, I say that we ought to shoot them like dogs. The Fourth regiment relieved one of the other regiments. Our troops behaved very well, charged on the enemy several times and drove them through the woods some distance; they were the Texan Rangers[149] and fought with great spirit. There were between twenty-five and fifty killed and quite a large number wounded, why yesterday Dr. Oakley[150] our Brigade Surgeon cut off six legs of the Zouaves. The batteries and gunboats did good service. After three o'clock in the afternoon the firing ceased pretty much, we were the reserve with two or three other regiments, at half past five we marched into the woods and relieved the fifth Maine,[151] right on the road where the fighting took place[;] the Rebels had fallen back some distance.[152] The trees and fence rails were cut in every direction with the balls and shells. Our whole Brigade relieved the other troops along the whole road where the others had been. I never saw pickets so strong before[;] the fence was perfectly lined with our troops[,] each man touched the other. I will write the rest in my other letter. I am very well. Give my love to Annie, Charley, Jos and Frank.

Your most affectionate son
Tom
2nd Lieut. Co. I. 3rd N.J.
Col. Brown

[Transcribed Copy]

West Point, Va.
May 10th 1862

Dear Jos,
Before I begin I must say that I have received no letter up to this morning because no mail has been received from Yorktown, it having been kept there because no arrangements have been made. The box I don't expect to get for a week at least. There is no office in Yorktown yet. I was there. Several times the rebels set up the most tremendous shooting attempting to drive our men on the left out but they did not succeed. Our troops kept perfectly cool and poured volley after volley into them and charged them two or three times. The 18th N.Y. volunteers[153] wonderfully escaped, no one being hurt, though that regiment was in advance and the enemy poured a heavy fire into them. But the 16th[154] lying down, returned the fire with deadly effect. Half a dozen times I thought we would make a rush to support the brigade of skirmishers in the woods but didn't. Hang being in reserve I say! About four the firing ceased and it became quiet. We were lying on the ground and it was nearly half past five. The orderly came up to acting General Taylor[,] who sent his aides to the different Colonels. In less than two minutes we were under way. Well, we marched, as I said in my letter to Ma, and took our positions behind a fence that we had occupied in the morning. We made ourselves comfortable. It was hardly long before half of Co. I were sound asleep. But every man slept on his arms. We divided the time between each platoon. The first to sleep two hours, the second two hours, and 60 through the night. There was some little firing on the left, which did not disturb us. At three in the morning we were under arms and stood until daylight as a precaution. At six I was sitting on a stump when I heard heavy crashing behind which I thought was a wagon down the road[,] but I just then heard the word "forward and through the fence" and we went pouring across the road and into the woods. We advanced about a mile and a half to a clearing or farm where we halted. We went in to the house. It was the farm house. Deserted. So as I was saying I went into it and obtained some candles, a tumbler, a ball of twine, a bottle of cologne, several other things. In fact I went over things pretty thoroughly. My men and those of other companies followed me and that is the way we do unto those who are in the rebel army. Well, the rebels had fallen back entirely. We found none about the farm and none of their pickets. At half past one we marched back to our camp through the woods and it was a sight to see, some trees crushed by the balls from our batteries and from our gun boats and others with their tops cut right off and others again cut in the center and the upper half hanging down. One ball from one of the gunboats cut in half and went in to the ground, bursting, made a place large enough to put a government wagon in. Yesterday afternoon we marched from our camp to a large plantation of 1100 acres. 200 slaves. If you will look on the map you will see our position. We are only two miles from West Point, above Eltham. Our other camp of Wednesday was three miles below our present position, on the river.

This farm is a beautiful place. It belongs to the rebel General Lee.[155] He has another place, fifteen miles from here. I have heard more from these slaves on this place than I ever supposed. The master is very wealthy and yet he could only afford to give to one old slave one pair of pantaloons in three years. And I do not believe that there is one piece of the original cloth left in them. And there is more that I could mention in this letter. I expect that we shall remain here for this day although it is uncertain. We have surrounded a part of the rebel army 11,000 strong it is said. We are on the road to Richmond. The railroad, as you will see on the map. We have Franklin's, Sedgwick's,[156] and one other division here. I suppose you have heard of the death of General Kearney's aides Captain Wilson and young Lieutenant Bernard.[157] They were killed at the battle at Williamsburg. The slaves tell us that the rebels are very much afraid of our gunboats. The mail has just come and I suppose that there is quite a little package for me. Well, is it possible! Here is but the one from you! Mailed on May 7th. I shall answer it as soon as possible. I suppose that there are letters in it also from Ma and Annie. It is quite warm now, in fact very warm. At night there is heavy dew. I am very well indeed. I have received no letters from Uncle Thomas's family. Give my love to all. Remember me to all my lady friends. Give my love to Ma and Annie and Charlie and Frank. Arch is going to be adjutant. I guess.

Your most affectionate brother
Tom

It is said that General Taylor and his aide, Bob Dunham, Lt Grubb, have been captured.[158] They have been away all night. I don't believe it though.

[Transcribed Copy]
Monday May 12th 1862

Dear Annie,
Last night we slept in the woods by the road. We are right on 9 miles from New Kent Courthouse and we will go on in the morning. There is very little news here except that about Norfolk which is certainly news.[159] A telegraph was formed yesterday afternoon to General Slocum's headquarters, three miles from West Point. Two miles of men placed about one hundred feet apart. They could pass a message from New Kent here in a half an hour. Nine miles. We marched yesterday morning four miles and such a march! Dusty, warm and tired! It was pleasant to get into the woods and sit down. Co. I and I have had nothing to do. I shall write again. We shall be in Richmond by Wednesday or Saturday[;] I will get the box by then. There is mail of a week that has not arrived yet. It will come today or tomorrow. I am very well, in fine spirits, anxious for a dash at those [illegible]. There is not a rebel within fifteen miles of us. McClellan's portion of the army has

arrived at New Kent and is going on. Remember me to all. Give my love to Ma, Charlie, Jos and Frank.

Your most loving brother and kisses
Tom
Write soon

[Original]
[Written at the top of the May 14th letter, below]
Col. Brown was put under arrest for interference with the Provost Guard day before yesterday, at any rate that is the Charge. I do not know whether that is the case or not. It is the second time he has been under arrest, so he cannot be Col. of the regiment. I think Col. Hatch[160] of the 4th will be our Col. without doubt.
Tom

Cumberland Va.
Wednes. May 14th '62

Dear Ma,
Yesterday morning we received orders, or rather Mon. Evening orders came to move at four in the morning; at the time appointed we sent tent and baggage to the wagons, and then marched to the cross roads a quarter of a mile above our old position, halted, stacked arms, and waited for the division to pass, instead of being first we are last; under Kearney we were the senior brigade, unde[r] Gen. Taylor we were the senior regiment of the brigade[;] you read the account of Col. Taylor's promotion, it is a great thing. He cares little for the Rebels; Last Wednesday, the day of our fight, late in the afternoon, having heard that the enemy had retreated I suppose, he marched to New Kent Court House ten or twelve miles ahead of the Division and without any permission. There he staid, Gen. Franklin was so worried that he sent two of his aides with cavalry out to look for him, it having been reported that he had been captured and the 1st and 2nd regiments cut to pieces. Well the long and short of the matter is, he is safe although he did have a skirmish. As I was saying we waited for the Division to march along; well Gen. Slocum's[161] brigade had passed and Gen. Newton's[162] Brigade was just coming up, when they halted for a rest, it was about five; pretty soon, I was standing near the road, I saw a large party of horsemen coming down one of the side roads, some one said there comes Gen. McClellan[;] sure enough, he did come, and as he turned into our road, such cheers that our regiment and the 8th N.Y.[163] gave him, well I never saw a man so much pleased as himself, he showed it in his face, he took his cap off and went down the road amid the most tremendous cheering I ever heard I think; he passed so near me that I could have touched his horse with my hand; You should have seen me waving my cap. He had his whole Staff with him, and his body guard, a regiment of cavalry, regulars, and his Infantry. In about two hours we commenced our march, and the two regiments, Fourth and Third, under Col. Simpson[164] of the 4th marched to N. Kent C. H. nine

miles, arrived there at two, instead of turning off and going to Cumberland[165] two miles to the right of New Kent, he marched us first to the Court House where we rested for an hour during which time something quite interesting occured; as we came out of the woods into a large field on the left of the road, a quarter of a mile from New Kent, we found the baggage train faced about, and the 4th which marched on before us drawn up in line of battle, on inquiring we found that as the train of wagons was going along the road a mile or two beyond New Kent a masked battery opened upon the escort of cavalry ahead[,] upon which they about faced and left *double* quick; pretty soon Gen. Sykes[166] of the Regulars dashed by with his Staff and escort, right after came his splendid Brigade the 12th, 11th, 10th, and 6th,[167] and Col. Warren's Zouaves, formerly Duryea's,[168] all at the double quick step, they had been up at Cumberland where we are now. I have not heard the result of their attack yet. I suppose the[y] fell back; there were only t[w]o bodies of Rebels within fifteen miles of us yesterday, there were fifteen hundred men and a battery at Cumberland, and those beyond New Kent; the Rebels at Cumberland were surrounded in a swamp and surrendered last night, they could do nothing, their battery was mired so it could not be handled, and we had the pleasure of taking it. We are encamped about three quarters of a mile from the river, which is crowded already with ships. It is uncertain whether we move to day or not, we may march over to New Kent again or go right on in the direction of Richmond. As for that box I do not think I will get it until we reach Richmond. I may received it before though. We have not received the back mail yet, it probably will get here to day some time. I am sorry but I don't think we will be paid for some weeks yet, it is very uncertain. Our march yesterday was the worst I have experienced or passed through yet, it seemed as if all the dust in Virginia was called on our road, and all the heat of the Sun right on us. In other words it was very warm and dusty. Remember me to all. Give love to Annie, Charley, Jos and Frank. I should like to be home this Summer but I expect we shall have to continue *our excursion* through most of the Southern States yet.

Your most affectionate son
Tom
2nd Lieut. Co. I. 3rd N.J. Inf.
Col. Brown. Gen. Taylor's Bri.

[Transcribed Copy]

White House Virginia
Friday May 16th 1862

Dear Jos,
I commenced a letter on Tuesday the 13th but getting orders to leave and join the other two regiments. We are at White House,[169] an immense farm owned by General Robert E. Lee. It was given him by Major Custis[,] the father in law of Washington. We are just 22 miles

from Richmond. The rebels have evacuated Richmond but there are some troops between here and that place to cover their retreat. There is no news of any kind here except that we have had a day and night of rain making the road from Cumberland to the White House perfectly awful. I received the box on Tuesday and nothing could have pleased me more. The stockings, the shoes, the carpet bag, the cake, the paper. It raised my spirits which were high anyhow, more than 80 degrees. I am in a great hurry to get this letter off. I received Ma's letter, and Annie's and Uncle Tom's letters all on Tuesday. You see they were delayed over a week. I have not heard from Sue and Annie yet. Give my love to Ma and Annie and Charlie and Frank. I am very well.

Your loving brother
Tom

Tell Annie that I am very much obliged to her for the stockings. They are very nice. That carpet bag came about the right time too for the officers' allowance is eighty pounds of baggage now. This place is a beautiful one indeed in fine weather. Mr Lee left only last Saturday. General Taylor arrived with the first and second cavalry a day and a half after he left. We will be in Richmond in a week if the roads permit, probably in three days.

[Original]

Camp at White House
Sun. Eve. May 18th '62

Dear Ma,
It is late and I am able to write only a few words. We march tomorrow at four and a half in the morning, How far we march I don't know, we may advance with in a few miles of Richmond; the enemy have only a few thousand troops in front of us, merely to cover their retreat, of course we must expect skirmishing and small fights but nothing *very extensive.* I hope to answer Annie's and Jos' letters from Richmond, date them from that place. This Evening Fanny Carpenters[170] letter arrived dated the 16th[;] I have been so busy, although it is Sunday[,] that I was unable to even read it, There is Sunday Inspection and Dress Parade which take some time besides other duties. I should like to spend *one more quiet Sunday* at home, and I hope I will very soon. I am in excellent health, and fine spirits. Anxious to finish or help finish this little affair in the South. I understand that we will be paid in about ten or twelve days. Give my love to Annie, Charley, Jos and Frank. Also to Uncle Thomas' family, all friends and relation, also much for yourself.

from your most affectionate son
Tom
2nd Lt. Co. I. 3rd N. J. Vol. Inf.
Lt. Col. Brown

[Transcribed Copy]

Wednesday May 21st 1862

My dear sister,
Your letter of the 16th came this evening. It was given to me while I was sitting under a large fruit tree. I am officer of the guard. Well, we have had a most fatiguing march today. We are encamped within twelve miles of Richmond exactly. I suppose we will march again early tomorrow morning. We may not March into Richmond tomorrow. In fact we might have a fight or something to prevent our enterring. Such a march! When we reached our camping ground I don't suppose there was half of the regiment there. The heat was awful. But I held out. Capt. Gibson[171] gave out and told the [illegible] that he could not go on. He followed afterward. I hope never to experience such a warm march again. It is so dark that I cannot write. I hope soon to appear at home and see my sweet sister. I shall write again soon. If I have time I will write tomorrow. Give my best to the best of mothers and to my dear brothers.

Your loving brother
Tom

[Original]

HeadQuarters 3rd Reg.
Thurs. May 22nd 1862

Dear Ma,
It being a beautiful morning, and I off duty, I thought you would like to hear from me in answer to your letter, although I was tired last night, still I knew you would like to get one of my *epistles* if only a few lines. I was not so tired yesterday on account of the walking as I was of the heat. It is very easy to march with the guard of a regiment, one can take his time generally. Before we started, Capt. Bryan,[172] the brother of that *"water Bryan"* of Camden,[173] well as I was endeavoring to say, although *I was interrupted,* ordered me to arrest all those who were found along the road. Well we found none of our regiment for a long time, but after we had marched about seven miles on a good road, but under the warmest, of *warm and* hot, sunshine that I ever experienced in my life, the road on both sides was almost lined with soldiers of our regiment, which was in advance of the other regiments of the brigade, and with the troops of the first two brigades of the Division, of course I knew it was useless to even attempt arresting the men, and I therefore said nothing to them; but I can tell you that when the regiment halted and encamped, I hadn't one half of my guards with me, they had fallen out, *worn out* by the head [heat] and the weight of their knapsacks. As the regiment stacked arms, Col. Brown called for the guard; he came up to me, and ordered me to post the guards around the camp. I told him that I had not one half of guards with me, he said that I must do the best I could, it was done, and nothing more was said. About six o'clock Capt. Bryan came to me and said that Col. Brown had been giving him the mischief, on account of my not being able to keep the guards to-

gether, well that made me angry, he also said that if the officer of the guard couldn't *keep* the *guard* together, the officer of the day would have to take it, well as I was attempting to say, *although I was interrupted again* that made me angry, and I plainly told the Capt. that if Col. Brown was not able to keep the regiment together, he must not expect the officer of the guard to keep his guard in good order, I said several other things that I will not put in; you must know that when I get angry, and I have not been really angry since I entered the army, I generally make a mire of *some sort, kind* and *class*. I have a great deal of the Howell blood as well as of the Carpenter in me, and I will have my rights no matter what Col. Brown or any other man says to the contrary. I know what is what, and also I have gained information enough since I entered the army *to have* and *keep* my rights that belong to me as a *son,* a *brother,* a *man* and a *soldier* &c. &c. This is a great deal of talk for a little boy of any size, standing and experience, but as I said before, I am a Howell. Lt. Col. Brown is disliked by all the men in the regiment, although he is not by the officers; there is no man they dislike more than Col. Brown. The only good news I can tell, is that we are encamped to day, only twelve miles from Richmond; I think myself that we will be in Richmond by Saturday. This morning Gen. Porter's division marched down the road in front of our camp[;] the sharpshooters (Col. Berdan) passed me after I was relieved from guard;[174] I was standing by the fence when they came along, and I really admired them, all good men. I think I shall have to stop, or I will have nothing to say to Jos' last letter, and all of Annie's. I had a letter from Uncle Ben about three weeks ago. Give my love to dear Annie, one of the best sisters, no mistake, Charley, Jos and Frank. I will tell you where the wrapper is in my next.

Your loving soldier son
Tom
2nd Lt. T. J. Howell Co. I. 3rd N. J. Vol. Inf.
Lt. Col. Brown

[Transcribed Copy]
Headquarters, Third Regiment
Thursday May 22nd 1862

My dear brother,
Before I begin to answer your letter of the 15th I will say that you must be careful to whom you show these letters. There is one thing I am certain of now. It's I have gained the goodwill of all my men. I am very strict when strictness is needed. But when off duty I am the quiet gentleman. In fact I always treat them as men should be treated. I am always gentle and manly in my contact toward them. That I am sure of, just as sure of as that I am now writing to you. As to my being 1st Lieutenant I hardly think I have a chance. I don't think that I should refuse if the position were offered to me. To speak of Mr. Harper[175] being shocked, I told him of the rumors that have been circulated about

him. He laughed but I could see that he did not like it, on account of his family I suppose. A thundershower has just come which will cool off the atmosphere and settle the dust and make things pleasant generally.

Quite a number of the officers in the brigade think of resigning when we reach Richmond, if they hear that our division will go south with the rest of the army. There is nothing new except the rumor of a victory won by Commander Halleck.[176] You will please tell Fanny Carpenter that I will send her a photograph as soon as I find time to write. Give my love to all of them at Uncle Thomas's. Also to my dearest of dear sister and Ma and Charlie and Frank. Remember me to the Potts and my young ladies.

Your most affectionate brother
Tom

[Original]
[Written at the top of the May 26th letter, below]
[A]bout the officer, that [h]as been my opinion ever since I entered the army, although I never experienced it before. In their intercourse with each other and with those *outside* of *themselves* they do not show themselves to be the polished gentlemen; they have given me no cause for *this feeling; it is only* what I have seen, everything is so coarse, it is not what I have been brought up to.
Tom

Head Quarters 3rd N. J. Vols.
Mon. May 26th 1862

My dear Mother,
Yesterday morning we marched from our encampment at Burnetts Cross Roads[177] at eight o'clock, and had a pleasant march from three to five miles to a large farm said by some to belong to the Rebel Gen. Lee.[178] I never saw in all my life such fields, breast high with oats and other grain; the road leading from the mansion to the highway was perfectly straight, and lined with fruit trees all the way; I suppose there were at least one hundred on a side, so you may know that it is *a road;* then on each side immense fields, no fences, of waving grains as I said before, I guess it is the finest farm we have seen yet. Well we marched to one part of the field near the woods and came to rest, when Col. Brown called together all the officers and informed them that the enemy were but three quarters of a mile off, and that there was to be no noise made, firing of guns &c. &c. After a while we stacked arms and pitched our tents. Nothing occured till about four o'clock when orders came for the 3rd Reg. to go out on picket, a duty that *sometimes* is very unpleasant, for instance when it rains, &c., but the weather was beautiful as out we went, through the narrow strip of woods surrounding the field in which our Division is encamped, out and down into the fields beyond; well after marching half way across, near to the old division pickets, we halted, stacked arms and rested, and had time to look at the Rebel pickets[,] the woods seemed to be full of them, and on a hill there

was a squad of their cavalry watching us; we had glasses and could make their uniforms, well we were within easy rifle shot range. Three or four of us went up to the top of a hill and could then see them more plainly; they could have shot some of us easily if *they* had been so inclined. We staid there about half an hour, when we went into camp again. It turned out that Gen. Stoneman[179] sent word to Gen. Taylor to connect his left *with* the *right*, I should say *to the right* of Gen. Smith's[180] Division; well Gen. Taylor ordered out the Third for that purpose, but found that a Vermont Regiment of Gen. Smith's Division had saved us the trouble, and had connected the right of Gen. Smith's pickets with the left of Gen. Stoneman's, so you see we were saved the trouble of watching all night. About seven last Evening the Rebels threw two or three shells into the woods near us, but could not get them into the camp[.] [A]lso this morning two burst about fifty feet off. We march "*in light marching order,*" that is without knapsacks or baggage, to Richmond over Rebel pickets and everything else. We are only *six* miles off from the City, Gen. McDowell[181] is not twelve miles, and I think that we will have no trouble whatever. I did not mention the day; we march from this camp on Wednesday. So I think that before long you will have a letter from me dated at Richmond. We will be paid off when we reach Richmond. There is something that I don't exactly like, which is the giving of whiskey to all the troops, officers and men; they get a gill each day, half in the morning, the same in the afternoon, it is not the amount, but many who did not use it are beginning to wish for it now, I have never touched a drop of anything stronger than beer since I have been in the army and knowing my promise don't intend to besides not liking any kind of brandy, whiskey, &c. The whole army gets it, it may be useful this very warm weather but to tell the truth it is a bad thing. And which prove the ruin of a great number. *I have been firm as a rock about my promise,* and intend keeping so, although I have been pressed to "take a drink" or a segar [cigar], *but it is not my style at all.* There is but one thing that I could wish now, that is to be able to see *my dear mother, sister, and brothers.* I am perfectly disgusted with the officers of this regiment as a class. I will mention no names; I consider some of them a *most miserable* set, and shall be glad when I am out of this reg't when this war is over. Give my love to all, Annie, Charley, Jos and Frank. I wrote to Uncle Ben last week also to Fanny Carpenter. Much love and many kisses.

Your most affectionate son
Tom
2nd Lt. Co. I. 3rd N.J. Vol. Inf.

[Transcribed Copy]
[Written at the top of the May 27th letter, below]
P.S. I have never been in better health or spirits than I am now. Remember me to all my friends in Camden. Mart has not answered my last letter yet. Tell Will and Bob Potts that I should like to hear from them. Remember me to their mother and sister[182] and also Mr. Potts.[183]

Tuesday, May 27th 1862

My dear Jos,

We are not in Richmond yet by a great deal. I had thought that we would have been in sight of the church spires by Sunday. I was mistaken however. I saw an order yesterday afternoon from General McClellan and it seems that he expects a fight to take place. He speaks of the approaching battle. Still we may have no fight. All yesterday we were under orders to march at a moments' notice. The cause of this order was the advancing of several collumns on General Keyes,[184] down near Bottom Bridge on the direct road to the city of Richmond. About six o'clock the order was countermanded. We have other orders today or rather they were received yesterday. These are that tomorrow maybe this afternoon we commence our march on Richmond, in light marching order. Probably we will see funny sights and have gay times. All baggage is to be left behind to come on afterward in a train of wagons. No wagons except ambulances will be allowed to march with the troops. The men and officers will have to carry three days provisions with them in their haversacks. The amunition wagons will be held in readiness. When sent for they will be able to join the troops immediately. As for the baggage wagons they will not move from our present encampment without orders. These orders come from General McClellan. Yesterday afternoon there was tremendous firing off in the direction of the James River. It ceased about half past six. I just heard that Proffessor Lowe[185] when he ascended up into the upper regions this morning saw the rebel troops retreating from Richmond. How true it is I do not know but I expect nothing else. I suppose that while the rebels have been wishing to play the mischief with us in their front they have been looking behind and off to their left. General McDowell has been coming down upon them. General McDowell's movements are slow but sure. No doubt he is merely keeping pace with our army for he could have been in Richmond long before this. He is now less than twelve miles from the city about half the same as ourselves. It is hard to believe that the rebels will stay and fight after having retreated so far. My opinion is that they will not, though we may have skirmishes. We had a very heavy rain last night. I'm afraid that if it should rain when we march it will be very uncomfortable as I shall carry nothing but my haversack and overcoat. At night roll myself up in my overcoat and go to sleep if possible. I have heard some officers say that they will not know how to sleep in feather beds when they go home. I can say that I am not one of those! I should always know what is what. I guess I have said enough in this letter. Please tell Grannie Carpenter[186] that I will send her my photograph in uniform if she wants it. I have not one in city clothes. Give my best love to Ma, Annie, Charlie and Frank. I wish Charlie would write. Tell Annie Carpenter that I have not had an answer to my letter yet. If I can I shall write to Sue today.

Your loving brother
Tom

[Transcribed Copy]

May 28th 1862

My dearest sister,

Ma's letter of the 24th and yours of the 25th came this morning. As we may possibly move tomorrow I thought I might as well answer both at once. One of the officers told me that there was a report in Camden about my being killed.[187] I can say that I am alive and kicking yet. Hope to continue the same for many years. I wrote to Will Potts and Jim Carpenter this morning after answering Ma's and your letters. I shall have only two to answer, Jos' and Sue's. If I am able I will try to reply to Sue's this evening. I'm afraid that Frank was so much pleased with my letter I shall have to try to write another one. There is something more that I wish to say in answer to your letter which is I hope that I may spend the fourth of July at home with you if possible. Be sure that I shall try my best to get home. The principle fighting should be over by that time. If it is I should think I might get a leave of absence to go home for a week or so. It depends of course on the state of affairs at that time. If I get home I shall expect every window to have about 25 candles both front and back so as to make quite an extensive light. I should like very much to see Uncle Samuel[188] again. I remember him very well although he may be quite changed since I saw him last. I don't know how many years. Don't you think Ma could send a tooth brush by the mail? Get Jos to fix it in a little bundle. As to pay day I expect we shall be paid off just as soon as we reach Richmond. If we move tomorrow I am certain that we will have a fight. How hard remains to be seen and if so you may be certain that I shall not be rash although you may be certain I shall not be backward, that is not my style. I think I can take care of myself. Dress parade will take place in a few minutes so I must hurry and finish. I think all the time about my Mother and sister and brothers. I wish you could be in Richmond with us that is when we enter. We will have great time no doubt. There are numerous rumors about Banks being defeated.[189] Tell Ma I should like her to send me the Inquirer[190] often. We don't get the papers here as often as we did at the White House. We have nothing to read. I could read them and let my men do the same. Give my love to Ma, Charlie, Jos and Frank. Remember me to Sally Potts and all my lady friends. And give me an account of everything going on in Camden. We have dress parade at six in the afternoon. A very pleasant time of day.

Your loving brother
Tom

[Transcribed Copy]

Head Quarters 3rd Reg.
Saturday May 31st 1862

Dear Jos,

*"Hot Work Soon Enough"* 113

As I have written to all it is your turn now. Sunday morning five o'clock. Yesterday at ten came in from picket. We had a great time. Nobody hurt. Yes. One was hit in the side by a piece of shell thrown by the enemy and one shot himself in the foot[191] but then most of all were wet. Such a storm as was to be seen only once in a great while. As I have but a short time to write I will say everything in a hurry. We were under orders to march all yesterday afternoon on account of heavy fighting down on our left, General Kearney's division and the other divisions. You never heard such firing. We did not march and this morning early we have orders that if the fighting commences again we are to cross the Chickahominy. The fighting has commenced and we will probably advance in less than a half an hour. Our troops have driven the enemy some distance[.] I expect that we will have a battle today as it is.[192] Give my love to Ma, Annie, Charlie and Frank.

Your most affectionate brother
Tom

[Original]
Head Quarters 3rd Reg.
Mon. June 2nd 1862

My dearest Mother,
Our orders for marching were countermanded yesterday, on account of our forces having driven back the enemy at all points. The enemy attacked our whole line on the left, but we swept them back, There were over eighty thousand men engaged, and although the nearest fighting was from four to five miles off, yet the firing, which was terrific, sounded as if it were only about a mile distant. It was very exciting; we stood with a large number of officers, upon a hill, about two hundred yards from camp, watching the shells bursting over the trees, and such a continued roll of musketry I never did hear; we knew that the enemy were falling back, from the fact that the firing which was a great way off to the left worked to the right slowly, very rapid I thought[,] towards Gen. Kearney's Division. Ma you should hear the heavy firing of musketry, and then think that a great number of those balls will *"take positions"* in the limbs and other parts of the body of our troops, and also in those of the Rebels, pleasant thoughts. But I believe that men hardly ever think, that they will be shot when going into battle. We had an order from Gen. Franklin, which said that "we had driven back the enemy where ever met;" The enemy however at one time were driving us having superior numbers but we were reinforced,[193] *and then* the *Rebels were defeated.* The men cheered tremendously when the news arrived. That is great news about Corinth's being evacuated;[194] it was said this morning that a great number of Rebel troops from Corinth would be immediately sent to Richmond, if that should happen, we will have our hands full, I don't say that they are not full now, but that Gen. McClellan would have a great deal more fighting to do, than if they kept the same force they have now there. We are having beautiful

weather but are pretty warm. If you could see your son now, this warm morning sitting in his tent with no coat on, and with the lower part of the tent raised up, you would say that he has not been hurt much by weather, marching or anything else, in fact I am perfectly well in *mind, body, soul* and *estate*. As for that wrapper I will not be able to get it until I return, it is stored away in Alexandria, if I find out the place I will write to that City and have it sent home. The only difficulty is in finding out the place where the wrapper was sent. There are over six field batteries that have been planted on the hill in front of us, and that are to cover our advance over the Chickahominy. Our Brigade goes first, so we will have the heaviest fighting to do; many a poor fellow full of life now, will bite the dust then, I hope I may escape, there is no telling how ever what will take place, still I hope I may *be prepared* for any thing that *may* take place. If a man gets hurt, he has the consolation to think that he was wounded, probably unto death, while fighting for his *country*; every man also runs a chance, of being killed or of escaping through everything; as soon as pay day comes I hope to be able to send home over a hundred dollars.

Remember me to Aunt Sarah and all in the City, also love to Uncle Thomas' family. Give my love to Annie, a better sister, a brother couldn't have, to Charley, Jos and Frank. Charley has answered none of my letters.

*I believe I am your most loving son*

Tom
2nd Lieut. Co. I. 3rd N.J. Vol. Inf.
Lt. Col. Brown

P.S. I shall finish my letter to Sam this morning, I thought I ought to answer yours first.
Tom


[Transcribed Copy]
[Written at the top of the June 3rd letter, below]
Private. a family letter

Camp near the Chickahominy
June 3rd 1862

My dearest sister,
Our brigade was paid off today. I send an order on Mr. Taylor, the sutler, on his organization in Philadelphia. I have placed on it Jos' name and he can draw on it by merely endorsing it on the back of the note. When receiving it I wish Jos to answer immediately. There is no news here of any account. The bridges are built and nothing remains but the orders for us to advance. We have been under orders to move over since twelve o'clock. I don't think that we will move for it has been raining very hard the last half hour. We are certainly upon the eve of TREMENDOUS BATTLE. There is no mistake about that. If we should move tomorrow the fields upon the other side of the river will

no doubt be covered with the bodies of our men. We have something to contend with now. There was quite a little battle of artillery this afternoon. A battery of field pieces appeared and opened upon one of ours. Three of ours replied and soon made them, the rebels, pretty quiet. One that came within three feet of Col. Simpson's fourth tent. We took it over to General Taylor's headquarters. I wrote a long letter to Sue yesterday. I hope that you will try to get Mary Harbert to exchange her photograph for one of mine. You may ask her if you want to. You would do me a great favor if you could send me the one she gave you! You will remember me to her. My best regards also to my other young lady friends. As for Uncle Jos,[195] he was in the fight the other day on our left. I have nothing more to think about, my dear sister, so I will cease firing. I am very well, having a very extensive appetite. Give my love to dear Ma, Charlie, Jos, Frank. I take great pleasure in being able to help support those dear ones at home.

Your loving brother,
Tom

P.S. I send another rebel banknote. Take care of it please.

[Original]
Camp near the Chickahominy River Va.
Thursday, June 5th 1862

My dear Mother,
I write a few words, so you may know that I am well. I was Officer of the Day for the first time yesterday. I will be relieved at nine this morning, it['s] only seven now; I guess that being Off. of Day is not so bad after all, a man can order the whole regiment to work or *do any thing else* that he thinks proper. I am *now* pretty certain that we are going to have a tremendous battle, after marching over the Chickahominy, Gen. McClellan seems to expect one, he has written an other order to his army. I will send home a copy in my next letter, it is *well written;* he is *the* man after all. One mile in our rear, there are ten thousand cavalry, that in case the rebels give way from before us, the cavalry may pressure and cut them up entirely, you know the enemy have to cross the James River, so we have a chance of capturing probably the whole army. I haven't time to say more. I wish you would send me one dollars worth of stamps. I will send a bank note to repay you for them, you see I don't want to be of any expense to you, but rather help, it is impossible to get stamps here for some reason. The letters are sent North and paid when they reach their destination.

I am very well, give my best love to dear Annie, Charley, Jos and Frank, remember me to Uncle Thomas' family.

Your loving son
Tom
2nd Lt. Co. I. 3rd N.J. Vol. Inf.
Lt. Col. Brown

I wrote to Sam this morning.

[Original]
[Written at the top of the June 7th letter, below]
$1. for Stamps

Camp at Mechanicsville Va.
Satur. June 7th 1862

My dear Ma,
Yesterday afternoon I received Jos' with your letter of the 1st. We left our old camp and came on to Mechanicsville[196] to relieve Col. Bartlett's[197] brigade. It was quite a pleasant march of two miles and a half across the country; we are just four miles from Richmond now having advanced two miles nearer that City. I never had a better time on picket that day before yesterday; I slept out with the outposts within speaking distance of the enemy. All night there was a constant rumbling of the cars upon the rail road, to and from Richmond, what they are doing I don't know. We see plenty of rebels, from the top of a hill upon which we are encamped yesterday as soon as we arrived, but the enemy commenced sending shells at us, when we struck tents and placed our camp at the foot of the hill[;] from the tops of the high trees we can see Richmond plainly, more *so* if we use a good glass; just when we think we are going to have a sharp fight, the rebels may take French leave of us. I don't [know] when we [will] have the fight, it must come some time[,] so the sooner the better I think. The houses of the town here are pierced and have been by our shells; in the last skirmish; the trees all are and have been cut, some have holes shot right through their trunks, others their tops cut off, then again others have been twisted, the use of the shell is a great institution and no mistake. When we cross, we will probably do so here, we connect the left of Gen. Porter's corps with the right of our own. Gen. Smith's division has crossed the Chickahominy, it marched over while we were on picket. The rebels did not like it and accordingly kept up a tremendous artillery fire upon the troops, but which did not hinder them in the least. That is splendid news from Gen. Halleck's army, you should have heard our Division cheer, when the news arrived[;] it could have been heard at least two miles within the rebel lines (that is the noise) [O]ne of my company[,] quite a young fellow, about sixteen, wanted to go down to the river bank and tell the rebel pickets across, the news[;] of course I wouldn't allow him to do it, being rather afraid of treachery. I have a number of such young soldiers in the company, the loss of whom would be a heavy blow. They are full of life and fun, and keep everything going. There is one thing that makes me very anxious, our Assistant Surgeon has not had much experience, and the result is that we have lost several men out of the company alone, one died this morning.[198] Dr. Madison[199] the surgeon is very ill in the hospital, and of course everything falls on Dr. Welling, he was in college with Charley, I wish you would ask C. about him, and tell me what he says.[200] It is a sad thing when men are taken sick,

go to the hospital and then are not well taken care of[;] if I get sick I will go to Dr. Oakley, or Dr. Clark[201] from Woodbury, the young doctor, I told Dr. Oakley he might expect a visit from [me] if I were to become sick. But I am now and hope to continue well; in this respect I thin[k] I have been fortunate, To never enjoyed better health, the army agrees with me. I Can't believe that about Uncle Jos. I saw no account of his being wounded in the N.Y. Herald, which gave a list of the killed, wounded and missing. I hope that he is safe at any rate. I send this dollar note so that you may get me those stamps. I have only five left and as I can't get them here, I should like to have a dollars worth. You have received that *order* from Sutler Taylor or rather Jos, I suppose some time ago, I should like to know. I guess the next letter I get will inform me. In answer to your letter now, Richmond has not been evacuated yet. You may be sure that Uncle's name in the newspapers as visitor to West Point has created some talking among the officers in camp.[202] There is one more thing I wish to speak about[,] that is my resolve as to drinking, smoking &c. You need have no fear of me my dear mother. Give my love to dear Annie, Charley, Jos and Frank. I will answer dear Jos' letter this afternoon. We see any quantity of the enemy all around us, *except in our rear,* which would be a *bad place for them*; please send the stamps by all means, I will have to stop writing if they don't come pretty soon. Remember me to aunt Sarah, with my love to her, and Aunt Anna's[203] family.

Much love and many kisses from your loving son
Tom
2nd Lieut. Co. I. 3rd N. J. Vol. Inf.

[Transcribed Copy]
Camp at Mechanicsville
Sat. June 7th 1862

My dear Fanny,[204]
Being in good health and fine spirits and having just finished quite a long letter to Ma I thought I would write to one of the best of cousins. Today we marched from our old camp to Curtis farm[,] which is six miles from Richmond in Mechanicsville, called a town but in reality merely a collection of miserable houses. One reason for my being disgusted with the south is that every ditch is called a river and every little collection of huts they call a town and each town with them is a city. They can boast of having a beautiful country to live in though. As to their rivers, when I was at my farm one day I saw a ditch someplace about the country, a ditch to drain fields, as large as the Chickahominy River. The Chickahominy becomes something like a creek where it enters the James River. At Mechanicsville a man can jump from one side to another. The houses in the town, so called, have been hit in many places by our shells. A number of trees in the woods are also torn and twisted by shot and shell. We pitched our tents upon the top of a hill in full view of the enemy two mile off. Pretty soon we saw the

smoke of the rebels and the shells commenced to fly and burst and allow me to tell you we struck tents and pitched down the hill. Meanwhile two of our batteries opened fire upon the enemy and one shell bursting directly above their battery they concluded to cease firing. I shouldn't be afraid to say that one shell did quite a good deal of damage. The seven batteries in our division are all good ones and when they get going the rebels have to be careful how they expose their miserable bodies. I could give them a number of hard names but I guess I will not trouble myself. We don't have to go far to see the enemy. One of my corporals climbed up to the top of a tall tree and with the aid of a pretty good glass could see plenty of the scamps. Also the spires in the city of Richmond. He could see that one was brown another white. I should like to know what the rebels think of our being four miles from their chief city. We will be nearer before long. More so than they will like I guess. When we advance I do not know[,] but we will have a fight I expect. I am prepared however to fight when the time comes. I have just received and read your father's letter. I have not heard yet of Uncle Joshua's being wounded or found any news of his being missing. I saw a sort of official account of the wounded officers also those who had been killed or said to be missing but Uncle Jos' name was not among them. I don't say that he is not wounded but I think not. There is no news of any account going about. I believe you have heard of General Halleck's victory and the rebels heard the cheers of our troops when the news arrived. We were out on picket and it was twelve o'clock at night and the way our division shouted, well, the rebels must have thought something of importance had occured. In my company a fellow 16 years of age wanted to go down to the river and inform the rebel pickets but I would not allow him to do it. I was afraid of treachery on the part of the enemy. They're mean enough I'm sure.

How do things progress in Woodbury? I would give a hundred dollars (if I had them) to be down at your house now, being the fishing season. I am disgusted, not with the army but with the south and everything belonging to it and will be glad to see the north once more. If I return from this war safe and sound I shall never travel in the south again. I hope that nothing has happened to Uncle Jos[,] because I have made up my mind that if he has been hurt or captured the enemy shall have little mercy from me!

Give my love to Aunt and Uncle Ben. I think that Master Ben Jr[205] might write to his soldier cousin. It would give me great pleasure to receive and answer letters from you all. I suppose Molly[206] is in school, Some of these days I may pay you a sudden visit. But we will fight a while first.

Much love from your affectionate cousin
Tom

[Original]

Camp at Mechanicsville Va.
Monday June 16th 1862

Dear Ma,

Yesterday morning was about one of the warmest that we have had; we had a march which I thought would have brought us into a fight with the enemy about three miles from Mechanicsville, but the rebels did not appear, so back we came. In the afternoon we had a very heavy thunder storm, which cleared the atmosphere, and now *this* morning it is quite cool and a fine day I think we will have. McClellan is commencing to play his old game over again,—*which game* is to take Richmond without a struggle, I don't mean to say that there will be *no* fighting, but at least nothing more than engagements and skirmishes along our lines. Our *whole army* has crossed the Chickahominy with the *exceptions* of *Porter's* and *Franklin's* Corps; *Porter* is on the *extreme* right, *then* comes *our Division of Franklin's* corps (Gen. Slocum's Division) which is said to be the finest troops in the *right wing*, the best troops are generally put in reserve. Turning back, I will say that Gen. McClellan is going to have Richmond no matter whether the rebels say "yes," or "no." His trains of *"big guns"* with great quantities of ammunition are now going to the front at the left, and in fact along the whole line, which gave rise to many strange reports[,] for Gen. McClellan gave orders that all provisions trains &c. should turn back to allow his siege trains to come up from the White House, where the[y] were and are now being landed. Well as I said, it gave rise to reports, one was that the rebel Gen. Jackson had escaped McDowell, and was rapidly advancing upon the Pamunkey River, had crossed with a large body, and had destroyed two schooners, a train of fifty wagons, fired into one of the rail-road trains &c. &c.[207] also that we would be attacked that night, of cours[e] we were under arms the greater part of the night; well the truth of the story is that a party of rebel cavalry appeared near the river and attacked a train of wagons sent out for forage and they captured some, Gen. Stoneman, receiving word of the fight went after, came across and attacked them[;] after having a severe sabre-fight Stoneman drove them away; one of Stoneman's Lieutenant's was *terribly cut up*, he still lives, but *I* think that it will be a miracle if he survives his injuries. The only thing that the enemy are afraid of is the plan that Gen. McClellan is sure to carry out, not withstanding all that the rebels do to frustrate it, which is exactly the same as at Yorktown[;] slowly but surely approaching their works, and then almost surrounding them they have to leave in a hurry; here at Richmond I believe he intends not only to approach but surround them and capture very near their whole force, time will show however. I think that as the rebels have collected together at and around Richmond a great part of their army, and also are so confident as to the result of the coming battle, that if we beat them[,] and I think that there can be no doubt of that, it will end the war, that is there will be no more extensive fighting, only the trouble of putting down the squads and small bands of men fighting upon their own hook; if it so turns out I resign and come home. I am not going to have myself burnt up with a sun the like of which has never been felt or seen in Camden; those are my sentiments[;] they are correct too that is more. My opinion is that a man no matter whether he be an officer or private is not benefitted by entering the army, when I get home I will give a number of instances. Since *I entered the army* I have taken particular notice of some and I know it to be a fact. There is one officer in the regiment who I like and admire quite a good deal. (his name is Capt. Buckley) [H]e is from Philadelphia[,] is and was quite a promising young lawyer; he reads his Bible every morning and often through the day when not having anything else to read in the shape of newspapers, besides he is not ashamed to be seen by others[;] I like that. I should choose such a man for a friend. I like him more than any other officer in the regiment just upon that account. An account of our march yesterday morning I will write to Annie this afternoon. I agree with you entirely about that photograph of Miss Mary Harbert. I find that it is always best to think twice before you act once; your letter is destroyed as you wished, I do hope that Charley will get into some business in Washington. *I don't want to see him in the army.* I also received Annie's letter of the 11th also two letters from Will and Bob Potts yesterday afternoon. I don't say that I am home sick, for that is not my style but I shouldn't mind getting home to see you dear Ma, and Annie, Jos and Frank. If you will give me Charley's direction, I shall write to him. I am very well and in high spirits[,] anxious for this miserable war to be *closed up*. Remember me to all my friends, and with much love to yourself, dear Ma, to my dear Sister, Jos and Frank.

I remain your loving son
Tom
Lieut. Co. I. 3rd N. J. Vol. Inf.
Lt. Col. Brown
Comd. Gen. Taylor's Brig.

[Transcribed Copy]
Camp at Mechanicsville
June 16th 1862

Dearest sister,
In the course of human events, it behooves every good brother to take care of his sister, I would demand [to know] who that Mr. Anderson[208] is, if you would excuse my curiosity. I thought that he was Mrs. Harbert's[209] brother. Is he? An orderly on horse back handed me a letter yesterday. And of course I wondered somewhat; but it is alright I suppose. Therefore I will now answer your welcome letters and I shall give you that account of our march of which I spoke in Ma's letter. Before I commence I will ask that that letter of Ma's be not taken out of our family. Saturday evening an order came around saying that in a sudden march by day or night the men should take their haversacks and canteens with them[,] also twenty extra rounds of cartridges in their pockets. I never supposed that we were going to march so soon. It was a little before two o'clock early Sunday morning and of course I was sound asleep when the officer of the day came to my tent and when he

had awakened me said that I must get my company up in time immediately[,] so I jumped up and in five minutes with belt, sword, revolver on and a pocket full of cartridges was out and had the orderly out getting the men up. Well after calling the roll I brought the company to a rest. Pretty soon an orderly from Colonel Brown came with the order to send two quarter masters for the extra rounds of amunition. I sent two men and soon had 1000 rounds of cartridges distributed. It was hardly done before we marched out and formed lines on the west side of the camp. We were dressed and after resting upon our arms five minutes we were under way. It was quite light before we had marched over a mile and a half from Mechanicsville. Well, we marched altogether about three miles to a farm. The regiment turned to the left into the farmyard and marched along the fence. Coming to a front we were ordered to lie down. After us came Captain Howe's regular battery.[210] I should have said two sections of it. They were pointed at the roads about three hundred yards off. One just at the side of the farmhouse. I was wishing that the rebels would open on us. The farmer's house would have gone for certain. Other dispositions of our forces were made down the road, the one on which we had come, about 80 yards, [J]ust at another road as straight as an arrow was posted one brass piece which could have swept it as nicely as one would have wished. Below that gun was a squadron of cavalry and below and to the right of that was the Second regiment. The First was on picket along the white line and the 4th N.J. was sent to assist the 1st. So to sum up our whole force we had two regiments of infantry, one battery and a squadron of cavalry also two companies of sharp shooters. These were deployed as skirmishers in front of us. Well, we waited for about two hours when an orderly came to Gen. Taylor. Pretty soon we had orders to fall in and were on our way back to camp. It was a hot although short march, I can tell you. The occassion of all this was that a cavalry picket thought the enemy were crossing the Chickahominy, they having heard a noise. Stoneman's pickets are stationed all along the roads leading to the river. So General Taylor of course took measures for giving them a warm reception. I think that they were tempted to cross. We had a fine position. The ground was elevated, in front of us was a meadow, beyond were woods and a little beyond ran the river. We could have commenced shelling them before they had even had time to cross[,] and then if they had pushed forward from the woods into the broad field they would have been cut to pieces by grape and shell. But they did not come. I will also say that the greater part of the regiment was behind a thin wood hill so that they would have caught rats[211] from us and would not have been able to return the compliment. It turned out to be all a humbug. So you see my dear sister we were spared a pretty heavy fight. While I am writing there is considerable artillery firing out left. It all amounts to nothing I guess. I can almost pity that farmer[,] for if the enemy had attempted to cross the distance which was short and of course the range was easy that it would have been merely the quickness in loading and I think that our troops are not behind hand in that business. I spoke about that photograph in Ma's letter and I have this to say. Please don't feel anxious on my account. I shall not be reckless but remembering those at home I will be careful. I am very much obliged to Ma for those toothbrushes and papers. I wish she would send more. I don't want dear Ma to be anxious about me. It is getting now quite dark so I must close. Give my love to Ma, Charlie, Jos and Frank.

Your loving brother
Tom

[Transcribed Copy]

Fair Oaks, Va.
Friday eve June 20th 1862
Private!

Dear Jos,
As it is pretty late I will write only a few words in answer to your letter of the 14th. We are now encamped near the battlefield of Fair Oaks having crossed the Chickahominy yesterday afternoon at New Bridge. It was a very fatiguing march all the way from Mechanicsville and by a round about way at that. At one time I had not fifteen men in the ranks, most having fallen out, but fortunately we halted for two hours. I will give all the particulars in Marts and Annie's letters. No one unless he could see for himself has any idea of the last fight. The trees are all cut up. One tree had in its trunk only two feet above the ground eighteen bullet marks. That is the way all through the woods. As to the graves, trenches are dug and the bodies of the enemy as well as those of our men are put in promiscuously. One grave had in it 11 corporals, two sergeants, 1 Lieutenant. Our division is a part of the second line. The army is divided into three. We will come in for a heavy part of the work. Hookers,[212] Kearney's, Smith's divisions are in the first line also many others. The 6th N.J.[213] has only 350 men for duty. One company has a corporal to command it. The Captain is dead, the 1st Lieutenant is wounded, the 2nd Lieutenant is sick and all the sergeants are killed. They had to place the 22nd. N.Y. Volunteers in the N.J. brigade to fill it up.[214] But it is certain that if the rebels attack us again they will repent it. Our men are working all the time. They have rifle pits and ports in every direction. Now then my reason for speaking to you concerning Lt. Col. Hatch is this. There is no one in our regiment that does not know that Lt. Col. Brown drinks. And he is to be our Colonel with a report started that Uncle Thomas is using his influence for Lt. Hatch. Of course Brown, knowing that Uncle has influence and also that he is a near relation of mine would in revenge turn on me.[215] And you know well enough how easily he could do that, so I wanted to know for certain. I think that Arch Taylor has something to do with it. He will be adjutant, certain, and to injure me has probably circulated this report. He says that Bob Dunham told him, someone having informed him, Bob. I know Arch Taylor like a book. He is a selfish ungenerous fellow. I keep on friendly terms with him but I know the man. There is nothing more than can disgust me than for one man to sponge upon another.

*"Hot Work Soon Enough"* 123

He does. I was tired of it so down I came and you see the consequence. He out of mere spite, it can't be anything else, creates such a report knowing that Brown if he wanted to might make it very uncomfortable for me. I shall be very careful and keep my eyes wide open and my ears. I can hold my own against Brown or any other man like him no matter who he is. As for Bob, I will not write anything concerning him. He has given way to what you said in your letter. I feel sorry for him. He is a fine fellow otherwise. I will have to stop as it is now quite late. I am very much obliged to you, my dear brother, for your little gift of the stamps. I also received those from Ma and the Recorder newspaper. We are ready for battle at any time. It may come soon and then again it may not. There is constant skirmishing. Be careful that Ma is not worried by this letter. You better not read it all to her. Can I have Charlie's address.

Your loving brother
Tom

P.S. I am in command at present as Lt Taylor is sick.

[Transcribed Copy]

Fairoaks, Va.
Sun aft. June 22nd 1862

Dear Annie,
As I was not able to write yesterday I will do so now. There are several things I wish to speak about. First you are probably very much surprised at Jos' last letter from me. It is the case and I might say more. You must understand that we are on perfectly friendly terms although I see more than Arch Taylor supposes. To tell the truth he has been what is called a spoilt child and it is so even now. Well we will let that drop altogether and turn to some more interesting subject which will be an account of our work yesterday. In the morning I had made up my mind to write letters but about seven an order came for our brigade to go out on fatigue duty at eight precisely[,] so at the time appointed the whole regiment marched out. Turning to the left we came to a halt at General Slocum's headquarters and here half the regiment after being supplied with axes and shovels and picks went to work. Those with axes went in to the woods to cut down trees, those with shovels and picks to form a road with ditches on each side of said road[,] which was to be wide enough for two wagons for siege trains as the road we made connected with one running to the trenches. Well it was an interesting sight to see trees falling in every direction[,] which after being cut up into the right sizes we carried out and put alongside the road where they were to be split. They were then put on the road, first two lines like a railroad and then pieces put across up and down the road. After putting down the timber the earth was thrown all over about eight inches thick[,] which formed and finished a road that will last fifty years. One could not have better roads made for hard service especially if they are to have heavy artillery pass over them. The heaviest guns

cannot smash this road. It took three whole days for our regiment to finish a part of the road half a mile in length. There were three or four regiments at work and you may imagine what a sight it must have been. It was just like three or four swarms of bees. Captain Hopkins[216] of the U.S. Army Engineers superintended the work. I had command of the detail. Lt. Taylor was very unwell and had to go into camp. It was nearly seven when we returned into camp. As the orderly was calling the roll I heard what I supposed to be a man kicking upon an empty barrel and of course paid no attention to it[,] but as it came nearer it turned out to be firing and before the orderly sergeant had finished the calling of the roll[,] the booming of the heavy guns and the constant crash of muskets told us all that we were in a fight. Just as my sergeant was giving the command to break ranks I stopped him and ordered him to stack arms again as I was pretty sure that we would be called upon. Well the company was dismissed and I went to my tent and sat down to supper. The noise was quite battlelike. I mean the musketry and the guns. I had hardly finished my supper before the order came to fall in and have twenty rounds of cartridges issued to each man and in other words get ready to fight. You must know that I did not hurry however. I was bound to get my supper not withstanding the rebels[,] allowing Lt. Taylor the pleasure of attending to the company. Well to tell the truth the third regiment was very much fatigued with the day's work and I must say that I was too having to stand all the time overlooking the work. To return however we rested on our arms for about a half an hour, our whole division, infantry, cavalry and artillery, and after some time the firing slackened until it finally ceased and then we broke ranks. Now I suppose my dear sister would like to know what all the fuss was about. Well it was simply this. The attack commenced a way down to the left at General Sumner's line and it came up to the N.J Brigade which is on the first line. We are on the second line a mile behind the first. Also the 2nd brigade is off to our left. Well it was merely skirmishing along the line until it reached the Jersey troops when instead of fighting in the roads the enemy came out, about four regiments, and made a rush for the ranks. Our artillery did not fire until the rebels were close. We let fly at them with grape and shell. It is said that we mowed them down by scores. The reason that we allowed, them to get so near was that our men were waiting for the pickets to get back in. They did not want to kill them of course. Well we had two men killed and five wounded. Our men say that it was awful the way our shells and grape burst among and through them all. The enemy broke and scattered in all directions. Today they say that there is not a rebel to be seen. The deserters say that they have fallen back two miles. We are going to throw out our pickets tonight more in advance. All last night the pickets were skirmishing, that is firing away at one another. No damage on our side I believe except some wounds. This is the way there is and will be constant firing until we drive them out. It is reported that the rebels are preparing to leave, that is evacuate Richmond. I shall have to stop I guess. The weather is very warm now, something like a furnace, but what's the odds. I'm perfectly well. I received your letter also Marts and Jos'. Annie dear tell Frank that I will write him but he must answer my last letter. I shall write Ma tonight as we might have out at any time. No one knows. Give my love to all.

I am still your loving brother no doubt about that
Tom

[Original]

*Private, only in the family.*

Fair Oaks Va.
Sunday Evening June 22nd

Dear Ma,
Being Officer of the Day I will say a few words about matters and things; Lt. Col. Brown has one bad practice, which will get him into trouble some day, this habit is drinking, and when he gets drunk he always makes a fuss. Once at Fort Worth being "under the weather" as it is called he went out and watching his opportunity ran up, seizing the musket from a guard took it off with him, next day he gave the sentry four hours extra; that man has tried this plan of troubling the guards several times, it will not do to try such a game here; again, Major Collet tried to play the same trick upon a sentry one dark night, but the guard sprang back and brought his bayonet close to the Major's breast. I can tell you my dear Mother the worthy Major did not try it a second time; Lt. Col. Brown has attempted it a half a dozen times, it is merely to try them and see whether they are attending to their duty, but there is no necessity for it, and does a great deal of harm[;] if he were to go around quietly it would be all right, but to meddle as he does sometimes will not pay as he will find to his sorrow. Well he wont do it tonight without being punished, for I have just sent a corporal around to instruct the guards that *in case any one, no matter who comes and fools with them such as snatching a gun &c. to shoot him down*, they *are* to have *caps upon* their *guns all night*[;] now then if Mr. Brown wishes to get shot he had better go around the men on post. I am perfectly right, for right in front of the enemy the greatest caution must be observed and no trifling allowed[;] these are my sentiments, I do not know whether Col. Brown's are the same as my own, I *only know* that he had better not play his pranks around me. I was quite pleased with something that took place this afternoon, it was this, Capt's Gibson, Stickney,[217] Buckley and two or three of the Lieutenants went to Chaplain Darrow and asked him if he thought that he did right in not having service, and also if his conscience did not rebuke, he has been doing nothing to show that he *is* Chaplain, and moreover Capt. Gibson asked Mr. Darrow if he would preach a sermon upon a subject that he (Gibson) would give him. Mr. Darrow said that he would preach upon any subject, text &c, that they might give him, accordingly Capt. Gibson gave him the three words "What is it." Well at half past six many of the men and most of the officers, among whom I saw Major Collet, were there in front of the Chaplain's tent, and had the Baptist service, he

preached and it was a good sermon; every body went away pleased, the singing was good, and to tell the truth it seemed more like home than anything else; but I don't believe Mr. Darrow is entirely to blame, if the officers had set a good example at first of course the men would attend[,] but as the Chaplain generally had about ten or twelve men to hear him preach of course it discouraged him, but I hope now that there will be a change, I shall use all my influence and by good example get my men to go, and by these means get everything straight again. I believe that is all I have to say upon these to subjects. Everything seems to go on just so, all is great pretty much along the lines, except a little skirmishing between the pickets sometimes. The whiskey ration has been discontinued by Gen. McClellan for the reason that Gen. Sickles Brigade[218] saved their whiskey in bottles and taking it out on picket, became intoxicated and raised the mischief out there[.] [O]n account of this I say, the whole army suffers, but it will not do them any harm. They can get along without very well[;] some say not however. There is nothing more I believe my dear mother, unless it be to thank you for those papers, and I wish you would send them as often as you can. Give my love dear ma to Aunt Sarah, all at Uncle Edward's, and Aunt Anna Jones',[219] please remember me to all my friends in Camden. Give my love to dearest Annie, Jos and Frank, also much love and many kisses for yourself. I refrain from saying anything about the little *skirmish* you had about property if you may call it such, nothing like independence after all. I am very well indeed and long to see you and all the dear ones at home.

Your most affectionate son
Tom
Lt. Co. I. 3rd N. J. Vol. Inf. Col. Brown
Gen. Taylors Brigade
Slocum's Div.

[Transcribed Copy]
Camp Lincoln Fair Oaks Va
June 24th 1862
Private!!!

My dearest sister,
I received your letter with thanks this afternoon and of course will answer. Keep it a secret but if I am spared through the coming battle I shall resign. Quite a number of officers in the brigade, as I have said before, are going to do the same thing after the arrival at Richmond. Although I would not do so now before the app[r]oaching fight for two hundred dollars unless I thought it was absolutely necessary. I would not do it for this reason. Some, not knowing the why or wherefore, would take it for cowardice or fear or any other hard word that they might think of much to my injury. I think that I may say with truth, or whatever you may call it (I am not gifted in that way) I can lead my men as far as they will want to go. These are my sentiments my dear

sister. Do you agree with me? Now then a few words in the other direction. We are constantly under arms because of the continued skirmishing of the pickets. For instance last night we had a tremendous storm with thunder and lightning and even in the midst of that the outposts were keeping up a fire, doing no harm however and thus an orderly came and we were out in line at half past three, all ready for anything, the whole division, infantry cavalry, artillery. Well we were under arms until the men's breakfast was ready when the ranks were broken and the men were allowed to eat their meal. As soon as this was accomplished we fell in again and did not stack arms until nearly seven o'clock. I believe an attack was expected but I advise the enemy to keep at a proper distance for our works are strong and extensive and also our guns are regular steam engines when they once get to work. It has been pretty quiet all day. All of yesterday and until 9 this morning Lt. Taylor and I were without a company, it being on picket with Capt. Gibson. On their return I was told what had happened out on the front. As I said in my last letter, the pickets and the rebels are out in a wheatfield within speaking distance. While the first string was [illegible] an attempt to exchange papers. A rebel came halfway bringing with him a newspaper. Arthur Merry,[220] one of the corporals of Co B, you know who he is[,] being from Camden, well he went out and they made an exchange. All things were going along in the right style when the field officer of the day came along and seeing that Merry had a rebel newspaper asked Merry how he obtained it. Of course Merry answered and Major Birney[221] put him in arrest. He will be reduced in ranks and fined, I suppose, for a general order was given out against it. It is a pity for Corporal Merry is a good soldier but it can't be helped. Most of the firing has been down at the railroad. The rebels can see straight down the road to our part, an immense hill of crackers boxes. Well that makes them both hungry and annoyed, I suppose, and accordingly they vent their wrath by attacking us at that point. On the railroad we have two guns loaded with grape and, when the enemy comes out of the woods we give it to them hot and heavy as they will witness. It is thought that in the little fight of Saturday evening they lost at least six hundred men. This morning a number of large guns arrived by the cars and are being put into position. I expect that before long the hills and woods will ring with the tremendous reports of heavy guns and batteries. As we will have to turn out tomorrow morning early I think that I shall have to close, dear Annie, by answering your epistle and Frank's. In the first place I get all the stamps Ma sends me but sometimes I forget to mention it in my letters. Wish she would send me the Recorder every week. The newspapers we get here one day and a half after being printed. As for Bob's staying in the army that is more than I know. I suppose he will stay until he leaves. This is all I know about it. Dearest sister, tell Frank to go ahead, Jim Carpenter and everything. He can do it if he wants to. Please tell him to remember me to Fred and James Dixon.[222] Tell Frank that I shaved the other day, or rather the operation was performed by the brigade barber. I now sport a remarkable goatee. It is quite extensive. I did make up my mind not to shave while I was in the army, but I found that that would not do at all. Dear Annie, remember me to all my friends, both sexes of course. When I leave for home I shall not let you know of it. Understand it will be when I reach Richmond or there abouts. I send my love to Ma, Charlie, Jos, and Frank. Much love to yourself.

Your loving brother,
Tom

[Original]

[Written in his mother's handwriting at the top of Howell's June 25th letter, below]

*The last letter of my noble loving boy. Was killed on the 27 of June before Richmond. The bravest of the brave in the cause of his country and glorious flag. He died as he lived a christian Soldier.*

Camp Lincoln, Fair Oaks Va.
Wednes. June 25th 1862

Dear Ma,
I sent off a letter to Annie this morning, and as we are under marching orders to go to the front, I thought that you would like to hear from me. There is one thing the people in the South have, and what we don't often see in the North, it is the thunder storm for violence not equaled, it comes with a *rush* and it does not rain but, *as I was going to say*, it is like *standing under the Niagra Falls, probably not so bad as that*. I never saw anything to equal the storms we have had in the last week. The other night when it poured down so, the pickets stood up in an open wheat field, with blankets and some had India-Rubber, some just with the common ones, rather rough that was, but one must not expect to have everything as he might wish or like, and according to his own idea. Life here is rather rough. if I had my own way, I think that I would detach this brigade to guard Richmond when we get there. I am not partial to the hot Sun &c. but if we have to march further South this Summer, of course it is all right. although I don't say that I will go. This morning the corps that Gen. Kearney's division is in advanced, and which brought on quite a sharp fight.[223] it is all over I believe now, and we hold our position too. there is nothing at present. love to dear Annie Jos and Frank, much love for yourself

Tom
Lt. Co. I. 3rd N. J. Vol Inf
Taylor's Brigade

PS. We are going out to the front immediately.
Tom

[Transcribed Copy]

Camp Lincoln. Fair Oaks
Thurs. June 26th 1862

Dear Jos,

We have just received glorious news. It is 10 o'clock at night. This afternoon the rebels crossed the Chickahominy River in force and attacked General Porter's corps.[224] Well, we drove them and are still driving them and you never heard such cheering in your life from way back in the rear out to the pickets and from the right to the left. Fifteen minutes ago Bob [Dunham] came over with the word that the regiment should turn out immediately and cheer. Well the whole brigade did turn out and the way we shouted was a caution. There is no doubt that the fight was a brilliant one. All the ambulances in our division were ordered to report at headquarters at once to proceed to Mechanicsville. There may be a general advance tomorrow and then again there may not be but we will probably see some sights. Yesterday General Sumner,[225] expecting an attack, thought that he was in need of more men so he asked of General Slocum one brigade[,] so one brigade marched out and down the railroad 250 yards from our works[,] which are of immense strength. No one has any idea of their magnitude until he sees them. They extend nearly from the James River to the Chickahominy with ports here and there all along the whole line. And let me tell you, if the enemy attacks us they will get the mischief. Well to return, after we had marched over we stacked arms and the[n] just walked around looking at the frame buildings pierced with balls and also the grave. We returned at eight. About four in the afternoon our troops opened a tremendous fire with one of our heavy guns at the enemy said to be approaching in force. Whether they were approaching or not all I know is that they did not come far for it is said that we did awful damage amongst the rebels just in front of Our pickets which were in some force. Understand that one two or three brigades go out to picket at once and in one place at one time in front of General Kearney's position to our left[,] and where their pickets were stationed in the woods all of a sudden we heard first one and then another and then burst out a tremendous roll of musketry the like of which people in the north have never heard. In less time than I can write the whole regiment made a grand rush for the stacks of arms but after the firing had lasted about 35 minutes we broke ranks. The same happened several times but we did not run for arms again. I guess we will hear of our victory tomorrow. Such playing of bands you never heard going in every direction. I will first be willing to say that the enemy hate us like everything for all this demonstration. I don't believe that they thought we had bands or any music for it was not allowed to play. They know now. I am very well and shall write soon. Give me love to Ma, Annie, Charlie, Frank. I received your last letter today. Also for yourself.

From your affectionate brother,
Tom
3rd Regiment
Taylor's brigade

# NOTES

1. The *John A. Warner* was chartered by the government from March 1, 1862, to March 4, 1864, then April 21, 1864, to June 5, 1865. Charles Dana Gibson and E. Kay Gibson, *The Army's Navy Series: Dictionary of Transports and Combatant Vessels Steam and Sail Employed by the Union Army, 1861–1868* (Camden, ME: Ensign Press, 1995), 177. According to Tom Howell, this was the sixth trip the ship was making to transport troops to the peninsula. Stephen Sears mentions that the government chartered every available steamer on the East Coast and that the 113 steamers were chartered at a cost of $24,300 per day. Sears, *To the Gates of Richmond*, 23.

2. Daniel P. Buckley to Father, April 20, 1862. D. Penrose Buckley Papers (#1775), HSP.

3. Tom Howell to Mother, April 24, 1862. H-41, Howell Family Collection, GCHS.

4. Tom Howell to Joshua Howell, April 20, 1862. Transcribed copy, author's collection.

5. Mark A. Snell, "'Very Crude Notions on the Subject': William B. Franklin's Amphibious Assault at Eltham's Landing," in *Union Combined Operations in the Civil War*, ed. Craig L. Symonds (New York: Fordham University Press, 2010), 33–35.

6. Daniel P. Buckley to Erin, April 22, 1862. D. Penrose Buckley Papers (#1775), HSP.

7. Tom Howell to Mother, April 24, 1862. H-41, Howell Family Collection, GCHS; Tom Howell to Annie Howell, April 26, 1862. Transcribed copy, author's collection.

8. Tom Howell to Joshua Howell, April 30, 1862. Transcribed copy, author's collection.

9. Daniel P. Buckley to Father, May 1, 1862. D. Penrose Buckley Papers (#1775), HSP.

10. Ibid.

11. McPherson, *Battle Cry of Freedom*, 419–20.

12. Ibid., 422.

13. Kearny took over Charles Smith Hamilton's division of the III Corps after Hamilton was relieved by McClellan on April 30, 1862. McClellan stated to President Lincoln that "General Hamilton is not fit to command a division." O.R. I, 11(3): 129, 185–86.

14. Tom Howell to Mother, May 2, 1862. H-41, Howell Family Collection, GCHS.

15. Daniel P. Buckley to Mother, May 16, 1862. D. Penrose Buckley Papers (#1775), HSP; emphasis in original.

16. Daniel P. Buckley to Mother, May 4, 1862. D. Penrose Buckley Papers (#1775), HSP.

17. Snell, "Very Crude Notions," 36.

18. Captain Buckley explained, "The vessel has become rather suspicious in the bug line, in fact a close inspection of clothing is frequently necessary." Daniel P. Buckley to Father, May 1, 1862. D. Penrose Buckley Papers (#1775), HSP.

19. Sears, *To the Gates of Richmond*, 84–85.

20. Snell, "Very Crude Notions," 36.

21. Tom Howell to Mother, May 5, 1862. H-41, Howell Family Collection, GCHS.

22. Ibid.

23. Daniel P. Buckley to Erin, May 6, 1862. D. Penrose Buckley Papers (#1775), HSP.

24. Sears, *To the Gates of Richmond*, 66.

25. Daniel P. Buckley to Erin, May 6, 1862. D. Penrose Buckley Papers (#1775), HSP.

26. O.R. I, 11(3): 143.

27. Rowena Reed, *Combined Operations in the Civil War* (Annapolis, MD: U.S. Naval Institute Press, 1978), 159.

28. O.R. I, 11(3): 143; Snell, "Very Crude Notions," 36.

29. O.R. I, 11(1): 615.

30. Tom Howell to Mother, May 8, 1862. H-41, Howell Family Collection, GCHS; Tom Howell to Joshua Howell, May 10, 1862. Transcribed copy, author's collection.

31. Tom Howell to Joshua Howell, May 10, 1862. Transcribed copy, author's collection.
32. Jeffrey D. Wert, *The Sword of Lincoln: The Army of the Potomac* (New York: Simon and Schuster, 2005), 80.
33. Tom Howell to Joshua Howell, May 10, 1862. Transcribed copy, author's collection.
34. Daniel P. Buckley to Father, May 9, 1862. D. Penrose Buckley Papers (#1775), HSP.
35. Sears, *To the Gates of Richmond*, 108.
36. Tom Howell to Mother, May 8, 1862. H-41, Howell Family Collection, GCHS.
37. Tom Howell to Annie Howell, May 12, 1862. Transcribed copy, author's collection.
38. Tom Howell to Joshua Howell, May 10, 1862. Transcribed copy, author's collection. Howell wrongly estimated that the plantation was eleven hundred acres.
39. O.R. I, 11(3): 162. Stoneman's cavalry was the lead element of McClellan's army as it moved up the peninsula from Yorktown.
40. Tom Howell to Joshua Howell, May 10, 1862. Transcribed copy, author's collection.
41. Tom Howell to Annie Howell, May 12, 1862. Transcribed copy, author's collection.
42. Tom Howell to Mother, May 14, 1862. H-41, Howell Family Collection, GCHS.
43. Ibid.
44. Tom Howell to Joshua Howell, May 16, 1862. Transcribed copy, author's collection.
45. Tom Howell to Mother, May 14, 1862. H-41, Howell Family Collection, GCHS; emphasis in original.
46. Daniel P. Buckley to Mother, May 16, 1862. D. Penrose Buckley Papers (#1775), HSP. White House was twenty-three miles from Richmond.
47. Sears, *To the Gates of Richmond* , 104. General Lee's wife was a Custis and granddaughter of Martha Washington. Mrs. Lee was staying at this place until a few days before the Union troops arrived.
48. Martin, *Peninsula Campaign*, 93.
49. Tom Howell to Mother, May 18, 1862. H-41, Howell Family Collection, GCHS; emphasis in original.
50. Daniel P. Buckley to Mother, May 16, 1862. D. Penrose Buckley Papers (#1775), HSP.
51. Martin, *Peninsula Campaign*, 96.
52. James I. Robertson Jr., ed. *The Civil War Letters of General Robert McAllister* (New Brunswick, NJ: Rutgers University Press, 1965), 161.
53. Sears, *To the Gates of Richmond*, 103.
54. Ibid., 110.
55. Ibid.
56. Tom Howell to Mother, May 22, 1862. H-41, Howell Family Collection, GCHS; emphasis in original.
57. Foote, *Gentlemen and the Roughs*, 79.
58. Tom Howell to Mother, May 22, 1862. H-41, Howell Family Collection, GCHS.
59. Tom Howell to Joshua Howell, May 27, 1862. Transcribed copy, author's collection.
60. Ibid.
61. Tom Howell to Joshua Howell, May 22, 1862. Transcribed copy, author's collection.
62. Sears, *To the Gates of Richmond,* 109; Tom Howell to Mother, May 26, 1862. H-41, Howell Family Collection, GCHS.
63. Tom Howell to Annie Howell, May 28, 1862. Transcribed copy, author's collection. I have been unable to find such account in the papers.
64. Ibid.

65. Daniel P. Buckley to Mother, May 27, 1862, and Daniel P. Buckley to Father, June 1, 1862. Both in D. Penrose Buckley Papers (#1775), HSP.
66. Ibid.
67. Ira M. Rutkow, *Bleeding Blue and Gray: Civil War Surgery and the Evolution of American Medicine* (New York: Random House, 2005), 117, 123.
68. Daniel P. Buckley to Father, June 1, 1862. D. Penrose Buckley Papers (#1775), HSP.
69. Ibid.
70. Leeson's pension records state that he received his wound on May 29, 1862, but Captain Buckley's letter of June 1, 1862, mentions Leeson's wound and says it was received while on picket duty on May 30, 1862. Leeson Pension File, National Archives. Washington, D.C.
71. Confederates refer to this battle as Seven Pines, since that is the name of the village where they enjoyed their biggest success. Federals call the battle Fair Oaks, because nearby Fair Oaks Station is where they too achieved great success, although the results of the battle were inconclusive as to which side had won.
72. Sumner's II Corps crossed the Grapevine Bridge, which was swaying under the heavy current, and bolstered the Union line south of the river.
73. Tom Howell to Mother, June 2, 1862. H-41, Howell Family Collection, GCHS; emphasis in original.
74. Daniel P. Buckley to Father, June 1, 1862. D. Penrose Buckley Papers (#1775), HSP.
75. Daniel P. Buckley to Father, June 3, 1862. D. Penrose Buckley Papers (#1775), HSP.
76. Tom Howell to Mother, June 2, 1862. H-41, Howell Family Collection, GCHS; emphasis in original.
77. Ibid.
78. The Eighty-fifth Pennsylvania was in the Second Brigade, Second Division, IV Corps. It was later determined that Colonel Howell was not wounded during the battle.
79. Tom Howell to Fanny Howell, June 7, 1862. H-41, Howell Family Collection, GCHS.
80. Ibid.
81. Order No. 9, January 9, 1862. Regimental Order Book 1, Third New Jersey Infantry Regiment, Record Group 94, National Archives, Washington, D.C.
82. Tom Howell to Mother, June 5, 1862. H-41, Howell Family Collection, GCHS.
83. Tom Howell to Mother, June 16, 1862. H-41, Howell Family Collection, GCHS.
84. Tom Howell to Mother, June 7, 1862. H-41, Howell Family Collection, GCHS.
85. Stryker, *Record of Officers and Men*, 177.
86. Tom Howell to Mother, June 7, 1862. H-41, Howell Family Collection, GCHS.
87. *A Catalogue of the Officers and Students of the College of New Jersey, For the Academical Year 1856–57* (Princeton, NJ: John T. Robinson, 1857), 8–9.
88. Tom Howell to Annie Howell, June 16, 1862. Transcribed copy, author's collection.
89. Tom Howell to Mother, June 16, 1862. H-41, Howell Family Collection, GCHS.
90. Ibid.
91. Charles M. Evans, *War of the Aeronauts: A History of Ballooning in the Civil War* (Mechanicsburg, PA: Stackpole Books, 2002), 71.
92. Ibid., 237.
93. Daniel P. Buckley to Father, June 18, 1862. D. Penrose Buckley Papers (#1775), HSP.
94. Tom Howell to Joshua Howell, June 20, 1862. Transcribed copy, author's collection.
95. Ibid.
96. Sears, *To the Gates of Richmond*, 148.

97. Tom Howell to Annie Howell, June 22, 1862. Transcribed copy, author's collection.
98. Ibid.
99. Tom Howell to Mother, June 16, 1862. H-41, Howell Family Collection, GCHS.
100. Tom Howell to Annie Howell, June 24, 1862. Transcribed copy, author's collection.
101. Tom Howell to Joshua Howell, June 20, 1862. Transcribed copy, author's collection.
102. Ibid. Brown was eventually promoted to colonel on February 28, 1863, but the appointment was dated back to May 15, 1862.
103. As quoted in Sears, *To the Gates of Richmond*, 159.
104. Tom Howell to Annie Howell, June 24, 1862. Transcribed copy, author's collection; Tom Howell to Joshua Howell, June 26, 1862. Transcribed copy, author's collection.
105. Sears, *To the Gates of Richmond*, 183.
106. Ibid., 183–89.
107. Tom Howell to Mother, June 25, 1862. H-41, Howell Family Collection, GCHS.
108. Tom Howell to Joshua Howell, June 26, 1862. Transcribed copy, author's collection.
109. Sears, *To the Gates of Richmond*, 195.
110. Correspondent, "The Third New Jersey Regiment," *West Jersey Press*, July 23, 1862.
111. Sears, *To the Gates of Richmond*, 208.
112. As quoted in ibid., 207.
113. Tom Howell to Joshua Howell, June 26, 1862. Transcribed copy, author's collection.
114. The *John A. Warner* was a 527-ton side-wheel steamer that was built in 1857 in Wilmington, Delaware. The ship was owned by the Delaware River Steamboat Company and was chartered by the United States government from March 1, 1862, to March 4, 1864, and also from April 21, 1864, to June 5, 1864, for three hundred dollars per day. "*John A. Warner*," Water Transportation Vessel Files, 1834–1900, Box No. 111, Record Group 92, Office of the Quartermaster General, National Archives. Washington, D.C.
115. Fort Washington was built along the Potomac River in 1809 to protect Washington, D.C.
116. Jonathan Cook (1812–1883) was from the state's adjutant general's office. Prior to the Civil War, Cook had been a prominent businessman in Trenton and a delegate from the state of New Jersey to the 1860 Republican National Convention. During the Civil War, he supervised the transmission of money between the New Jersey soldiers in the field and their families back home. He frequently accompanied paymasters on their visits to the regiments. Richard F. Miller, ed. *States at War*, Vol. 4: *A Reference Guide for Delaware, Maryland, and New Jersey* (Hanover: University Press of New England, 2015), 673; *Annual Report of the Adjutant General of the State of New Jersey for the Year 1861* (Trenton, NJ: True American Office, 1862), 14.
117. Howell is referring to Martin Gray.
118. Mount Vernon was the home of George Washington. It is located along the banks of the Potomac River.
119. Yorktown is located near the end of the peninsula formed by the York and James Rivers in Virginia. It was the site of the surrender of the British army in 1781. For more about Yorktown during the Peninsula Campaign, see John V. Quarstein and J. Michael Moore, *Yorktown's Civil War Siege: Drums along the Warwick* (Charleston: History Press, 2012).
120. Captain Leonard H. Regur (1820–1915) never returned from recruiting duty. See Part I, n. 47.
121. It is unclear who Howell is referring to. There is no one with the name Bernard in the Howell or Carpenter families.

122. Howell is most likely referring to William K. Mackey (1852–1923) of Camden. 1870 United States Federal Census.

123. Benjamin Paschall Howell Jr. (1847–1925) was Tom Howell's cousin and the son of Dr. Benjamin Paschall Howell. Howell, *Book of John Howell and His Descendants*, 2: 594.

124. Howell is likely referring to the battle for Dam No. 1 that took place on April 16, but his description is not accurate. Five Vermont regiments under the command of Brig. Gen. William T. H. Brooks attacked the Confederate defenses behind the Warwick River. Yankee soldiers were able to occupy Rebel rifle pits, but Union commanders failed to send the Vermont soldiers support and a Confederate counterattack pushed them back at a loss of 165 men. For more on the attack on Dam No. 1, see Sears, *To the Gates of Richmond*, 55–56; Quarstein and Moore, *Yorktown's Civil War Siege*, 102–104.

125. Gloucester Point is opposite Yorktown, across the York River.

126. Howell most likely possessed a Smith & Wesson Model 1, which was a seven-shot .22-caliber revolver.

127. This Confederate note is in the Malcolm Lloyd Collection (#1618), HSP.

128. The First U.S. Cavalry was part of Col. George A. H. Blake's Brigade of Brig. Gen. Philip St. Cooke's Cavalry Reserve. Sears, *To the Gates of Richmond*, 363.

129. John E. Bedell (1839–1864) was the orderly sergeant, or first sergeant, of Co. I, Third New Jersey. He was killed in action near Spotsylvania, Virginia, in May 1864. Stryker, *Record of Officers and Men*, 177.

130. McClellan's Dragoons were Companies H and I, Twelfth Illinois Cavalry. These companies were organized in Chicago. *Report of the Adjutant General of the State of Illinois* (Springfield, IL: Phillips Bros., 1900), 1: viii.

131. First Connecticut Heavy Artillery Regiment.

132. Charles Tyler (1815–1899) was the captain of the *John A Warner*. He was the husband of Mary Ann Cone, whose brother, Jonathan Cone, owned the Delaware River Steamboat Company. William Whitney Cone, *Some Account of the Cone Family in America, Principally of the Descendants of Daniel Cone, Who Settled in Haddam Connecticut in 1662* (Topeka, KS: Crane & Company, 1903), 400–401.

133. Samuel W. Caldwell was eighteen years old and lived a few blocks from Howell on Sixth Street in Camden. 1860 United States Federal Census; Camden City Directory, 1863, 28.

134. These Confederate notes are also in the Malcolm Lloyd Collection (#1618), HSP.

135. The Confederates did not evacuate Yorktown until May 3, 1862. Quarstein and Moore, *Yorktown's Civil War Siege*, 133–35; Sears, *To the Gates of Richmond*, 61–62.

136. Howell did not mention the clash between the "Iron monsters" CSS *Merrimack* and the USS *Monitor* on March 9, 1862. He must have believed that another battle between the two occurred; however, this was not the case.

137. Edward B. Titsworth (1817–1898) of Plainfield, New Jersey, mustered into service on May 30, 1861, as a sergeant. 1860 United States Federal Census; Stryker, *Record of Officers and Men*, 176.

138. Edward Burd Grubb (1841–1913) was a second lieutenant in Co. C, Third New Jersey, then became first lieutenant of Co. D. Stryker, *Record of Officers and Men*, 158.

139. Kearny took over Charles Smith Hamilton's division of the III Corps after McClellan relieved Hamilton on April 30, 1862. See Part II, n13.

140. 1st Lt. Charles Wilson of Company A. Stryker, *Record of Officers and Men*, 152.

141. Joshua Blackwood Howell (1806–1864) was a brother of Richard W. Howell, who was Tom Howell's father. Joshua Blackwood Howell had been a lawyer in Uniontown, Pennsylvania, before the war. When the war began, he became colonel of the Eighty-fifth Pennsylvania Regiment. At Yorktown the Eighty-fifth Pennsylvania was in the Second Brigade, Third Division, IV Corps. Warner, *Generals in Blue*, 240.

142. McClellan's plan was to have Franklin's division steam up the York River to West Point and disembark. McClellan hoped that Franklin could cut off the retreating

rebels from Yorktown. The plan did not work, because McClellan put Franklin into motion two days too late. Sears, *To the Gates of Richmond*, 84–85.

143. Louis Loeb (1838–1874) was from Camden, New Jersey. He was born in Germany and moved to the United States with his family in 1842. He enlisted as a private in Co. I, Third New Jersey, on September 11, 1861. 1860 United States Federal Census; Stryker, *Record of Officers and Men*, 177.

144. West Point was on the York River and was the terminus of the Richmond and York River Railroad. It occupied a piece of land where the Pamunkey and Mattapony Rivers join to form the York River. Sears, *To the Gates of Richmond*, 85.

145. Potopotank Creek is located along the York River. There is no village there.

146. Second United States, Battery D was attached to Franklin's division. Sears, *To the Gates of Richmond*, 362.

147. Gosline's Zouaves was the Ninety-fifth Pennsylvania Regiment. They were in the Third Brigade of Franklin's division. The brigade was under the command of Brig. Gen. John Newton. O.R. I, 11(1): 625; Sears, *To the Gates of Richmond*, 362.

148. The Ninety-fifth Pennsylvania reported sixteen casualties in the battle. O.R. I, 11 (1): 618.

149. Brig. Gen. John Bell Hood's Texas Brigade, which consisted of the First, Fourth, and Fifth Texas Regiments plus the Eighteenth Georgia Regiment (which the Texans referred to as the "Third Texas"). The brigade was part of Brig. Gen. William Henry Chase Whiting's First Division of Reserves. O.R. I, 11(1): 629–30.

150. Lewis W. Oakley (1828–1888) became the surgeon of the Second New Jersey Regiment on January 6, 1862. He received his medical degree in 1852 from the College of Physicians and Surgeons, New York. He practiced medicine in Elizabeth, New Jersey until the beginning of the Civil War. New Jersey Historical Society, *Proceedings of the New Jersey Historical Society*, Second Series, Vol. 9, 1886–1887 (Newark, NJ: Daily Advertiser Printing House, 1887), 46.

151. Fifth Maine Regiment was in Brig. Gen. Henry W. Slocum's Second Brigade, First Division, I Corps. The New Jersey Brigade was the First Brigade, First Division, I Corps. Sears, *To the Gates of Richmond*, 362.

152. The battle described by Howell was the Battle of Eltham's Landing, which was fought on May 7, 1862. Franklin's division battled men from Chase Whiting's division, which was part of Johnston's rearguard. Confederate losses amounted to forty-eight men. Federal losses totaled 186 men. For more on the battle, see Sears, *To the Gates of Richmond*, 85–86.

153. The Eighteenth New York Regiment was in Brig Gen. John Newton's Third Brigade, First Division, I Corps. As Howell mentioned, the regiment did not suffer any casualties in the Battle of Eltham's Landing. As stated in Brig. Gen. Newton's report, O.R. I, 11(1): 624.

154. The Sixteenth New York Regiment was in Brig. Gen. Henry W. Slocum's Second Brigade, First Division, I Corps. The regiment suffered thirteen casualties at Eltham's Landing. O. R. I, 11(1): 618.

155. Howell is most likely referring to the 4,656 acre Romancoke plantation, which is on the Pamunkey River. The plantation was originally owned by George Washington Parke Custis, who was Robert E. Lee's father-in-law. Custis died in 1857 and bequeathed Romancoke to Lee's son, Robert E. Lee Jr. There is no mention of how many slaves lived on this plantation. Bruce Chadwick, *1858: Abraham Lincoln, Jefferson Davis, Robert E. Lee, Ulysses S. Grant and the War They Failed to See* (Naperville, IL: Sourcebooks, 2008), 53.

156. Brig. Gen. John Sedgwick (1813–1864) was in command of the Second Division, II Corps. Sears, *To the Gates of Richmond*, 359.

157. Capt. James M. Wilson and Lt. William C. Barnard were killed during the Battle of Williamsburg, May 5, 1862. Kearny mentions the death of the two men in his official report. O.R. I, 11(1): 493.

158. This is not true.

159. Union troops occupied Norfolk on May 10, 1862. Sears, *To the Gates of Richmond*, 90–91.

160. William B. Hatch (1838–1862) was lieutenant colonel of the Fourth New Jersey Regiment. Hatch was from Camden and lived at 544 Cooper Street. He was promoted to colonel of the Fourth New Jersey in August 1862 and died in December 1862 from the wounds he received during the Battle of Fredericksburg. Stryker, *Record of Officers and Men*, 182; Philadelphia City Directory, 1861, 1242.

161. Brig. Gen. Henry W. Slocum (1827–1894) commanded a brigade (Second Brigade) in Franklin's division. He was from New York and was a graduate of the West Point class of 1852. After Franklin was promoted to corps commander, Slocum took command of the division. Warner, *Generals in Blue*, 451–53.

162. Brig. Gen. John Newton (1822–1895) commanded a brigade (Third Brigade) in Franklin's division. Newton was a Virginian and graduated second in his class at West Point in 1842. Warner, *Generals in Blue*, 344–45.

163. Howell likely meant the Eighteenth New York Regiment from Newton's Brigade, not the Eighth New York.

164. James H. Simpson (1813–1883) was from New Brunswick, New Jersey, and was a graduate of the West Point class of 1832. Prior to the Civil War, Simpson served in the U.S. Army's Topographical Engineers. After the war began, he was commissioned as colonel of the Fourth New Jersey Regiment in August 1861. Dan L. Thrapp, *Encyclopedia of Frontier Biography*, vol. 3: *P-Z* (Glendale, CA: A. H. Clark Co., 1988), 1311–12.

165. Cumberland Landing is on the Pamunkey River and was used as a supply depot by the Union army during the Peninsula Campaign. Sears, *To the Gates of Richmond*, 103.

166. Brig. Gen. George Sykes (1822–1880) was born in Dover, Delaware, and graduated from West Point in 1842. He was a major in the Fourteenth U.S. Infantry Regiment when the Civil War began. Sykes was promoted to brigadier general in September 1861 and commanded the Infantry Reserve until the middle of May 1862 when the V Corps was created. He was then given command of the Second Division, V Corps. Warner, *Generals in Blue*, 492–93.

167. The Infantry Reserve, commanded by Brig. Gen. George Sykes, was composed of the Second U.S. Infantry Regiment, Third U.S. Infantry Regiment, Fourth U.S. Infantry Regiment, Sixth U.S. Infantry Regiment, Tenth U.S. Infantry Regiment, Eleventh U.S. Infantry Regiment, Twelfth U.S. Infantry Regiment, Fourteenth U.S. Infantry Regiment, and Seventeenth U.S. Infantry Regiment. Sears, *To the Gates of Richmond*, 363.

168. Howell is referring to the Fifth New York Infantry Regiment. The regiment formed in April 1861 and was commanded by Col. Abram Duryée (1815–1890). After Duryée was promoted to brigadier general in August 1861, Gouverneur K. Warren (1830–1882) became the colonel of the regiment. Terry L. Jones, *Historical Dictionary of the Civil War*, vol. 1: *A-L* (Lanham, MD: Scarecrow Press, 2002), 441–42.

169. White House was a four-thousand-acre plantation owned by William H. F. "Rooney" Lee, the son of Robert E. Lee. Like the Romancoke plantation, White House was originally owned by George Washington Parke Custis, who was Robert E. Lee's father-in-law. It was left to "Rooney" Lee after the death of Custis in 1857 and was the site where George Washington courted Martha Custis. Robert E. Lee's wife, who was a Custis, had been staying in the house until a few days before the arrival of the Yankee troops. Sears, *To the Gates of Richmond*, 104.

170. Frances "Fanny" Mary Carpenter (1844–1933) was Tom Howell's cousin. She was the daughter of Samuel Tonkin Carpenter, the brother of Mary Tonkin Carpenter Howell. Carpenter and Carpenter, *Samuel Carpenter and His Descendants*, 100.

171. Henry C. Gibson (1819–1883) was from Camden, New Jersey, and was the captain of Co. B, Third New Jersey. Stryker, *Record of Officers and Men*, 154; Philadelphia City Directory, 1861, 351.

172. Capt. William E. Bryan. See Part I, n. 158.

173. Howell is likely referring to Isaiah Bryan (1817–1864) of Camden. Camden City Directory, 1863, 26.

"Hot Work Soon Enough" 137

174. Howell is referring to the First Division, commanded by Brig. Gen. George W. Morell, of Brig. Gen. Fitz John Porter's V Corps. Col. Hiram Berdan's First U.S. Sharpshooters was attached to that division. Sears, *To the Gates of Richmond*, 372.

175. It is unclear whom Howell is referring to here. This may be a mistake in the transcription of the letter. There is no record of anyone named Harper in the regiment or brigade. It is likely that he was referring to Samuel C. Harbert, who was the regimental quartermaster, and an error was made in the transcription of the letter.

176. Howell is likely alluding to the fighting of Maj. Gen. Henry W. Halleck's army around Corinth, Mississippi, but Halleck did not score a great victory until May 30, 1862, when the Confederate Army of Tennessee, under the command of Gen. Pierre G. T. Beauregard, abandoned Corinth and withdrew to Tupelo, Mississippi. James Scythes, "Siege of Corinth, Mississippi," in *American Civil War: The Definitive Encyclopedia and Document Collection*, ed. Spencer C. Tucker (Santa Barbara, CA: ABC-CLIO, 2013), 438.

177. Howell is referring to Burnett's Inn, located in the crossroads village of Old Cold Harbor. Sears, *To the Gates of Richmond*, 221.

178. General Lee did not own a farm in this area. Howell may be referring to the plantation owned by Dr. William Gaines, which was described in a letter written by Lt. Col. Robert McAllister of the First New Jersey on May 25, 1862, as being "twelve hundred acres and ... beautiful, even better than Lee's White House farm." Robertson, *Civil War Letters of General Robert McAllister*, 165.

179. Brig. Gen. George Stoneman (1822–1894) was from New York and was a graduate of the West Point class of 1846. During the Peninsula Campaign, Stoneman commanded the Advance Guard of the Army of the Potomac. Warner, *Generals in Blue*, 481–82; Sears, *To the Gates of Richmond*, 374.

180. Brig. Gen. William F. "Baldy" Smith (1824–1903) was from Vermont and graduated from West Point in 1845. During the Peninsula Campaign, he commanded the Second Division of Franklin's VI Corps. On May 24, just two days before Howell's letter, "Baldy" Smith's division pushed the Confederates out of Mechanicsville, which was only five miles from Richmond. Warner, *Generals in Blue*, 462–64; Sears, *To the Gates of Richmond*, 110.

181. Unbeknownst to Howell, McDowell's I Corps was no longer heading to the peninsula. On May 24 President Lincoln countermanded the order to send McDowell to the peninsula because of the threat posed by Stonewall Jackson's troops in the Shenandoah Valley. *O.R.* I, 11(1): 30.

182. Sallie H. Potts was the sister of William and Robert Potts of Camden. She was fifteen years old in 1862. 1850 United States Federal Census.

183. Robert B. Potts (1817–1865) was the father of William, Robert, and Sallie Potts. He worked as a chemist. 1850 United States Federal Census.

184. Brig. Gen. Erasmus D. Keyes (1810–1895) was from Massachusetts. He graduated from West Point in 1832. During the Peninsula Campaign, Keyes commanded the IV Corps. Warner, *Generals in Blue*, 264–65.

185. Thaddeus Sobieski Constantine Lowe was born on August 20, 1832, in Jefferson Mills, New Hampshire. As a young boy, he was interested in scientific investigation and claimed that at a young age his "mind was centered on the possibility of an airship." In 1850 Lowe became an assistant to Professor Reginald Dinkelhoff, who toured around the North giving scientific lectures. By 1852 Lowe began giving scientific lectures of his own and people began referring to him as "Professor" Lowe. In 1856 he purchased a balloon capable of carrying him into the air, and by 1859 he began constructing a balloon that he could use to travel across the Atlantic Ocean. At the beginning of the Civil War, President Lincoln made Lowe the head of the Union Army Balloon Corps, which was a civilian unit, so he never received a commission. During the Peninsula Campaign, Lowe had two balloons in operation around Richmond, one near Mechanicsville and the other near Dr. Gaines's farm. Evans, *War of the Aeronauts*, 36–39, 50.

186. This is unclear. His grandmother Sarah Carpenter died in February 1852. He likely wrote Fanny Carpenter and an error was made in transcribing the letter. He mentioned in his May 26 letter that he planned to send Fanny a photograph.

187. There is no record of this in any of the Camden newspapers.

188. Samuel Tonkin Carpenter (1810–1864) was a younger brother of Mary Tonkin Carpenter Howell, Tom Howell's mother. Carpenter studied in the Episcopal Seminary at Alexandria, Virginia, and became a reverend. In 1860 he lived in Illinois, which would explain why Howell said he had not seen Carpenter in years. During the Civil War, Samuel Carpenter was a chaplain in the U.S. Army, visiting men in military hospitals. While visiting the sick, he contracted a fever in a hospital in Cincinnati and died on December 6, 1864. Carpenter and Carpenter, *Samuel Carpenter and His Descendants*, 99–100.

189. Maj. Gen. Nathaniel P. Banks was routed by the Confederate forces under the command of Stonewall Jackson on May 25, 1862, at the First Battle of Winchester. Banks was forced to cross the Potomac River into Maryland after his army was defeated. This defeat, along with Banks's defeat at Front Royal on May 23, 1862, led to President Lincoln's decision to countermand McDowell's order to join McClellan on the peninsula, since Jackson now posed a threat to Washington. For more on Jackson's defeat of Banks, see S. C. Gwynne, *Rebel Yell: The Violence, Passion, and Redemption of Stonewall Jackson* (New York: Scribner, 2014), 274–98; Sears, *To the Gates of Richmond*, 110.

190. The *Philadelphia Inquirer*.

191. Pvt. Landric Leeson, of Company C, accidentally shot himself in the left foot and had to have the second toe amputated. Landric Leeson Pension File, National Archives, Washington, D.C.

192. The fighting mentioned by Howell is the Battle of Fair Oaks, also known as the Battle of Seven Pines, which took place on May 31 and June 1, 1862. The Confederates hoped to destroy the two Union corps (III and IV) that were south of the Chickahominy River. Since the Confederate generals failed to coordinate their attacks, the rebels made no significant gains and were not able to succeed in crushing the two isolated Union corps. The two sides suffered a total of eleven thousand casualties during the two-day fight. Sears, *To the Gates of Richmond*, 111–47.

193. Troops from the II Corps crossed the Chickahominy on May 31, 1862, to support the III and IV Corps. Sears, *To the Gates of Richmond*, 135–36.

194. Fearing the town of Corinth, Mississippi, would fall to invading Union soldiers, Gen. P.G.T. Beauregard stealthily evacuated his Confederate troops to Tupelo, Mississippi. Scythes, "Siege of Corinth," 438.

195. Col. Joshua Blackwood Howell's Eighty-fifth Pennsylvania was in Brig. Gen. Henry W. Wessells's Brigade in Keyes's IV Corps. They were engaged in fighting around Seven Pines on May 31, 1862, and suffered seventy-six casualties, but Colonel Howell was not wounded during the battle. O.R. I, 11(1): 762.

196. Mechanicsville is a village located on the Chickahominy River five miles north-northeast of Richmond. Sears, *To the Gates of Richmond*, 110.

197. Col. Joseph J. Bartlett (1834–1893) was born in New York. He was a lawyer before the Civil War and enlisted in the Twenty-seventh New York when the war began. He became the colonel of the regiment in September 1861. During the Peninsula Campaign in 1862, he commanded the Second Brigade of Slocum's First Division, in the VI Corps. Warner, *Generals in Blue*, 23–24.

198. Pvt. Henry Berga died of disease near Mechanicsville on June 7, 1862. Stryker, *Record of Officers and Men*, 177.

199. John V. Mattison (1826–1896) enlisted as the surgeon of the Third New Jersey on May 6, 1862, after Lorenzo Coxe resigned. Mattison was a graduate of the University of the State of New York, receiving his medical degree in 1846. He lived in Washington, Warren County, New Jersey, before the Civil War. Stryker, *Record of Officers and Men*, 150; *University of the State of New-York, College of Physicians and Surgeons of the City of New-York, Annual Catalogue of the Regents of the University, and of the Trustees, Faculty,*

*and Students of the College, 1845–6* (New York: Daniel Adee, 1846), 7; 1860 United States Federal Census.

200. Edward L. Welling (1835–1897) was from Hopewell, Mercer County, New Jersey. He graduated from the College of New Jersey (Princeton University) in 1857. As Howell mentioned, Charles (Charley) Howell also attended the College of New Jersey; he was one year behind Welling. Welling enlisted as the assistant surgeon of the Third New Jersey on June 25, 1861. *Catalogue of the Officers and Students, 1856–57,* 8–9; Stryker, *Record of Officers and Men*, 150.

201. Henry C. Clark (1832–1904) was from Woodbury, New Jersey. He received his medical degree from the University of Pennsylvania in 1855. He mustered in as the assistant surgeon of the Second New Jersey on October 17, 1861. *Catalogue of the Trustees, Officers, and Students, of the University of Pennsylvania. Session 1854–55.* (Philadelphia: T. K. & P. G. Collins, 1855), 18; Stryker, *Record of Officers and Men*, 102.

202. In the May 28, 1862, edition of the *West Jersey Press* (Camden, NJ) it was reported that "among the names of those appointed by the President as visitors to the Military Academy at West Point, for the annual examination of 1862, we find that of Thomas P. Carpenter, Esq., of this City."

203. Anna Carpenter (1818–1883) was the wife of Edward Carpenter, the brother of Mary Howell. Edward and Anna were married on November 16, 1837. Carpenter and Carpenter, *Samuel Howell and His Descendants,* 100.

204. Frances "Fanny" Howell (1839–1901) was a daughter of Dr. Benjamin Paschall Howell and his wife, Rachel. Dr. Howell lived in Woodbury, New Jersey, and was a brother of Richard W. Howell, Tom Howell's father. Howell, *Book of John Howell and His Descendants,* 2: 594.

205. Benjamin Paschall Howell, Jr. (1847–1925) was the youngest child of Dr. Benjamin Paschall Howell and his wife, Rachel. Howell, *Book of John Howell and His Descendants,* 2: 594.

206. Mary "Molly" Howell (1846–1909) was the youngest of three daughters of Dr. Benjamin Paschall Howell and his wife Rachel. Howell, *Book of John Howell and His Descendants,* 2: 594.

207. Howell was wrong in crediting Stonewall Jackson with this destruction. This was part of the destruction caused by Confederate cavalry under the command of Brig. Gen. J.E.B. Stuart. Stuart conducted his "Ride around McClellan's army" between June 12 and June 15. At Garlick's Landing, near White House on the Pamunkey River, Stuart's men burned two schooners and destroyed seventy-five wagons. Sears, *To the Gates of Richmond,* 172.

208. It is unclear who Howell is referring to here. Mrs. Georgianna Harbert's maiden name was Smith, so Mr. Anderson would not have been her brother. There were a number of people in the city of Camden with the last name of Anderson. Without more information from Howell, it is impossible to know specifically to whom he is referring.

209. Georgianna Wishart Harbert (1821–1892) was the wife of Samuel C. Harbert.

210. Howe's battery was the Fourth U.S. Artillery, Battery G, under the command of 1st Lt. Charles H. Morgan. The battery was in the Second Brigade of the Artillery Reserve. Rudolph J. Schroeder III, *Seven Days before Richmond: McClellan's Peninsula Campaign of 1862 and Its Aftermath* (New York: iUniverse, 2009), 520.

211. As with his earlier use of the word "rats," Howell most likely means hell.

212. Brig. Gen. Joseph Hooker (1814–1879) was born in Massachusetts and graduated from West Point in 1837. He fought in the Mexican-American War and was brevetted as a lieutenant colonel. When the Civil War began he received a commission as a brigadier general, and during the Peninsula Campaign he commanded a division in the III Corps. Warner, *Generals in Blue,* 233–35.

213. The Sixth New Jersey Regiment was in Col. Joseph B. Carr's brigade in Brig. Gen. Joseph Hooker's division of the III Corps. The Sixth New Jersey was part of the Second New Jersey Brigade, which consisted of the Fifth, Sixth, Seventh, and Eighth New Jersey Regiments. Sears, *To the Gates of Richmond,* 380.

214. This is not accurate. The Second New York Regiment was added to Col. Joseph B. Carr's brigade on June 6, 1862, not the Twenty-second New York Regiment as Howell suggested. Sears, *To the Gates of Richmond*, 380.

215. As mentioned earlier, Brown became colonel of the Third New Jersey with his appointment dated from May 15, 1862. Stryker, *Record of Officers and Men*, 150.

216. Howell is likely referring to Capt. Woolsey R. Hopkins, who was a quartermaster on the staff of Brig. Gen. Henry W. Slocum. Hopkins was not an engineer as Howell suggested. *O.R.* I, 11(2): 436.

217. James W. H. Stickney (1820–1915) lived in Camden, New Jersey, at the beginning of the Civil War. He was commissioned as captain of Co. F, Third New Jersey Regiment on May 28, 1861. Camden City Directory, 1863, 122; Stryker, *Record of Officers and Men*, 167.

218. Brig. Gen. Daniel E. Sickles's brigade was also known as the "Excelsior Brigade." It was composed of the Seventieth, Seventy-first, Seventy-second, Seventy-third, and Seventy-fourth New York Regiments. During the Peninsula Campaign, the brigade was in Brig. Gen. Joseph Hooker's Division of the III Corps. Sears, *To the Gates of Richmond*, 380.

219. Anna Maria Jones (1795–1865) was a sister of Richard W. Howell, Tom Howell's father. She married Joseph H. Jones, D.D., in 1825. Joseph and Anna Jones lived at 524 Spruce Street in Philadelphia. Howell, *Book of John Howell and His Descendants*, 2: 586.

220. Arthur H. Merry (1840–1862) was born in England and moved to the United States with his family in 1849. The Merry family settled in a house located at 426 Market Street in Camden, New Jersey. When the Civil War began, Merry enlisted as a corporal in Co. B, Third New Jersey Regiment on May 25, 1861. 1860 United States Federal Census; Philadelphia City Directory, 1861, 1246; Stryker, *Record of Officers and Men*, 157.

221. Maj. William Birney (1819–1907) was the elder brother of Brig. Gen. David Bell Birney. When the Civil War began, Birney received a commission as captain of Co. C, First New Jersey Regiment. He was promoted to major of the Fourth New Jersey Regiment on September 27, 1861, and by the end of the war had risen to the rank of brevet major general. Warner, *Generals in Blue*, 35.

222. Attempts at identifying these two men have proven to be unsuccessful.

223. The Battle of Oak Grove on June 25, 1862, marked the beginning of the Seven Days' Battles. The two divisions of the III Corps, supported by one brigade from the II and IV Corps, attacked the Confederates at Oak Grove. This was part of McClellan's plan to push forward his line south of the Chickahominy so that he could move his heavy artillery closer to Richmond. The battle was indecisive, as the Union troops advanced only six hundred yards. Sears, *To the Gates of Richmond*, 183–89.

224. The Battle of Mechanicsville on June 26, 1862, was the second of the Seven Days' Battles. General Lee sent a force of 55,800 Confederates to attack Brig. Gen. Fitz John Porter's V Corps. Porter's corps was the only Union corps north of the Chickahominy River and Lee hoped to destroy it. Porter's men had built a strong defensive position behind Beaver Dam Creek, and the Confederates suffered heavily in their attacks on this position. Confederate losses numbered 1,475 men to only 361 casualties for the Union. Sears, *To the Gates of Richmond*, 208.

225. Brig. Gen. Edwin V. Sumner (1797–1863) was born in Boston and entered the military in 1819. He fought with distinction in the Mexican-American War. When the Civil War began, Sumner became a brigadier general. During the Peninsula Campaign, he commanded the II Corps of the Army of the Potomac. Warner, *Generals in Blue*, 489–90.

# Conclusion

On the morning of June 27, the third of the Seven Days' Battles, General McClellan, believing he was facing an enemy of superior numbers, decided to change his base from White House Landing to the James River, which signaled the end of his attempt to capture the Confederate capital.[1] He ordered General Porter's V Corps to fall back from Mechanicsville and take up a defensive position to protect the bridges crossing the Chickahominy River. Porter placed his corps in a line behind Boatswain's Swamp. The left of his line sat on the eastern bank of Boatswain's Swamp on a plateau fifty feet above the stream; the right covered the road from Old Cold Harbor to the Grapevine Bridge. The men did their best to strengthen their position with field fortifications, abatis, and other obstacles.[2] Porter would have to hold this position without significant reinforcements from McClellan. The army commander ordered only one division, Henry Slocum's, from the VI Corps to support Porter if needed, but that division was still on the south side of the river that morning.[3] With the addition of Slocum's division, Porter could count only thirty-six thousand men to defend his position against General Lee's force of fifty-seven thousand men.

The New Jersey Brigade was sent around 8:45 a.m. to support Porter's corps, but they never crossed the Chickahominy River. The troops rested south of the river until noon and marched back to their camp, since there was no sign of any action north of the Chickahominy River.[4] Around 2:00 p.m. the Confederates commenced their assault on Porter's front, starting the Battle of Gaines's Mill (fig. 3.1). After a series of attacks, however, the Southerners were unable to break the Union line, but the Yankees were hard-pressed and Porter sent for Slocum's division to reinforce his line around 2:30 p.m.[5]

Thomas Howell remained on the south side of the river along with the rest of Taylor's brigade and Slocum's division during the early hours of the Battle of Gaines's Mill. After the order to reinforce Porter was received, Slocum later reported that the "movement was executed at once" and that his division marched to the Chickahominy River and began crossing around 3:00 p.m.[6] Brig. Gen. John Newton's brigade had already crossed the Chickahominy earlier in the afternoon. Taylor's brigade crossed the river at the Woodbury-Alexander Bridge (usually labeled as Alexander's Bridge on most maps of the battlefield) and was followed by the last brigade in the division under the command of Col. Joseph J.

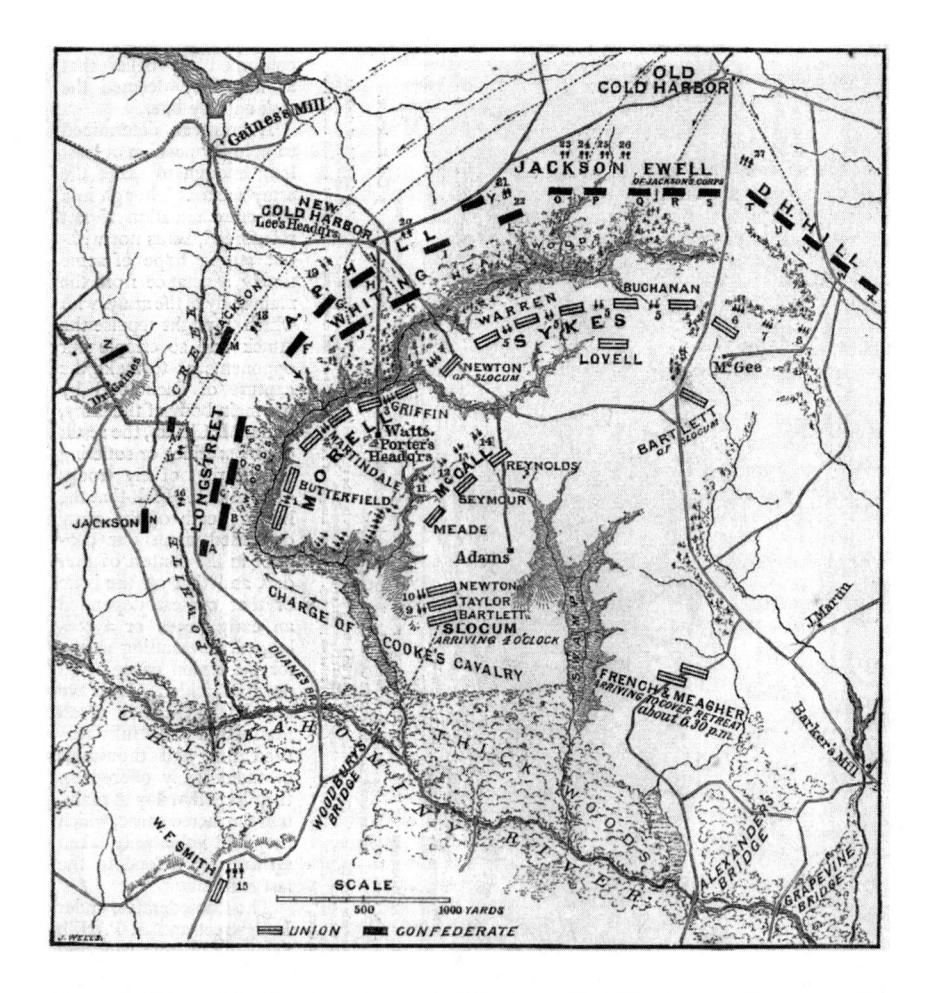

**Figure 3.1** Map of the Battle of Gaines's Mill, June 27, 1862. *Source*: Courtesy of the Library of Congress.

Bartlett. Lieutenant Howell was finally going to participate in his first battle.

After crossing the Chickahominy, the men of the New Jersey Brigade, according to a correspondent, seemed determined and eager to meet the enemy.[7] The brigade formed in line of battle, with the Third and Fourth New Jersey in the front and the First and Second New Jersey behind, and moved at the double-quick toward the front. The day was very warm and dust completely enveloped the troops. As they moved closer to Porter's line, the soldiers could hear the roar of battle and began to see the wounded.[8]

Taylor's brigade reached Porter's position around 5:00 p.m. (fig. 3.2).[9] The men were positioned in a field of clover a few hundred yards from the front, but they were close enough to the action that "spent balls were flying around us."[10] The troops were lying down as ordered until General Porter rode up and in a loud, clear voice spoke a few words of encouragement to the men: "Now, boys! strike boldly, for your State, your Country, and your God; Jersey is a little State, but she is a big one. Go in with three hearty cheers!"[11] After the three cheers were given, General Taylor ordered the "Third Regiment, under the command of Lieutenant-Colonel Brown . . . to advance forward into the woods, where a fierce combat was raging. Colonel Brown immediately formed his regiment in line of battle, led it into the woods, and began a rapid fire upon the enemy."[12]

General Taylor's command, along with the rest of Slocum's troops, was used to support weak points in Porter's line. The Comte de Paris, who was on McClellan's staff, took the Fourth New Jersey into the woods to support Brig. Gen. George A. McCall's beleaguered troops.[13] Taylor ordered one of the members of his staff, Edward Burd Grubb, to go with the Comte de Paris to see where he put the regiment and then report back to Taylor.[14] The First New Jersey entered the woods about a half an hour after the Third New Jersey while the Second New Jersey, which numbered only four companies on the field, remained behind the woods with the Fourteenth New York and the Fourth Michigan of Brig. Gen. Charles Griffin's brigade from Porter's corps.[15]

With the New Jersey brigade divided, General Taylor entered the woods with his old regiment, the Third New Jersey. One soldier recalled, "Entering the woods we had mud and brush to pass through, which broke the ranks a little, and the colors got in the advance, but as soon as we got through a line was formed."[16] The regiment went into position along Boatswain's Swamp between the Ninety-fifth Pennsylvania ("Gosline's Zouaves") and the Eighteenth New York of Brig. Gen. John Newton's brigade.[17] Just as these men were placed in line, the Confederates attacked. The Third New Jersey was "exposed to the murderous fire of a vastly superior force, as the bullets flying thick and fast; bombs bursting and solid shot cutting large trees off all around us; bushes and branches falling in all directions; but not for one moment did our troops waver," explained one New Jersey soldier as he attempted to describe the situation in the woods.[18] General Taylor stood with his sword in his hand, encouraging his men, and yelled to them, "Boys, let us give them a little touch of the bayonet. Charge!"[19] The Southern troops were pushed out of the woods, and the Jerseymen pursued them a short distance before being driven back by heavy fire from Confederate reserves positioned in an open field beyond.[20]

The Third New Jersey returned to its original position in the woods and was struck again by the enemy. "During the fight, while cheering on my men to the deadly work, I accidentally caught sight of a gray suit in a pine tree some twenty yards in advance of our lines," a sergeant in the

144                                   Conclusion

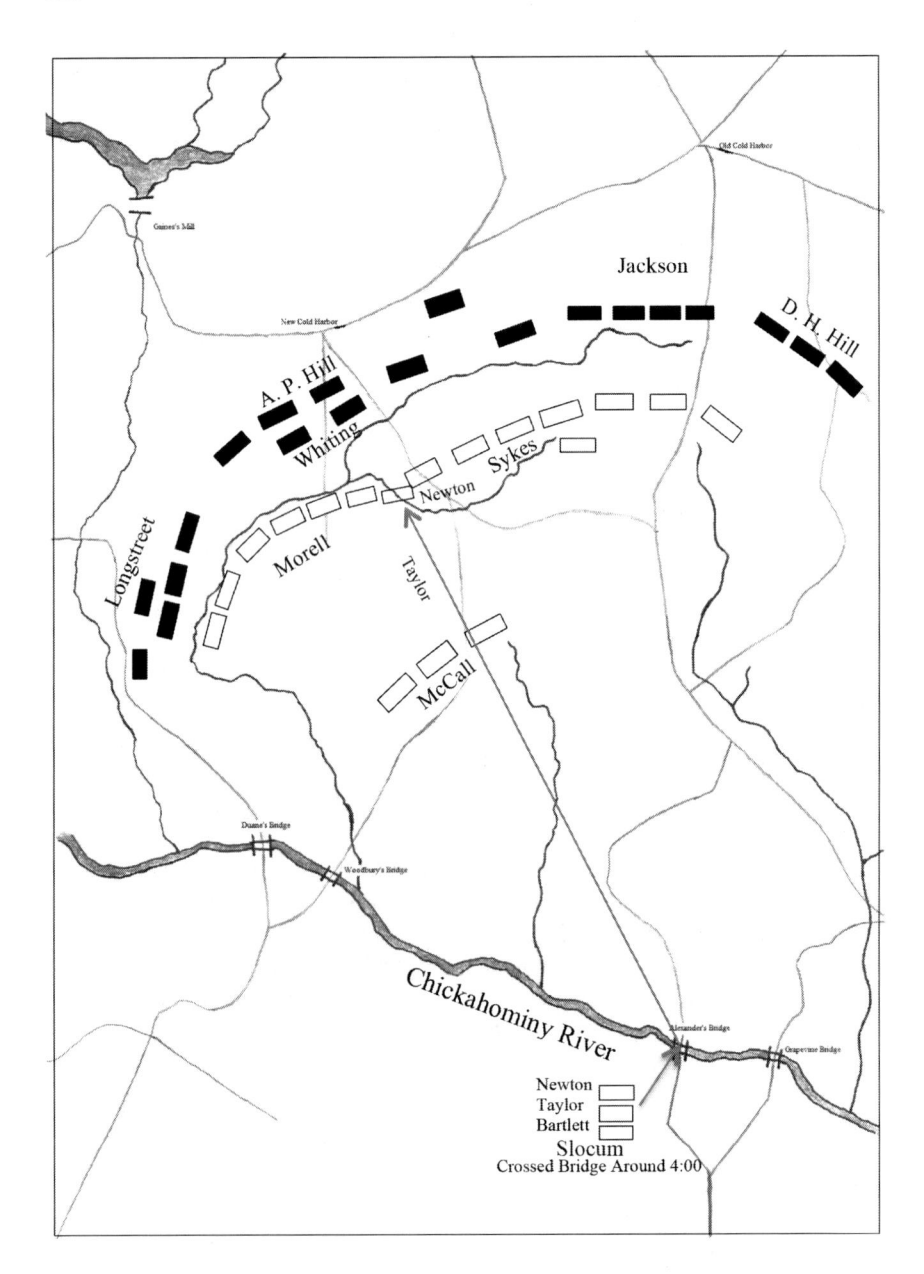

*Figure 3.2* **Map of the placement of Taylor's command along Boatswain's Swamp during Battle of Gaines's Mill.** *Source*: **Courtesy of the author.**

Third New Jersey later reported. "He was fast ramming home the bullet that would soon perhaps have slain some noble volunteer, when I snatched a rifle from one of my men, and taking deliberate aim, I sealed his doom for all time, for with the crack of my rifle he was a corpse."[21] Soldiers commented after the battle that as the fighting continued it became difficult to distinguish the Confederate dead and wounded from those of Union regiments, because upon being hit many of the men became covered in mud after rolling into the swamp.[22]

For over two hours the Northern troops held out against successive Confederate attacks. By this point every Yankee soldier was covered with powder and mud, and large beads of perspiration dripped from their faces as they repulsed each advance. "The firing now became general, and as it was 'bushwhacking,' we took the best positions we could get, behind trees, &c.," recalled one soldier. "In it all no one shrank from duty. Every man seemed anxious to do his share, and officers were at their posts, cheering on their men."[23] According to Arch Taylor, Tom Howell was one of those officers. Lieutenant Taylor said of Howell, "Oh, I shall never forget, nor the brave men who fought under us on that memorable day, how he cheered them onward to deeds of bravery and valor."[24] One can only imagine the young Howell moving up and down the line, encouraging his men and taking aim at the approaching Confederates with his new revolver. Based on his earlier letters to prove himself an able leader, he surely would have wanted to take full advantage of the opportunity.

By 7:00 or 7:30 p.m. the Third New Jersey, with the First New Jersey to its right, remained in position along Boatswain's Swamp with the other Union troops from Porter and Slocum's commands. The Confederates again attacked. However, the rebel troops were not only attacking from directly in front of the Third New Jersey's position; some rebels had made their way into the woods and set up about forty-five yards away in a sunken road that ran parallel to the right of the New Jersey men's position. The Confederates began to pour a deadly crossfire into the Union line, but according to General Taylor, the men "maintained their ground."[25]

Taylor realized that his line was in danger of being flanked by the rebels and sent his aides to look for reinforcements, but none could be found. Adjutant Dunham was sent to General Porter with a message from Taylor, which most likely reported that Taylor needed support if he was to be expected to hold his position. Just as Dunham delivered his message to Porter, the two men watched as a rebel shell shrieked over their heads and exploded twenty yards away, killing a group of five men.[26] Porter likely informed Dunham that he did not have any troops to send to Taylor's aid.

Lieutenant Grubb rejoined the Third New Jersey in the woods around the same time the Confederates attacked. He found General Taylor near the left of the regiment, "parading up and down the line like a wounded lion."[27] The smoke of battle was so thick in the woods that "it was impossible to see twenty yards."[28] The men were lying on the ground, loading and firing, but Taylor realized that the firepower of the troops was not very effective, because they could not see the enemy. The general gave the order to cease fire so that the smoke could clear. Taylor also realized that many of the men were running low on ammunition, having expended most or all of the sixty shots each man was given at the beginning of the battle, and he wanted to make every shot count. He commanded Grubb to go down the line and tell the officers of the regiment to order their men to cease fire. As Grubb did so he noticed "a great many of the poor fellows dead and hurt," evidence of the carnage produced by over two hours of fighting.[29] While moving about the line, Grubb found his cousin Capt. Daniel Penrose Buckley wounded on the ground, "pressing a bloody handkerchief to his left hip. . . . I said to him: 'How is it with you, Penn?' and he said: 'Not bad, Ned, only a buckshot in my hip.'"[30] Grubb left his cousin and continued passing the order down the line until the firing ceased.

As some of the smoke cleared and the Confederate fire subsided, "Our men, doubtless glad to be relieved from their cramped positions, arose from the ground, some on their knees, and some standing erect peering through the smoke."[31] While the Northern troops paused, an order was heard from the Confederate lines: "Fire!" The volley from the Southern troops sent the Union men into disarray. The men were not prepared for this hail of bullets and the line broke. Union troops to the left of the Third New Jersey withdrew, exposing the regiment's left flank. "The enemy had us on both flanks, and in five minutes would have surrounded us," reported one soldier. "The wonder is, not that so many fell, but that so many escaped. The balls would fly past us, fall by our side, tear trees near us, and cut limbs that would fall against us."[32] Around this same time, the Confederates achieved other breakthroughs in Porter's line. Farther to the left, Brig. Gen. John Bell Hood's Confederates pierced the Union line along Boatswain's Swamp while other units from Stonewall Jackson's command drove back the Yankees to the right of the Third New Jersey.

As Taylor's men fled from the woods, an attempt was made to rally the troops, but it was unsuccessful.[33] A soldier from the regiment recalled, "We halted after getting the colors out and tried to rally the men, but there were few who came round them, for but few were left."[34] When Captain Buckley's command, Company C, emerged from the woods, a sergeant noticed that only seven of the sixty-eight men that went into the battle were still alongside him, but Buckley himself was not among the survivors. He had been left in the woods as the regiment retreated, and after the battle it was believed the captain had been taken prisoner by the Confederates. Grubb wrote to a relative: "I saw him myself *perfectly, unhurt* not *five minutes* before the enemy drove us out of the woods. . . . *There is no reason to believe Pen killed*[.] I hope and *believe* that he is in good hands in Richmond."[35] Why Grubb did not tell his family that Buckley was wounded when he saw him in the woods is unknown. Maybe the captain's nonchalant description of his wound left Grubb to believe it was not too severe.

A few weeks after the battle Grubb learned that Buckley had been mortally wounded shortly after the two men spoke in the woods. Sgt. John Stewart of Company C, who was also wounded in the woods and lying near Buckley, saw the captain get into a hand-to-hand fight with two Confederate soldiers. Buckley killed one of the rebels, but the other one shot him in the chest.[36] The captain would lie on the battlefield suffering from his wounds until he finally succumbed on July 4, 1862.[37] "He died gloriously . . . fighting in the rear of a retreat," Grubb wrote about his fallen cousin. "What grieves us most is that he, and all those brave *gentlemen*, who fell at Gaines Hill . . . were *sacrificed* by the *tremendous incompetency* of our *political generals*. . . . The brigade has lost one of the most genial and polished of its *few* gentlemen and I have lost my cousin and my best friend."[38]

Pvt. Louis Loeb, Tom Howell's servant, was also wounded during the fighting along Boatswain's Swamp. He was hit in the left leg by a shell fragment that broke his bone. An attempt was made by another soldier to help him to the rear, but the soldier was shot dead. As they retreated, men from the regiment saw Loeb lying facedown on the ground, groaning from the pain caused by his wound.[39] Loeb's family did not know his fate and believed he was dead, but near the end of July they learned he was alive and was a prisoner in Richmond. Private Loeb recounted in his diary the ordeal he endured after being wounded in the battle and left in the care of the Confederates:

> I laid on the Battle Field 2 Days and nights. taken on a Litter to the Ambulance. while putting me in the Ambulance my foot struck the other Litter and doubled it up and pained me very much. was taken to the Hospital and Laid there 2 more days without any thing to eat and very little water to drink and the maggetts eating me up alive. on Tuesday afternoon Dr. Palmer came to see me and ask me if i was Soldier enough to have my leg cut off. i told him i was so he ordered four Rebs to take and lay me on the Table. they done so, so the Doctors came and commenced to Cut & Slash, without giving me any Chloroform, for they had none. i stood it like a Soldier and in a half hour all was over, which was the painfullest Operation ever i went through, so they took me and laid me and laid me [sic] under a Tree and the next morning it commenced raining and they left me laying out in the rain till afternoon, then they come and put me down the Cellar.[40]

The Confederate doctor amputated Loeb's left leg just above the knee. He would be returned to the North in a prisoner exchange later that summer.

After withdrawing from the woods around Boatswain's Swamp, the New Jersey troops and others from Porter's command headed for the Chickahominy and the bridges that crossed it. As they approached the river, a new line started to form and General Taylor was able to rally his men, who were joined on the right by Brig. Gen. Thomas F. Meagher's Irish Brigade from the II Corps.[41]

Tom Howell played an instrumental role in the rallying of the troops near the Chickahominy River. According to a correspondent for the *New York Tribune*, Tom Howell, whom the correspondent incorrectly identified as "Lieut. J. Howell," "had gone down upon the plain, found a portion of Company H, of his regiment, and with them, as a nucleus, was rallying to his colors a provisional regiment from the mass of stragglers."[42] It is apparent that the troops responded to his actions. As the young lieutenant pointed to the flag of the Third New Jersey and addressed the men in "stirring words," he was able to gather several hundred soldiers in this makeshift line.[43]

As the sun began to set, Union soldiers trickled into the line near the Chickahominy River as they retreated from the front. This line was composed of a hodgepodge of troops as men from many other regiments headed toward the Chickahominy as well. The Confederates did not pursue the Yankee troops, and after dark the order was given to withdraw all of the Union troops across the bridges.

Lieutenant Grubb noted that there was only one bridge behind the entire left of the new line to accommodate the troops, the Woodbury-Alexander Bridge (fig. 3.3). The order to withdraw the New Jersey brigade was given to General Taylor around 8:45 p.m.[44] As the Jerseymen prepared to cross the bridge, the Confederates continued to fire their artillery in an attempt to destroy it. Tom Howell and the rest of the men of the Third New Jersey attempted to organize their ranks to cross the Chickahominy.

At 9:00 p.m. the Third New Jersey started crossing the bridge. Tom Howell had survived the heavy fighting in the woods along Boatswain's Swamp and helped rally the troops after the retreat from the woods. General Taylor noted in his official report of the battle that Lieutenant Howell behaved "very well" and performed with "distinguished merit."[45] Howell's friends, Bob Dunham and Arch Taylor, also survived the battle. According to General Taylor, Arch Taylor acted cool under fire and behaved "very well." The general also recommended Arch for promotion.[46]

While standing near the Woodbury-Alexander Bridge waiting to cross, Howell saw General Taylor and Lieutenant Grubb. According to Grubb:

> Just before we came to the bridge-head, Lieutenant Howell of Company I, of the Third Regiment, who was one of my dearest personal friends, came out of the ranks and shook hands with me, saying how glad he was that we were both alive. He walked a few paces and turned to say something else to me or to some of his company, and a

*Figure 3.3* **Photograph of the Woodbury-Alexander Bridge.** *Source:* **Courtesy of the Library of Congress.**

    round shot that was fired by the enemy's gun struck him full in the breast and literally tore him to pieces.[47]

After only six months in the army, Tom Howell was killed in his first battle. He was the youngest officer in the New Jersey Brigade and the last New Jersey casualty of the battle.[48]

    With the continuation of the Confederate artillery fire and the need to withdraw all of the Union troops from their positions north of the Chickahominy by daybreak, Tom Howell's men had no choice but to leave his body on the battlefield. Dr. Edward Welling (fig. 3.4), the assistant surgeon of the Third New Jersey, attempted to carry the young lieutenant's body across the Woodbury-Alexander Bridge before the bridge was blown up, but was unable to do so. As he told Howell's sister Annie years later, "I was a small man and . . . Howell was so tall. I stood at the bridge and begged for help to get him onto a gun carriage, to carry a litter between horses, but everyone was running and everyone shouted 'We are blowing up the bridge. You will be captured.' I *had* to leave him."[49] Before leaving Howell's body, Welling removed the dead lieutenant's bloodstained belt, sash, prayer book, and epaulettes, which were later sent to the family (fig. 3.5).[50] Taylor's men finished crossing the Woodbury-Alexander Bridge around 10:00 p.m. and the brigade returned to its camp at the Courtney House.

Shortly after the Battle of Gaines's Mill, reports and casualty lists made their way to the Northern cities. Initially the fate of young Tom Howell was unknown. One neighbor of the Howells in Camden wrote her sister in England, "We have been having such dreadful news from the seat of war the past week. . . . Mary Howell's son is believed to be killed. . . . It is truly awful the waste of human life by those remorseless rebels."[51] Howell's family was unsure if he had been killed in battle or had been taken prisoner. His uncle Thomas Preston Carpenter recounted, "Mary almost sank after the first report of poor Tom's death, or that he was wounded and probably a prisoner before the truth became certainty, so uncertain, conflicting & unreliable were the first reports."[52] Louis Henry Carpenter, who was on the peninsula with the Sixth U.S. Cavalry, wrote on July 10, "Poor Tom Howell! I saw his name in the list of killed in the 3rd N.J. Regiment. I sympathize with Aunt Mary if the news are true."[53]

The news was true and the family soon received confirmation. In the July 9, 1862, edition of the *West Jersey Press*, Howell was listed among those killed in the Battle of Gaines's Mill. A small article titled "The Brave Lieut. Howell" described the events surrounding his death:

> Among the sad casualties in the late terrible battle on the Peninsula, which have made our community mourn, is that which resulted in the death of Lieut. THOMAS J. HOWELL, of this city. He was attached to Co. I, of the 3d N.J. Regiment, and which, we believe, he commanded during the great struggle of Friday the 27th, in consequence of the sickness and absence of his superior officers. He had, as we are informed, gone unscathed through the action, and after the active fight had ceased, was preparing to retire, according to others. Whilst the roll of his company was being called, and he was addressing his men, a cannon ball struck him, killing him instantly. It is said to have been the last shot fired by the rebels at his regiment. Strange that after the great dangers of battle had been passed, he should have fallen by a mere chance shot at the close.
>
> He was quite young when he met so gloriously his untimely fate; but by his gallant and noble conduct had won the approbation of his superior officers. His death is a great loss to the service, and inflicts great grief on his family and friends. He was a son of the late Richard W. Howell, of this city.[54]

*Figure 3.4* Photograph of Dr. Edward Welling, assistant surgeon of the Third New Jersey. *Source*: Courtesy of New Jersey State Archives; Department of State.

*Figure 3.5* **Photograph of Tom Howell's prayer book and epaulettes.** *Source*: **Courtesy of Gloucester County Historical Society.**

"I saw some of the men in poor Tom Howell's company who saw him die," Louis Henry Carpenter wrote in a letter home to the family. "There is no doubt about his death. He was killed by a cannon ball toward the close of the action."[55] To another relative Carpenter wrote:

> Poor Tom Howell! To be cut off in the bloom of youth seems a cruel fate to most men, although there can be but little doubt that in this case the precepts and teachings of pious parents were not entirely thrown away. Ned [Carpenter's brother Edward] and I feel very sorry for Aunt Mary, but I hope by this time she is resigned to her loss, and is more composed. There is one thing to consider. He was not mangled in limb or body, so that death would be at last a relief from suffering, but life was extinct instantly.[56]

The correspondent to the *Newark Daily Advertiser* described the events of Howell's death in the following manner:

> Lieut. Thomas Howell, of Company I, 3d Regt, went all through the fight uninjured, and acted with great bravery. But after his regiment came out of the woods, and was forming to cross the bridge on its return to camp, he was struck in the stomach by a chance and nearly spent cannon ball, which went clear through him, killing him instantly. The Lieutenant was but seventeen years old and a talented and worthy young man.[57]

Another member of the Third New Jersey recounted the events associated with Tom Howell's death in the July 16, 1862, edition of the *West Jersey Press*, but added "sad news for his widowed mother, and the other members of his family. But let the fact that 'He died, where the brave die, / On battle's red breast' Fighting for his God and his country, mitigate the anguish that must wring their hearts."[58]

Tom Howell's obituary appeared in the July 15, 1862, edition of *The Constitution*:

> Killed on the battle-field, at Gaines Mill, Va., on Friday, June 27th, 1862, while encouraging and rallying his men, Lieutenant THOMAS J. HOWELL, of Company I, 3d N. J. Volunteers, son of the late Richard W. Howell, Esq., of this city.
>
> Among the many young men of our city who, at the call of the President, rather more than a year since, prepared to buckle on their armor for the fight, none were more earnest and enthusiastic than poor HOWELL. Young, brave, chivalric, noble and self-sacrificing, his whole soul became enlisted in the cause of his country, and though he did not depart with the rest of his young friends for the seat of war, his heart was with them, and we were not surprised, therefore, at his acceptance, a few months since, of an appointment to a vacant Lieutenancy in the Third New Jersey. We cannot forget the boyish enthusiasm with which he left us for the army—his buoyant, brave spirit yearning for distinction, eager for the field of fame and glory—to him alas the field of death. Cut off in his first engagement, in the very spring-time of life, death falls on him like an untimely frost. From the field of strife and carnage his brave and gentle spirit is summoned to an eternal rest and peace with HIM who gave it, and far away from home, from kindred and from friends, upon a hostile soil his body fills a soldier's grave on the banks of the Chickahominy. While we have tears for his sad fate, let us not forget to add his name to the list of heroic Jerseymen who have laid down their lives for the preservation of our beloved Union.[59]

It is interesting that the obituary referred to Howell as a "chivalric, noble and self-sacrificing" young man. This is exactly what Howell described in the essay on chivalry he had written at Mr. Fewsmith's school in 1860: a man surrendering his life for a noble cause.

The Battle of Gaines's Mill was the largest and bloodiest of the Seven Days' Battles. On the Union side, out of the 36,000 men under General Porter's command there were 6,837 casualties. Slocum's division suffered 1,971 casualties, the most of any Union division on that day. The Third New Jersey sustained a loss of 215 men, including Tom Howell, Daniel Penrose Buckley, and Louis Loeb.[60] On the Confederate side, General Lee's forces suffered 8,700 casualties out of the 57,000 men engaged. Lee scored his first battlefield victory over the Union Army on that bloody Friday, and over the next few days his army continued attacking in an attempt to push McClellan's army away from the Confederate capital. By early July 1862 the Union Army reached its new base along the James River at Harrison's Landing, where it remained until late August when it was withdrawn to Washington to reinforce Maj. Gen. John Pope's Army of Virginia.

As the American Civil War dragged on for another two years and eight months, with thousands more young men being sacrificed in the cause for liberty, Tom Howell's family struggled to come to grips with his death. His mother, Mary Howell, was distraught after losing her fifth child. She also suffered financial troubles after her son's death, since she had relied on Tom sending home part of his pay from the military. Mrs. Howell filed an application to receive her son's pension on the grounds that she had limited means and that Tom had helped support the family. On February 14, 1863, her application was approved and she received fifteen dollars per month, beginning from the date of Tom's death, for the remainder of her life.[61]

As the reality of Tom's death sank in, his family began to wonder what fate had befallen the young lieutenant's remains. Thomas Preston Carpenter wrote: "He was a fine, generous noble hearted young fellow & I feel proud as well as grieved at his untimely fate. He was left on the opposite side of the Chickahominy near Woodbury Bridge when his regiment crossed. . . . I am uncertain whether he was buried by his friends or was left in the expectation that that office would be performed for him by the enemy."[62] In an article in the July 16, 1862, edition of the *West Jersey Press*, it was announced that a "deputation of gentlemen . . . have gone to Virginia to endeavor to recover the body of the late lamented Lieut. Howell. We sincerely hope they will be successful in their mission."[63] There is no evidence indicating whether the men ever made it to Virginia to search for Howell's remains, but since his body was never recovered, it is clear that this mission ended in failure.

On August 4, 1862, the Howell family received a letter from Arch Taylor. Taylor told Howell's mother that he had not been present when Tom died and was shocked to hear what had happened to him. "One can readily imagine what must have been his feelings when told Tom was killed only twenty minutes after parting company. . . . Then alive and uninjured, now mangled and lifeless," Tom's brother Joshua wrote his sister Annie, referring to Lieutenant Taylor's correspondence.[64] Taylor would not survive the war either. At the Battle of Salem Heights on May 3, 1863, Arch Taylor, then the captain of Company I, was seen at the head of his company urging his men to stand firm and keep in line when he was struck by enemy fire and killed. He was just one month shy of his twenty-first birthday.[65]

After the Battle of Gaines's Mill, Louis Loeb and other wounded Union troops were taken to Savage's Station, and the bumpy wagon ride caused him much discomfort. He stayed at this location until July 27, when he was transported to City Point and exchanged under a flag of truce. Private Loeb was taken on board the *Elm City* and sailed down the James River to Harrison's Landing, where General McClellan talked with some of the men on the ship, including Loeb. "Gen'l McClellan came on Board to see the sick and wounded. he went to every man and Shook Hands and talked, he also came to me and talked and Shook Hands with me. i ask him a great many questions. he was very Socialbly and Stayed with me about 20 minutes."[66] Loeb was then taken to Chester, Pennsylvania, and admitted to U.S.A. General Hospital on August 13, 1862, where he remained until he was discharged on September 29, 1862.

Loeb's ordeal would not end there. After being taken prisoner by the Confederates and having his wounded leg amputated, then being part of a prisoner exchange with the North, he received an artificial leg on January 1, 1863. However, he could not wear it, because his stump was always sore and never fully healed. Blue spots, similar to boils, appeared on the stump, and pieces of bone would come out of these spots. Loeb continued to work, trying to support his mother, but this proved increasingly difficult as time went on. Soon his right calf started aching and sores frequently appeared on his right leg. Doctors said the condition was a result of blood poisoning. It was not until around 1873 that the sores finally dried up. Loeb's mother later reported that her son had no appetite and was weak, but he also suffered from pain in his kidneys and had trouble urinating. She stated that he "made water often and little at a time—The water didn't look right. It was too dark and there was much sediment in it."[67] Louis Loeb died from blood poisoning on March 21, 1874.

The death of Tom Howell especially devastated his younger sister Annie (fig. 3.6). She had been "immensely proud" of her brother when he left New Jersey to join his regiment in Virginia in early 1862, and after the report came that he was among those killed outside Richmond, she continually thought of him and described him as "the idle [sic] of my young life."[68] Her brother Joshua tried to console her in a letter a month after Tom's fate was realized. He took Annie back to the last day Tom had spent in Camden, saying that he remembered Tom

> as if yesterday, standing in the front office six months ago immediately after getting appointed. Tom, Frank and myself were in the front office admiring the new uniform, the sword, the outfit generally, while Uncle was hurrying through some business to come out and talk to him. There he stood with his ruddy cheeks, beaming with fun and good humor, his fatigue cap set in the most stylish manner on his glossy brown hair, overcoat on and open just enough to catch a glimpse of scarlet sash amongst the glittering buttons and setting off a handsome figure which did not need the foreign aid of ornaments to set it off. It completed the picture which gave us all the pleasantest feeling to look at and admire. . . . Poor fellow! His absence causes a very great gap. Whenever the house wanted brightening up, whenever anyone was in

low spirits, he if no one else with his cheery roistering laugh warmed everything into sunshine and mirth.[69]

Annie continued to grieve, however, and in a letter in March 1863, she told her uncle Col. Joshua Blackwood Howell that she could not accept that her brother's body was "lying far away on the banks of a Southern river."[70] She could only hope that "some kind hand even among the enemy may have pitied the young face, the beautiful face, and laid him in a grave."[71] In his reply to his niece the following summer, Colonel Howell summed up his feelings about what had happened to Tom:

> In the glorious death of the gallant boy dear boy Tom, your family have offered up to the cause of country a sacrifice, without blemish, and, God knows, great indeed & great enough, without asking that any others of my beloved brother's children should be offered up. I will fight this fight out. I don't want any more of my family in it. God

*Figure 3.6* **Photograph of Annie Howell from 1862.** *Source:* **Courtesy of Gloucester County Historical Society.**

giving me strength & my country giving me rank, I will see it through.[72]

The colonel was unable to make it to the end of the war, however. Just two months after he wrote to Annie, Joshua Blackwood Howell died. In September 1864 he was commanding William Birney's division in front of Petersburg, Virginia. Shortly after midnight on September 12, Colonel Howell was leaving X Corps Headquarters to return to his own quarters when his horse reared back and fell on him. He was taken to the Eighty-fifth Pennsylvania's hospital but never regained consciousness, having suffered from "violent contusions of his stomach and head."[73] Joshua Blackwood Howell died on September 14, 1864.

After the Civil War, Annie Howell married Malcolm Lloyd of Philadelphia on May 10, 1869, at her mother's home in Camden and started a family, but her heart continued to ache for years over the loss of her brother and the absence of a grave for him. Her daughter wrote, "Pictures and letters of his, mementoes of those days, were kept by my Mother till the day of her death. In all the activities and responsibilities of her later life she never forgot this beloved brother."[74]

Determined to recover her brother's body, Annie went to see Dr. Welling, the assistant surgeon of the Third New Jersey, who was visiting in Camden on March 21, 1886. He did not tell her anything she did not know except "the sadder fact that the lovely gentle handsome fellow only seventeen years old, had been left lying on the ground alone."[75] Over the next few weeks, Annie and her husband went over letters and maps of the Gaines's Mill battlefield searching for clues that might lead them to Tom Howell's body. She wrote the remaining officers of the Third New Jersey, hoping someone could give her more information, but she did not receive the answers she had wished for.

Annie and Malcolm planned a trip to Virginia in 1886 to search for Howell's body, but because of delays, caused mostly by illnesses of their children, the journey was not taken until four years later. In March 1890 they landed at Fort Monroe and made their way to Richmond, where they stayed in Ford's Hotel. Annie's heart bothered her when she reached the city, effects from the childhood illness that had hit the Howell house in the early 1850s, so Malcolm made the trip alone to the National Cemetery at Cold Harbor and searched the lists of dead for Howell's name. He then

> engaged a man to guide him over the Gain's Mills battle fields. Left at 8 A.M. . . . After a toilsome day they lost their way in the Chickahominy swamp and did not get home until 8 A.M. after making their way to a colored man's house where they got some supper and hired a team to get back to Richmond. . . . They tried to trace the ending of the corduroi road leading from the Woodbury Bridge and partly succeeded in the matter.[76]

It seems that Malcolm and his guide may have come across the corduroy road built by Tom Howell and other Union troops shortly before the Battle of Gaines's Mill. Thus, they were close but were unable to find the remains of the young lieutenant. Annie would make no further attempts at recovering her brother's body, and her weak heart finally gave out in 1913.

The story of Tom Howell is a tragic one. His death represents just one of the 750,000 lives lost during the American Civil War and the effect a death can have on the family the soldier left behind. The inability of Howell's family to recover his remains plagued them for the rest of their lives, particularly his sister Annie. His story brings to mind the Civil War song titled "The Faded Coat of Blue":

> My brave lad he sleeps in his faded coat of blue;
> In a lonely grave unknown lies the heart that beat so true;
> He sank faint and hungry among the famished brave,
> And they laid him sad and lonely within his nameless grave.
> *Chorus*
> No more the bugle calls the weary one,
> Rest noble spirit, in thy grave unknown!
> I'll find you and know you, among the good and true,
> When a robe of white is giv'n for the faded coat of blue.
>
> He cried, "Give me water and just a little crumb,
> And my mother she will bless you through all the years to come;
> Oh! tell my sweet sister, so gentle, good and true,
> That I'll meet her up in heaven, in my faded coat of blue.[77]

Today the life of Thomas James Howell is all but forgotten to history. As a silent reminder of his sacrifice, his name appears on the Civil War monument in Camden, New Jersey, dedicated in 1873, which lists the names of all of those men from Camden County who paid the ultimate price in the defense of the Union. His name also appears on the Howell family plot in Evergreen Cemetery in Camden. This was likely done so that the family could have a place to mourn his loss, since his body was never recovered from the battlefield. The epitaph on the family tombstone under Tom Howell's name reads, "A Kind and dutiful Son and a / Christian Soldier his rest / shall be glorious." Shortly after Tom's death, his mother, Mary Howell, wrote on the front of the letter book where she kept all of the letters he wrote her during his time in the army that her son "lies on the banks of the Chicahomony far from home. He was the bravest of the brave, and 'stood first in his Reg. as a christian [,] 2nd to none as an Officer[,] beloved by all.'"[78] It is apparent from the quote above and the epitaph on the tombstone that Mary Howell saw her son as a Christian soldier and believed his death was a noble sacrifice in the cause for liberty. According to historian Reid Mitchell, "Portraying the soldier as Christ reassured the legitimacy of the Union cause and the meaningfulness of Union deaths—a cause that the Christlike soldier would die for was manifestly a holy one and one worth dying for."[79] The young Howell lived as a "Christian Gentleman" and died as a Christian soldier.

Many young men filled the ranks of Civil War armies, and as historian Bell I. Wiley stated, the greatest cost of America's bloodiest war was the "slaughter of youths . . . whose potential for leadership represented the nation's best hope."[80] Tom Howell is just one example of the thousands of young soldiers sacrificed in "The Boys' War." Howell entered the army hoping his service would aid him in his transition from boyhood to manhood. Perhaps if he had survived the war, he could have become a respected lawyer like his father and uncle. Instead, after just six months of service, his life was cut short at the age of seventeen by a Confederate cannonball on the banks of the Chickahominy River.

## NOTES

1. Sears, *To the Gates of Richmond*, 210–11.
2. Burton, *Extraordinary Circumstances*, 87.
3. According to Gen. Order No. 15, issued by General Slocum on June 27, 1862, his division was to "move at 5:30 o'clock AM." Regimental Order Book, 3rd New Jersey Infantry Regiment, Record Group 94, National Archives, Washington, D.C.
4. Correspondent, "Report of the 'Jersey Blues,'" *Newark (NJ) Daily Advertiser*, July 9, 1862. McClellan halted Slocum's movement across the Chickahominy that morning after he saw no action in Porter's front.
5. *O.R.* I, 11(2): 432.
6. Ibid.
7. Correspondent, "Report of the 'Jersey Blues.'"
8. Burton, *Extraordinary Circumstances*, 112.
9. *O.R.* I, 11(2): 438. Taylor reported that they arrived at the front around 4:00 p.m., but other accounts have the arrival closer to 5:00 p.m.
10. Correspondent, "The Third New Jersey Regiment," *West Jersey Press*, July 23, 1862.
11. Ibid.
12. *O.R.* I, 11(2): 438.
13. The commander of the Fourth New Jersey stated that it was the Duc de Chartres, who was also on McClellan's staff, who took the regiment. Burton, *Extraordinary Circumstances*, 435, n.14.
14. Burton, *Extraordinary Circumstances*, 112.
15. Gaines's Mill map #7, 5:00–7:00 p.m., Gaines's Mill National Battlefield Park. The other six companies of the Second New Jersey were on picket duty on the other side of the Chickahominy.
16. Correspondent, "Third New Jersey Regiment."
17. The First New Jersey took position behind the Third New Jersey along with the other two of Newton's regiments. Correspondent, "Third New Jersey Regiment."
18. Frank Coles, letter dated July 5, 1862, appearing in *The Constitution* (Woodbury, NJ), July 22, 1862.
19. Correspondent, "Report of the 'Jersey Blues.'"
20. Joseph Bilby, "Some of Us Will Never Come Out: An Account of the 1st New Jersey Brigade at Gaines Mill," *Military Images* 14 (Nov./Dec. 1992): 12.
21. Frank Coles, letter dated July 5, 1862.

22. Ibid.
23. Correspondent, "Third New Jersey Regiment."
24. Howell, *Book of John Howell and His Descendants*, 2: 422.
25. *O.R.* I, 11(2): 438.
26. Correspondent, "Report of the 'Jersey Blues.'"
27. Baquet, *History of the First Brigade*, 317.
28. Ibid.
29. Ibid., 318.
30. Ibid. Louis Loeb noted in his diary that Buckley was "shot in the privates." Pocket Diary of Louis Loeb, Pension Records, National Archives, Washington, D.C.
31. Ibid.
32. Correspondent, "Third New Jersey Regiment."
33. Baquet, *History of the First Brigade*, 319.
34. Correspondent, "Third New Jersey Regiment."
35. Edward Burd Grubb to cousin, July 15, 1862. D. Penrose Buckley Papers (#1775), HSP.
36. Baquet, *History of the First Brigade*, 318.
37. Ibid. In Louis Loeb's pocket diary, Private Loeb mentions that Captain Buckley died on July 3, 1862. Pocket Diary of Louis Loeb, Pension Records, National Archives. Washington, D.C.
38. Edward Burd Grubb to Mother, July 29, 1862. D. Penrose Buckley Papers (#1775), HSP; emphasis in original.
39. Susanna Loeb to Kate, July 24, 1862. Louis Loeb Pension Records, National Archives, Washington, D.C.
40. Pocket Diary of Louis Loeb, Louis Loeb, Pension Records, National Archives, Washington, D.C.
41. Baquet, *History of the First Brigade*, 321.
42. Correspondent, "Attack on Porter's Corps," *New York Tribune*, July 4, 1862. The *Tribune* issued a correction of Howell's name in its July 15, 1862, edition with an article "Lieut. Thomas J. Howell, 3d N. J. V."
43. Ibid.
44. Baquet, *History of the First Brigade*, 321.
45. "Report of Com'd Officers and Enlisted Men who were engaged in action at Gaines Farm who behaved meritoriously—27 June 1862," Record Group—Department of Defense, Adjutant General's Office, Civil War, 1861–1865, Regimental Records 1861–1865, 3rd Regiment, Box 6, New Jersey State Archives, Trenton, New Jersey; *O.R.* I, 11(2): 439.
46. Ibid.
47. Baquet, *History of the First Brigade*, 322.
48. Bilby and Goble, *"Remember You Are Jerseymen!"* 71.
49. Anna Howell Lloyd Hayward, "Howells—Grandmother and Uncle Tom," author's collection; emphasis in original. Mrs. Hayward did not record the name of this man in her article, but Dr. Welling is identified as the one who tried to secure Tom's body in "Howell, Thomas J.," Memorials of Officers, Record Group—Department of Defense, Adjutant General's Office, Civil War, 1861–1865, Regimental Records 1861–1865, 3rd Regiment, Box 6, New Jersey State Archives, Trenton, New Jersey.
50. Ibid. The belt and sash were either lost or are still held by a family member. It is possible that the family buried these two items in the family burial plot in Evergreen Cemetery in Camden, but the records from the cemetery are incomplete, so there is no evidence to substantiate this theory. The prayer book and the epaulettes are in H-41, Howell Family Collection, GCHS.
51. Letter from Sarah Barnard to Beulah, July 7, 1862. Author's collection.
52. Thomas Preston Carpenter to Edward, July 20, 1862. Carpenter Family Papers (#0115), HSP.
53. Louis Henry Carpenter to Father, July 10, 1862. Carpenter Family Papers (#0115), HSP.

54. "The Brave Lieut. Howell," *West Jersey Press*, July 9, 1862.
55. Louis Henry Carpenter to Sallie Carpenter, July 16, 1862. Carpenter Family Papers (#0115), HSP.
56. Louis Henry Carpenter to Annie Carpenter, July 24, 1862. Carpenter Family Papers (#0115), HSP.
57. Correspondent, "Report of the 'Jersey Blues.'"
58. "Letter from Third N.J. Reg. Camp near James River," July 5, 1862, *West Jersey Press*.
59. *The Constitution* (Woodbury, NJ), July 15, 1862.
60. O.R. I, 11(2): 40. The breakdown of the losses of the Third New Jersey is as follows: 2 officers killed, 5 wounded, and 1 captured or missing; 33 enlisted men killed, 131 wounded, and 43 captured or missing.
61. Thomas J. Howell Pension Records, National Archives, Washington, D.C. Mary Howell received the pension until her death on May 3, 1893.
62. Thomas Preston Carpenter to Edward, July 20, 1862. Carpenter Family Papers (#0115), HSP.
63. "The Body of Lieut. Howell," *West Jersey Press*, July 16, 1862.
64. Joshua Howell to Annie Howell, August 5, 1862. Transcribed copy, author's collection.
65. "Taylor, Archibald S." Memorials of Officers, Record Group—Department of Defense, Adjutant General's Office, Civil War, 1861–1865, Regimental Records 1861–1865, 3rd Regiment, Box 6, New Jersey State Archives, Trenton, New Jersey. Arch Taylor's grave is in the Clinton Presbyterian Churchyard next to the grave of his uncle Gen. George W. Taylor, who died on September 1, 1862, from the wounds he received in the Second Battle of Bull Run.
66. Pocket Diary of Louis Loeb, Pension Records of Louis Loeb, National Archives, Washington, D.C.
67. Deposition of Henrietta Loeb, Pension Records of Louis Loeb, National Archives, Washington, D.C.
68. Diary of Annie Howell Lloyd, March 21, 1886. Howell Family Collection, GCHS.
69. Joshua Howell to Annie Howell, August 5, 1862. Transcribed copy, author's collection.
70. Annie Howell to Joshua Blackwood Howell, March 30, 1863. H-30, Howell Family Collection, GCHS.
71. Diary of Annie Howell Lloyd, March 21, 1886. Howell Family Collection, GCHS.
72. Joshua Blackwood Howell to Annie Howell, July 22, 1864. Howell Family Collection, GCHS.
73. Deposition of Edward Campbell, October 5, 1866, Joshua Blackwood Howell Pension Records, National Archives.
74. "Anna Howell," *Genealogical Charts, Lineage Papers, Notes and Letters Regarding the Howell Families of Gloucester County, New Jersey, Bertha McGeehan Collection* [FC Ho], HSP.
75. Diary of Annie Howell Lloyd, March 21, 1886. Howell Family Collection, GCHS.
76. Ibid., March 1890. Annie did not write the events of individual days during this month. The details of her trip to Virginia are in a paragraph.
77. J. H. McNaughton, "The Faded Coat of Blue," in Francis Trevelyan Miller, ed., *The Photographic History of the Civil War in Ten Volumes* (New York: Review of Reviews Co., 1912), 9: 349–50.
78. Mary C. Howell on front of letter book. H-41, Howell Family Collection, GCHS.
79. Mitchell, *Vacant Chair*, 147.
80. Wiley, "Boy Lieutenant in Blue," 30.

# Bibliography

*Primary Sources*

Author's Collection

    Anna Howell Lloyd Hayward Recollections
    Sarah Barnard Letter
    Thomas James Howell Transcribed Letters

Burlington County Historical Society, Burlington, New Jersey

    Benjamin H. Wiley Papers

Camden County Historical Society, Camden, New Jersey

    Alice B. Doughten Collection
    Richard W. Howell Collection

Gloucester County Historical Society, Woodbury, New Jersey

    Civil War Letters Collection
    Howell Family Collection

Historical Society of Pennsylvania, Philadelphia, Pennsylvania

    D. Penrose Buckley Papers (#1775)
    Carpenter Family Papers (#0115)
    Malcolm Lloyd Collection (#1618)
    *Genealogical Charts, Lineage Papers Notes and Letters Regarding the Howell Families of Gloucester County, New Jersey* (Call number: FC Ho—No collection number)

National Archives, Washington, DC

    Letter Book. Third New Jersey Infantry Regiment, Record Group 94
    Pension Records
    Regimental Order Book. Third New Jersey Infantry Regiment. Record Group 94

New Jersey State Archives, Trenton, New Jersey

    Letters to Governor Charles S. Olden. Record Group—Department of Defense, Adjutant General's Office, Civil War, 1861–1865, Regimental Records 1861–1865, 3rd Regiment, Box 6, Folder 30
    Memorials of Officers. Record Group—Department of Defense, Adjutant General's Office, Civil War, 1861–1865, Regimental Records 1861–1865, 3rd Regiment, Box 6

## Secondary Sources

Annual Report of the Adjutant General of the State of New Jersey for the Year 1861. Trenton, NJ: True American Office, 1862.

Baquet, Camille. *History of the First Brigade, New Jersey Volunteers.* Trenton: State of New Jersey, 1910.

Barton, Michael. *Goodmen: The Character of Civil War Soldiers.* University Park: Pennsylvania State University Press, 1981.

Beatie, Russel H. *Army of the Potomac: McClellan's First Campaign, March 1862–May 1862.* New York: Savas Beatie, 2007.

Bilby, Joseph G. "An Officer and a Gentleman . . . sort of." *Military Images* 13 (Jan./Feb. 1992): 24–25.

———. "Some of Us Will Never Come Out: An Account of the 1st New Jersey Brigade at Gaines Mill." *Military Images* 14 (Nov./Dec. 1992): 10–15.

Bilby, Joseph G., and William C. Goble. *"Remember You Are Jerseymen!": A Military History of New Jersey's Troops in the Civil War.* Hightstown, NJ: Longstreet House, 1998.

Burton, Brian K. *Extraordinary Circumstances: The Seven Days Battles.* Bloomington: Indiana University Press, 2001.

Bushman, Richard L. *The Refinement of America: Persons, Houses, Cities.* New York: Alfred A. Knopf, 1992.

Carpenter, Edward, and Louis Henry Carpenter. *Samuel Carpenter and His Descendants.* Philadelphia: J. B. Lippincott, 1912.

*A Catalogue of the Officers and Students of the College of New Jersey, For the Academical Year 1856–57.* Princeton, NJ: John T. Robinson, 1857.

*Catalogue of the Trustees, Officers, and Students, of the University of Pennsylvania. Session 1854–55.* Philadelphia: T. K. & P. G. Collins, 1855.

*Catalogue of the Trustees, Officers, and Students, of the University of Pennsylvania. Session 1858–59.* Philadelphia: Collins, 1859.

*Catalogue of the Trustees, Officers, and Students of the University of Pennsylvania. Session 1860–61.* Philadelphia: Collins, 1861.

Catton, Bruce. *Mr. Lincoln's Army.* Garden City, NY: Doubleday, 1951.

Chadwick, Bruce, *1858: Abraham Lincoln, Jefferson Davis, Robert E. Lee, Ulysses S. Grant and the War They Failed to See.* Naperville, IL: Sourcebooks, 2008.

Cone, William Whitney. *Some Account of the Cone Family in America, Principally of the Descendants of Daniel Cone, Who Settled in Haddam Connecticut in 1662.* Topeka, KS: Crane & Company, 1903.

Cooling, Benjamin Franklin, III, and Walton H. Owen II. *Mr. Lincoln's Forts: A Guide to the Civil War Defenses of Washington.* Shippensburg, PA: White Mane Publishing, 1988.

Cullen, Joseph P. "The Battle of Gaines's Mill." *Civil War Times Illustrated* 3, no. 1 (1964): 10–17, 24.

———. *The Peninsula Campaign, 1862: McClellan & Lee, Struggle for Richmond.* New York: Bonanza Books, 1973.

DePeyster, J. Watts. *Personal and Military History of Philip Kearny, Major-General United States Volunteers.* Elizabeth, NJ: Palmer & Co., 1870.

Draper, Sarah H. *The Howells of Fancy Hill.* Stonington, CT: Draper, 1978.

*Eleventh Annual Announcement of the Homeopathic Medical College of Pennsylvania. Session 1858–59.* Philadelphia: King & Baird, 1858.

Elson, Ruth Miller. *Guardians of Tradition: American Schoolbooks of the Nineteenth Century.* Lincoln: University of Nebraska Press, 1964.

Erickson, Charlotte. *Invisible Immigrants: The Adaptation of English and Scottish Immigrants in 19th-Century America.* Ithaca, NY: Cornell University Press, 1972.

Evans, Charles M. *War of the Aeronauts: A History of Ballooning in the Civil War.* Mechanicsburg, PA: Stackpole Books, 2002.

Foote, Lorien. *The Gentlemen and the Roughs: Violence, Honor, and Manhood in the Union Army.* New York: New York University Press, 2010.

Foster, John Y. *New Jersey and the Rebellion: History of the Services of the Troops and People of New Jersey in Aid of the Union Cause.* Newark, NJ: Martin R. Dennis & Co., 1868.

Fox, William F. *Regimental Losses in the American Civil War, 1861–1865.* Albany, NY: Albany Publishing Company, 1889.

Gallagher, Gary W., ed. *The Richmond Campaign of 1862: The Peninsula & the Seven Days.* Chapel Hill: University of North Carolina Press, 2000.

Gibson, Charles Dana, and E. Kay Gibson. *The Army's Navy Series: Dictionary of Transports and Combatant Vessels Steam and Sail Employed by the Union Army, 1861–1868.* Camden, ME: Ensign Press, 1995.

Goode, Charles E., and Peter Leach. *Archaeological Evaluation for the Proposed Chapel of the Ages at the Virginia Theological Seminary Alexandria, Virginia.* Alexandria, VA: John Milner Associates, 2013.

Gottfried, Bradley M. *Kearny's Own: The History of the First New Jersey Brigade in the Civil War.* New Brunswick, NJ: Rutgers University Press, 2005.

Gould, Benjamin Apthorp. *Investigations in the Military and Anthropological Statistics of American Soldiers.* New York: U.S. Sanitary Commission, 1869. Reprint, New York: Arno Press, 1979.

Gwynne, S. C. *Rebel Yell: The Violence, Passion, and Redemption of Stonewall Jackson.* New York: Scribner, 2014.

Hareven, Tamara K. "The Last Stage: Historical Adulthood and Old Age." In *Adulthood*, edited by Erik H. Erikson, 201–15. New York: W. W. Norton, 1978.

Hauptman, Laurence M. *Between Two Fires: American Indians in the Civil War.* New York: Free Press, 1995.

Haydon, F. Stansbury. *Military Ballooning during the Early Civil War.* Baltimore: Johns Hopkins University Press, 1941.

Heaps, Willard A. *The Bravest Teenage Yanks: True Stories of Extraordinary Heroism in the Civil War.* New York: Duell, Sloan, and Pearce, 1963.

Hess, Earl J. *The Union Soldier in Battle: Enduring the Ordeal of Combat.* Lawrence: University Press of Kansas, 1997.

Howell, Frances. *The Book of John Howell and His Descendants.* New York: Frances Howell, 1897.

Jackson, William J. *New Jerseyans in the Civil War: For Union and Liberty.* New Brunswick, NJ: Rutgers University Press, 2000.

Jones, Terry L. *Historical Dictionary of the Civil War.* Vol. 1: *A–L.* Lanham, MD: Scarecrow Press, 2002.

Keesee, Dennis M. *Too Young to Die: Boy Soldiers of the Union Army, 1861–1865.* Huntington, WV: Blue Acorn Press, 2001.

Kett, Joseph F. *Rites of Passage: Adolescence in America, 1790 to the Present.* NewYork: Basic Books, 1977.

Kilmer, George Langdon. "Boys in the Union Army." *Century* 70 (June 1905): 269–75.

Lender, Mark Edward. *One State in Arms: A Short Military History of New Jersey.* Trenton: New Jersey Historical Commission, 1991.

Long, E. B. *The Civil War Day by Day: An Almanac, 1861–1865.* New York: Da Capo, 1971.

Lossing, Benson J. *Pictorial History of the Civil War in the United States of America.* Hartford: T. Belknap, 1868.

Lubin, Thomas T. "Colonel Joshua Ladd Howell Letters, 1762–1818." Unpublished paper. Stewart Collection. Campbell Library. Rowan University. Glassboro, NewJersey.

Marks, J. J. *The Peninsula Campaign in Virginia.* Philadelphia: J. B. Lippincott & Co., 1864.

Marten, James. *Children for the Union: The War Spirit on the Northern Home Front.* Chicago: Ivan R. Dee, 2004.

Martin, David G. *The Peninsula Campaign, March–July 1862.* Conshohocken, PA: Combined Books, 1992.
McNaughton, J. H. "The Faded Coat of Blue." In *The Photographic History of the Civil War in Ten Volumes*, edited by Francis Trevelyan Miller, 9: 349–50 (New York: Review of Reviews Co., 1912).
McPherson, James M. *Battle Cry of Freedom: The Civil War Era.* New York: Oxford University Press, 1988.
———. *For Cause and Comrades: Why Men Fought in the Civil War.* New York: Oxford University Press, 1997.
Melville, Herman. *Battle-Pieces and Aspects of the Civil War.* Gainesville, FL: Scholars' Facsimiles and Reprints, 1960.
Miller, Francis Trevelyan, ed. *The Photographic History of the Civil War in Ten Volumes.* New York: Review of Reviews Co., 1912.
Miller, Richard F. ed. *States at War, Vol. 4: A Reference Guide for Delaware, Maryland, and New Jersey.* Hanover: University Press of New England, 2015.
Mitchell, Reid. *Civil War Soldiers.* New York: Viking, 1988.
———. *The Vacant Chair: The Northern Soldier Leaves Home.* New York: Oxford University Press, 1993.
New Jersey Historical Society. *Proceedings of the New Jersey Historical Society.* Second Series, Vol. 9, 1886–1887. Newark, NJ: Daily Advertiser Printing House, 1887.
Nofi, Albert A. *The Civil War Notebook: A Collection of Little-Known Facts and Other Odds-and-Ends about the Civil War.* New York: Da Capo, 1993.
*Official Register of the Officers and Cadets of the U.S. Military Academy, West Point, New York, June 1861.*
Oller, John. *American Queen: The Rise and Fall of Kate Chase Sprague, Civil War "Belle of the North" and Gilded Age Woman of Scandal.* Boston: Da Capo Press, 2014.
Palm, Ronn, Richard Sauers, and Patrick A. Schroeder. *The Bloody 85th: The Letters of Milton McJunkin, a Western Pennsylvania Soldier in the Civil War.* Daleville, VA: Schroeder Publications, 2000.
Prowell, Geo. R. *The History of Camden County, New Jersey.* Philadelphia: L. J. Richards & Co., 1886.
Quarstein, John V., and J. Michael Moore. *Yorktown's Civil War Siege: Drums along the Warwick.* Charleston: History Press, 2012.
Reed, Rowena. *Combined Operations in the Civil War.* Annapolis, MD: U.S. Naval Institute Press, 1978.
*Report of the Adjutant General of the State of Illinois.* Vol. I. Springfield, IL: Phillips Bros., 1900.
Roberts, Robert B. *Encyclopedia of Historic Forts: The Military, Pioneer, and Trading Posts of the United States.* New York: Macmillan, 1988.
Robertson, James I., Jr., ed. *The Civil War Letters of General Robert McAllister.* New Brunswick, NJ: Rutgers University Press, 1965.
———. *Soldiers Blue and Gray.* Columbia: University of South Carolina Press, 1988.
Rotundo, A. Anthony. *American Manhood: Transformations in Masculinity from the Revolution to the Modern Era.* New York: Basic Books, 1993.
———. "Learning about Manhood: Gender Ideas and the Middle-Class Family in Nineteenth-Century America." In *Manliness and Morality: Middle-Class Masculinity in Britain and America, 1800–1940*, edited by J. A. Mangan and James Walvin, 35–51. New York: St. Martin's, 1987.
Rudolph, Jack. "The Children's Crusade: Youth in the Civil War." *Civil War Times Illustrated* 21, no. 3 (1982): 10–17.
Rutkow, Ira M. *Bleeding Blue and Gray: Civil War Surgery and the Evolution of American Medicine.* New York: Random House, 2005.
Schroeder, Rudolph J., III. *Seven Days before Richmond: McClellan's Peninsula Campaign of 1862 and Its Aftermath.* New York: iUniverse, 2009.

Scythes, James. "Siege of Corinth, Mississippi." In *American Civil War: The Definitive Encyclopedia and Document Collection*, edited by Spencer C. Tucker, 436–38. Santa Barbara, CA: ABC-CLIO, 2013.
Sears, Stephen W., ed. *The Civil War Papers of George B. McClellan: Selected Correspondence, 1860–1865*. New York: Da Capo, 1992.
———. *George B. McClellan: The Young Napoleon*. New York: Ticknor and Fields, 1988.
———. *To the Gates of Richmond: The Peninsula Campaign*. New York: Ticknor and Fields, 1992.
Selcer, Richard F. "Youthful Innocence Shattered." *America's Civil War* 1, no. 6 (1989): 27–32.
Siegel, Alan A. *Beneath the Starry Flag: New Jersey's Civil War Experience*. New Brunswick, NJ: Rutgers University Press, 2001.
Snell, Mark A. "'Very Crude Notions on the Subject': William B. Franklin's Amphibious Assault at Eltham's Landing." In *Union Combined Operations in the Civil War*, edited by Craig L. Symonds, 32–43. New York: Fordham University Press, 2010.
*St. Mary's Hall: Register*. Philadelphia: King & Baird, 1862.
Stryker, William S. *Record of Officers and Men of New Jersey in the Civil War, 1861–1865*. Trenton, NJ: John L. Murphy, Steam Book and Job Printer, 1876.
Styple, William B., ed. *Letters from the Peninsula: The Civil War Letters of General Philip Kearny*. Kearny, NJ: Belle Grove Publishing, 1988.
Swinton, William. *Campaigns of the Army of the Potomac: A Critical History of Operations in Virginia, Maryland, and Pennsylvania, From the Commencement to the Close of the War 1861–5*. New York: Charles B. Richardson, 1866.
Thrapp, Dan L. *Encyclopedia of Frontier Biography*. Vol. 3: P–Z. Glendale, CA: A. H. Clark Co., 1988.
*University of the State of New-York, College of Physicians and Surgeons of the City of New-York, Annual Catalogue of the Regents of the University, and of the Trustees, Faculty, and Students of the College, 1845–6*. New York: Daniel Adee, 1846.
U.S. War Department. *An Act Establishing Rules and Articles for the Government of the Armies of the United States*. Albany, NY: Websters and Skinners, 1812.
———. *Revised Regulations for the Army of the United States, 1861*. Philadelphia: J. G. L. Brown, Printer, 1861.
———. *The War of the Rebellion: A Compilation of the Official Records of the Union and Confederate Armies*. 128 vols. Washington, DC.: U.S. Government Printing Office, 1880–1901.
Warner, Ezra J. *Generals in Blue: Lives of the Union Commanders*. Baton Rouge: Louisiana State University Press, 1992.
Weinert, Richard P., Jr., and Colonel Robert Arthur. *Defender of the Chesapeake: The Story of Fort Monroe*. Shippensburg, PA: White Mane Publishing, 1989.
Wert, Jeffrey D. *The Sword of Lincoln: The Army of the Potomac*. New York: Simon and Schuster, 2005.
Wiley, Bell I. "Boy Lieutenant in Blue." *Civil War Times Illustrated* 19, no. 6 (1980): 24–30.
———. *The Life of Billy Yank: The Common Soldier of the Union*. Baton Rouge: Louisiana State University Press, 2008.
Winterer, Caroline. *The Culture of Classicism: Ancient Greece and Rome in American Intellectual Life, 1780–1910*. Baltimore: Johns Hopkins University Press, 2002.
Young, Kenneth Ray. *The General's General: The Life and Times of Arthur MacArthur*. Boulder, CO: Westview Press, 1994.

## Newspapers

*The Constitution* (Woodbury, NJ)
*Newark (NJ) Daily Advertiser*
*New York Tribune*
*Philadelphia Inquirer*

*Trenton Times*
*West Jersey Press* (Camden, NJ)

## City Directories

Camden City Directory, 1863–1864
Philadelphia City Directory, 1861

## Census Reports

1850 United States Federal Census
1860 United States Federal Census
1870 United States Federal Census

# Index

Alexandria, VA, 23, 36
Allison, Thomas S., 69, 89
American Anti-Slavery Society, 8
American Colonization Society, 5, 8
American Revolution, 4
ammunition wagons, 111
amputation, 147
Ann (Dunham's sister), 67
Army Engineers, U.S., 87
Army of the Potomac, 73

Fort Monroe base for, 33

Franklin, W., division commander of, 22, 34

Howell, T. J., experiences in, 11–12

McClellan, G., commanding, 32, 33

*Arrowsmith* (ship), 71, 99
artillery battle, 115

baggage wagons, 111
Balloon Corps, 86
Banks, Nathaniel, 80, 138
Baquet, Camille, 67
Barnard, William C., 68, 135
Bartlett, Joseph, 82, 84, 138, 141–142
battlefield graves, 86
battles, 115, 134, 143

of Fair Oaks, 82–83, 87, 122, 132, 138
of Mechanicsville, 140
of Oak Grove, 88–89, 140
of Salem Heights, 154

Seven Days', 88–89, 140, 141
Shiloh, 35

of Williamsburg, 103. *See also* Gaines's Mill, battle of

Baxter, E. G., 3
bayonet exercises, 24, 38, 49
Beauregard, P. G. T., 73, 138
Bedell, John E., 134
Berga, Henry, 85, 138
Birney, David Bell, 52, 69, 126–128, 140
Birney, William, 140, 157
blood poisoning, 155
Boatswain's Swamp, 141, 143, 144, 148
body recovery, of Howell, T. J., 154, 157–158
"Boys in the Union Army," 2
boy soldiers, 3
"The Boy's War," 159
Bristoe Station, 36, 59, 70
Brooks, William T. H., 134
Brown, Henry W., 64

drinking habit of, 125

fierce battle of, 143

Howell, T. J., angered by, 107–108
Howell, T. J., fed up with, 87

as mean-spirited, 26–27

photo of, 28

Brown, John, 15n65
Browning, Abraham, 25, 69
Browning, Elizabeth, 69
Browning, George, 55, 70
Browning, Gertrude ("Gert"), 25, 69, 91, 98
Bryan, Isaiah, 136
Bryan, William E., 68, 80, 107, 136

170 Index

Buckley, Daniel Penrose, 29, 48, 67, 70, 79, 82, 130

death of, 160n37

letter to father by, 83

as mortally wounded, 146–147, 153

photo of, 30

Rebel Army position reported by, 75

Bull Run, 22, 31, 48, 67, 68
Burke's Station, 45, 66
Burnett's Inn, 109, 137
Burnside, Ambrose E., 66
Butler, Benjamin, 73
Butler, Charles T., 9

Caldwell, Samuel W., 134
Camden Court House, 10
Captain prospects, 44
Carpenter, Anna Stratton, 64, 69, 139
Carpenter, Annie, 47, 94, 111
Carpenter, Edward, 4, 70, 139
Carpenter, Frances ("Fanny") Mary, 106, 109, 117–118, 136
Carpenter, James Edward, 19, 50, 112, 126–128
Carpenter, James Hopkins, 68
Carpenter, James Stratton (uncle), 3–4
Carpenter, Louis Henry (cousin), 18, 19, 150, 152
Carpenter, Mary Tonkin. *See* Howell, Mary Tonkin Carpenter
Carpenter, Rebecca Hopkins, 68
Carpenter, Samuel, 138
Carpenter, Sarah, 4, 138
Carpenter, Susan Mary, 69
Carpenter, Thomas Preston (uncle), 3–4, 64, 68, 87, 139, 154

background of, 6–7

Howell, T. J., departure and, 20
Howell, T. J., motivations and, 11

lieutenant vacancy and, 17

resolutions drafted by, 9–10

Virginia visit of, 60

Carpenter family, emigration of, 4
Carr, Joseph B., 139
Cassady, Peter, 70
Catlett's Station. *See* Colvin's Station
Centreville, VA, 46, 67
Chartres, Duc de, 159n13
Chickahominy fever, 82, 85
chivalry, 7
Christian Gentleman, 6, 25–26, 29, 81, 158
Civil War
"The Faded Coat of Blue" and, 158

Fort Sumter beginning of, 9

Gould's study of, 2–3

Howell, T. J., body left behind in, 149–150
Howell, T. J., death in, 148–149, 150, 152–153
Howell, T. J., first witnessing, 31
Howell, T. J., near fighting in, 71–73

romanticized view of, 7

sacrifice and pain of, 154
slaughter of youth in, 159
soldier's life in, xiv

young person's opportunity in, 2

Clark, Henry C., 85, 117, 139
Collett, Mark Wilkes, 67
Colvin's Station, 35, 57, 70
combat experiences, 76
commissioned officers, 3
commission order, 23–24, 24–25
company drills, 43
Comte de Paris, 143
Cone, Jonathan, 134
Cone, Mary Ann, 134
Confederate Army. *See* Rebel Army
Confederate States of America, 9
Cook, Jonathan, 133

# Index

corduroy road, 87
Corinth, 73, 75, 113–114, 138
Courtney House, 150
Coxe, Lorenzo Lewis, 67, 69
Cumberland Landing, 78–79
Custis, George Washington Parke, 105, 135

Dam No. 1 battle, 134
Darrow, George R., 67, 125
Davis, Jefferson, 82
Dayton, James B., 27
De Haven, Charlie, 55, 70
diary, of Howell, Annie, xiv
Dinkelhoff, Reginald, 137
Dixon, Fred, 126–128
Dixon, James, 126–128
Draper, Sarah, xiii
dress parade, 112
drinking problem, 26–27, 125
drum and fife corps, 93
Dunham, Robert T. ("Bob"), 34, 35, 37, 39, 42, 92

as assistant adjutant general, 73

background of, 64
battle survived by, 148

Howell, T. J., friends with, 27

rebel shell exploding and, 145

second Lieutenant request of, 49
sisters of, 67

tents gotten by, 40

Duryée, Abram, 136
18th N.Y. volunteers, 102, 135

Eighty-fifth Pennsylvania Volunteer Infantry Regiment, 20
Eighty-third Article of War, 27
*Elm City* (ship), 71, 99, 154
Eltham's Landing, 75, 77, 135
England, 4
epaulettes, 152
erysipelas, 62

Evergreen Cemetery, 160n50
expenses, during military service, 39
"The Faded Coat of Blue," 158

Fairfax Court House, 36, 45, 59
Fairfax Station, 31, 44, 66
Fair Oaks, battle of, 82–83, 87, 122, 132, 138
faith, of Howell, T. J., 34
Fancy Hill estate, 5, 13n31
farmhouse, looting, 76–77
Farragut, David, 73
fatigue party, 34, 53, 59, 123
Fewsmith, Catharine, 7, 14n50
Fewsmith, William, 7, 14n50, 14n51, 20
Fifth New York Infantry Regiment, 136
First New Jersey Brigade, 22
First New York Cavalry, 31
First U.S. Cavalry, 134
Fort Donelson, 35, 64
Fort Henry, 35, 64
Fort Monroe, 50, 56, 90–91, 96, 157

Army of Potomac base at, 33

McClellan, G., and, 32–36, 68

Union Army destination of, 33

forts, map of, 23
Fort Sumter, 1, 9
Fort Washington, 90
Fort Worth, 22, 38, 45, 57–59, 61, 125
Fourth New Jersey, 77
Fourth U.S. Artillery, 139
Franklin, William B., 59, 79, 100, 104

as Army of Potomac commander, 22, 34

background of, 66

Gloucester Point and, 46

retreating Rebels cut off by, 74

Fugitive Slave Act of 1850, 8–9

Gaines, William, 86, 137

## Index

Gaines's Mill, battle of, 11, 142, 147, 157, 159n15

casualties of, 150, 153

Howell, T. J., body left behind after, 149–150
Howell, T. J., death in, 148–149, 150, 152–153

Taylor, G., location in, 141–143, 144

Garlick's Landing, 139
Garrison, Joseph F., 65
Geary, Edward V., 3
Geary, John W., 3
General Order No. 55, 99
gentlemanly behavior, 27
gentleman's education, 8
Gibson, Henry C., 107, 125, 136
Gloucester County Historical Society, xiii–xiv
Gloucester Point, 46, 72, 92, 94, 99
Gosline's Zouaves, 101, 135
Gould, Benjamin, 2, 2–3
Grant, Ulysses S., 35
Grapevine Bridge, 132
graves, mass, 122
Gray, Martin, 39, 65
Gray, Philip J., 68
Gray, Samuel, 65
Gray, Sarah W., 68
Grey, Mart, 92
Griffin, Charles, 143
Grubb, E. Burd, 67, 73, 86, 97, 134

Howell, T. J., death observed by, 148–149

Third New Jersey rejoined by, 145–146

Halleck, Henry, 84, 109, 118, 137
Hamilton, Charles Smith, 130, 134
Hamilton, Ellis, 3
Harbert, Georgianna Wishart, 139
Harbert, Mary, 25, 42, 47, 53, 98

background of, 65

discussion about photo of, 115, 120

father of, 66

Harbert, Samuel, 25, 66
Harper's Ferry, 15n65
Harris, Thomas S., 70
Harrison's Landing, 153
Hatch, William B., 79, 136
Hayward, Anna Howell Lloyd (aunt), 13n23, 160n49
*Hero* (ship), 71, 97, 99
Hess, Earl, 7, 33
Hidden, Henry, 31, 66
Higgins, John D., 65
Hill, A. P., 68, 88
Hill, Daniel Harvey, 88
*History of the First Brigade* (Baquet), 67
Hoelle, Edith, xiii
Honnor, Moses, 9
Hood, John Bell, 75, 135, 146
Hooker, Joseph, 122, 139
Hopkins, Susan Barton, 69
Hopkins, Woolsey R., 123–125, 140
hot work soon enough, 94
Howell, Anna Blackwood (grandmother), 4
Howell, Annie (sister), 6, 13n20, 61

death of, 158
donated diary of, xiv

Howell, T. J., death devastating, 155–156

marriage of, 157

photo of, 156
prayer book given by, 20. *See also* letters, of Howell, T. J.

Howell, Benjamin Paschall, 65, 91, 98, 139
Howell, Benjamin Paschall, Jr., 139
Howell, Charley (brother), 6, 9, 13n20, 67, 139
Howell, Edward Carpenter, 13n20
Howell, Frances ("Fanny"), 139
Howell, Francis Lee, 13n20

# Index

Howell, Frank (brother), 6
Howell, John Ladd, 4
Howell, John Paschall, 13n20
Howell, Joshua Blackwood (uncle), 64, 83, 134, 138, 156

background of, 19–20
Burnside assistance information and, 66

death of, 157

Howell, Joshua Ladd (brother), 6, 13n20, 155. *See also* letters, of Howell, T. J.

Howell, Joshua Ladd (grandfather), 4
Howell, Maria ("Minnie"), 6, 65
Howell, Mary ("Molly"), 139
Howell, Mary Tonkin Carpenter (mother), 3, 4, 5, 138

children of, 13n20
Christian soldier belief of, 158

military pension received by, 154. *See also* letters, of Howell, T. J.

Howell, Richard (brother), 6, 13n20
Howell, Richard Washington (father), 3–4, 4–5, 13n20, 134, 150
Howell, Samuel (brother), 6, 8, 13n20, 64, 65
Howell, Sarah ("Sallie") Carpenter Howell, 6, 13n20
Howell, Thomas James, 17–18, 20, 21, 24, 71–73, 148

Army of Potomac experiences of, 11–12

battlefield graves observed by, 86
body left behind of, 149–150
body recovery failed of, 154, 157–158
Brown, H., angering, 87, 107–108

Carpenter, T. P., and, 11, 20
combat experience of, 34, 76
commission order for, 23–24, 24–25

death of, 148–149, 150, 152–153
Dunham friends with, 27

faith of, 34
first combat witnessed by, 31

gentleman's education of, 8
Grubb observing death of, 148–149

Harbert, M., inquiry of, 25
Howell, Annie, devastated by death of, 155–156
Howell, J. L., remembering, 155

last letter of, 128

McClellan, G., impressing, 49, 85–86
military experience hopes of, 10
money motivating, 10–11

obituary of, 153

as Officer of Guard, 41, 107, 115

original letters of, xiii, 12

parents of, 3–4
prayer book and epaulettes of, 152

Rebel Army described by, 77

as second lieutenant, 1

siblings of, 64
slaughter of youth and, 159
South loathed by, 84, 117

Taylor, A., comments on, 145
tombstone epitaph of, 158
transcribed letters of, xiii

Huger, Benjamin, 88

India Rubber, 93, 128
*Intrepid* (balloon), 86
*Investigations in the Military and Anthropological Statistics of American Soldiers* (Gould), 2
Iron monsters, 96

174 *Index*

Italian War of Independence, 22

Jackson, Andrew, 5
Jackson, Thomas J. ("Stonewall"), 68, 80, 88, 138, 139, 146
Jane (Dunham's sister), 67
*John A. Warner* (ship), 73, 89, 90, 134
photo of, 72

as side-wheel steam ship, 71, 133
as transport ship, 71, 74, 94, 99, 130

Johnston, Albert Sidney, 35
Johnston, Joseph E., 1, 31, 33, 67, 82
Jones, Anna Maria, 140
Jones, Joseph H., 140

Kansas-Nebraska Act, 15n65
Kearny, Philip, 44, 49, 50, 92, 97

background of, 22, 66

division advancing of, 128

General Order No. 55 by, 99

Hamilton, C. S., division taken over by, 134
heavy fighting with, 113

Oak Grove battle of, 88

promotion of, 73–74

Rebel Army discards and, 32
Regur's letter to, 62

Sangster's Station move of, 31
skirmish drill ordered by, 54

Third New Jersey praised by, 56

Keesee, Dennis M., 2, 3
*Kent* (ship), 71, 97, 99
Keyes, Erasmus D., 111, 137
Kilmer, George Langdon, 2, 3
King, Rufus, 52, 69
Kirkbride, Thomas, 67
Knap, Joseph M., 3

Knight, Franklin L., 65
knives, 42

leadership, 26
Lecompton Constitution, 15n65
Lee, Robert E., 1, 82, 88, 102, 131, 136
Lee, Robert E., Jr., 77
Lee, William H. F. ("Rooney"), 79, 136
Leeson, Landric, 82, 138
letters, of Howell, T. J.
to Carpenter, F., 117–118
to Howell, Annie, Apr 2 1862, 55–56
to Howell, Annie, Apr 19 1862, 90–91
to Howell, Annie, Apr 26 1862, 94–95
to Howell, Annie, Feb 11 1862, 37
to Howell, Annie, Feb 21 1862, 39
to Howell, Annie, June 3 1862, 114–115
to Howell, Annie, June 16 1862, 120–122
to Howell, Annie, June 22 1862, 123–125
to Howell, Annie, June 24 1862, 126–128
to Howell, Annie, Mar 6 1862, 42–43
to Howell, Annie, Mar 8 1862, 43–44
to Howell, Annie, Mar 19 1862, 47
to Howell, Annie, Mar 24 1862, 49–51
to Howell, Annie, Mar 26 1862, 51–52
to Howell, Annie, Mar 29 1862, 52–53
to Howell, Annie, May 1 1862, 96
to Howell, Annie, May 12 1862, 103–104
to Howell, Annie, May 21 1862, 107
to Howell, Annie, May 28 1862, 112
to Howell, J. L., Apr 2 1862, 54–55
to Howell, J. L., Apr 20 1862, 92–93
to Howell, J. L., Apr 30 1862, 95
to Howell, J. L., Fed 16 1862, 37–38
to Howell, J. L., June 20 1862, 122–123
to Howell, J. L., June 26 1862, 128–129
to Howell, J. L., Mar 15 1862, 45–46
to Howell, J. L., Mar 21 1862, 47–48
to Howell, J. L., May 3 1862, 97–98
to Howell, J. L., May 10 1862, 102–103
to Howell, J. L., May 16 1862, 105–106
to Howell, J. L., May 22 1862, 108–109
to Howell, J. L., May 27 1862, 111
to Howell, J. L., May 31 1862, 112–113
to Howell, M. T., Apr 2 1862, 56–57

## Index

to Howell, M. T., Apr 4 1862, 57
to Howell, M. T., Apr 11 1862, 57–59
to Howell, M. T., Apr 12 1862, 59–60
to Howell, M. T., Apr 15 1862, 60
to Howell, M. T., Apr 18 1862, 89–90
to Howell, M. T., Apr 19 1862, 91–92
to Howell, M. T., Apr 24 1862, 93–94
to Howell, M. T., Feb 26 1862, 40–41
to Howell, M. T., Feb 28 1862, 41
to Howell, M. T., Fed 19 1862, 38–39
to Howell, M. T., Jan 12 1862, 36–37
to Howell, M. T., June 2 1862, 113–114
to Howell, M. T., June 5 1862, 115
to Howell, M. T., June 7 1862, 116–117
to Howell, M. T., June 16 1862, 118–120
to Howell, M. T., June 22 1862, 125–126
to Howell, M. T., June 25 1862, 128
to Howell, M. T., Mar 5 1862, 41–42
to Howell, M. T., Mar 11 1862, 44–45
to Howell, M. T., Mar 15 1862, 46–47
to Howell, M. T., Mar 22 1862, 48–49
to Howell, M. T., Mar 28 1862, 52
to Howell, M. T., Mar 31 1862, 53–54
to Howell, M. T., May 2 1862, 96–97
to Howell, M. T., May 3 1862, 98
to Howell, M. T., May 5 1862, 99–100
to Howell, M. T., May 8 1862, 100–101
to Howell, M. T., May 14 1862, 104–105
to Howell, M. T., May 18 1862, 106
to Howell, M. T., May 22 1862, 107–108
to Howell, M. T., May 26 1862, 109–110

Lincoln, Abraham, 9, 20, 34, 80, 137
little drummer boy, 55
Lloyd, Eleanor, xiii
Lloyd, Malcolm, 157–158
Lloyd, Morris, Jr., xiii
Lloyd, Thomas, xiii
Loeb, Louis, 29, 135, 147, 153, 155
Longstreet, James, 88
Louisiana Territory, 15n65
Lowe, Thaddeus S. C., 86, 137
Lybrand, Joseph M., 4
Lyons, Richard Bickerton Pemell, 34, 69

MacArthur, Arthur, 3
Mackey, William K., 91, 134
Magruder, John B., 88

Manassas, 66, 67, 99

Third New Jersey first to, 46
Third New Jersey march to, 44–45, 50, 57

manhood, transition to, 1–2
map of forts, 23
Marcy, Randolph, 68
Markly, Albert W., 54, 69
Mattison, John V., 85, 116, 138
McAllister, Robert, 79, 137
McClellan, George B., 1

Army of Potomac addressed by, 33
as Army of Potomac commander, 32

background of, 67

Fort Monroe and, 56, 68

Howell, T. J., impression of, 49, 85–86

Oak Grove attack of, 88–89
orders from, 46, 77

Peninsula Campaign of, 11
plan devised by, 87–88

Rebel Army evacuation and, 99–100
Rebel Army plan of, 134
Richmond capture ended by, 141
Richmond without struggle goal of, 119–120

with Third New Jersey, 51

troop miscount by, 63
Tunstall's Station march of, 79

Union army reorganized by, 79

Washington, DC, defended by, 34–35
whiskey rations discontinued by, 126
wounded soldiers and, 154–155

McClellan, Mary Ellen Marcy, 68
McClellan's Dragoons, 94, 134
McDowell, Irvin, 22, 33, 68, 79, 110, 111

McPherson, James M., 24
Meagher, Thomas F., 147
mean-spirited, 26–27
Mechanicsville, 119, 138

battle of, 140

march from, 120–122

New Jersey Brigade march to, 84, 85

Third New Jersey arriving at, 116

Merry, Arthur, 126–128
Mexican-American War, 17, 32
military pension, 154
military service, 10, 24, 29, 39
miserable conditions, 35–36
Missouri Compromise, 15n65
Mitchell, Reid, 10, 158
Morgan, Charles H., 139
Mount Vernon, 90, 94
Munson's Hill, VA, 22

Napoleon, 32
New Jersey Brigade, 22, 34, 35–36, 59, 71, 78

eager to engage enemy, 142

Mechanicsville march of, 84, 85
movements of, 76

picket duty of, 80
Porter corps support by, 141

Taylor, G., new commander of, 73

White House stay of, 79

in woods and divided, 143

New Kent Court House, 78, 103, 104
Newton, John, 75, 104, 136, 141, 143
Newton, Richard, 68
Nine Mile Road, 87

Oak Grove, battle of, 88–89, 140
Oakley, Lewis, 85, 101, 117, 135

obituary, of Howell, T. J., 153
Officer of the Guard, 41, 107, 115
officers, xiv, 29

commissioned, 3

drinking and swearing of, 26

not gentlemen, 25–26

Old Capitol Prison, 69
Old Cold Harbor, 80
Olden, Charles S., 18
Old Tavern, 88
original letters, xiii, 12

parents, of Howell, T. J., 3–4, 26
patriotism, 10
Peninsula Campaign, 11, 86
Penn, William, 4
phonographic prayer book, 55
photographs, 115, 120

of Brown, H. W., 28
of Buckley, D. P., 30
of Howell, Annie, 156
of Howell, T. J., 20, 21
of *John A. Warner* (ship), 72

picket duty, 80, 82
Pope, John, 153
Poquoson River, 71
Porter, Fitz John, 79, 88, 129, 140, 141
Potts, Bob, 48, 68, 96
Potts, Sallie H., 137
Potts, Will, 48, 68, 96, 97, 112
Potts family, 65
prayer book, 20, 152

Ravinus, Esther, xiv
Rebel Army, 31

battle defeat of, 113
Buckley reporting position of, 75

Corinth evacuated by, 75, 113–114

Dunham near exploding shell of, 145

# Index

Franklin, W., cutting off retreating, 74

Howell, T. J., describing, 77

Kearny and discards of, 32

McClellan, G., and evacuation of, 99–100
McClellan, G., plan for, 134

New Jersey Brigade eager to engage, 142

pickets of, 109–110
Porter's corps attacked by, 129

retreat of, 75
Richmond defense of, 81
Richmond evacuation by, 105–106, 111

Third New Jersey skirmishes with, 102, 120–122, 143–146

Union Army skirmishes with, 74, 145
Union casualties from, 83

Regur, Leonard H., 24, 27, 62
reinforcements, 145–146
Richardson, Israel B., 88
Richmond, VA, 1, 80, 81

battle for, 126

McClellan, G., ending capture of, 141
McClellan, G., goal for, 119–120

Rebels evacuation of, 105–106, 111, 117

struggle anticipated for, 83

Third New Jersey four miles from, 118
Third New Jersey twelve miles from, 108

road building, 123–125
Rogers, Lizzie, 37, 47
Romancoke plantation, 77, 135, 136
rubber blankets, 66
Runyon, Theodore, 22

Salem Heights, battle of, 154
Sangster's Station, 31, 44, 62, 66
Savage's Station, 154
Sears, Stephen W., 77, 130
second lieutenant, 1, 17, 49
Second New York Regiment, 140
Seven Days' battle, 88–89, 140, 141
Seven Pines battle. *See* Fair Oaks
Shields, James, 79
Shiloh battle, 35
Ship Point, 73, 100
ships, transport, 71, 72, 75, 99
. *See also specific ships*
siblings, of Howell, T. J., 64
Sickles, Daniel E., 140
Sickles Brigade, 126
side-wheel steam ship, 71, 133
Simpson, James H., 104, 115, 136
Sixteenth New York Regiment, 135
Sixth New Jersey Regiment, 139
skirmish drill, 54
slavery, 9

abolition of, 5

contempt for, 77

expansion of, 15n65

Slocum, Henry W., 76, 104, 123, 129, 140

command changed and, 79

Porter being supported by, 141

regiments of, 135, 136

Smith, William F. ("Baldy"), 110, 137
Smith & Wesson, 35, 92, 134
soldier's life, xiv, 2
Southern states, 84, 117
Spence, William, 68
Spencer, Lewis C., 53, 64, 98
Stanton, Edwin, 34
Stewart, John, 147
St. George Hall, 43, 65
Stickney, James W. H., 140
Stickney, Richard, 55, 70

Stoneman, George, 77, 110, 137
Stratton, Charles, 7, 65
streptococcus infection, 6
Stuart, J. E. B., 85, 88, 139
Summers, Anna C., 65
Sumner, Edwin V., 129, 140
surgeons, 116
Sykes, George, 105, 136

target practice, 35
Taylor, Archibald ("Arch") S., 24, 27, 29, 34, 38, 40

background of, 64

Captain prospects of, 44, 91

death of, 154, 161n65

as fine boy, 53

first platoon command of, 54

Howell, T. J., comments of, 145

knives of, 42

phonographic prayer book and, 55

as selfish and ungenerous, 122

Taylor, Charlotte, 68
Taylor, George W., 17, 27, 31, 64, 66, 97, 99

battle of Gaines's Mill location of, 141–143, 144

letter from, 19

promotion of, 104

reinforcements sought by, 145–146

Sangster's Station march of, 62

troops rallied by, 147–148
Taylor, Henry, 44, 66
Taylor, Jane Taitt, 70

Taylor, Sutler, 49
Taylor, William Johnston, 47, 56, 66
teenage officer, xiv
temperance movement, 5
tents, 40
Third New Jersey Volunteer Infantry Regiment, 1

Alexandria, VA arrival of, 36

Boatswain's Swamp fighting and, 148

at Camp Fort Worth, 22

casualties of, 161n60
company drills of, 43
corduroy road built by, 87

at Fort Worth, 22

Grubb, E., rejoining, 145–146
grueling march of, 86

heavy fighting facing, 114, 114–115
Howell, T. J., joining, 17–18
Howell, T. J., rallying, 148

Kearny praising, 56

Manassas arrival of, 46
Manassas march of, 44–45, 50, 57
McClellan, G., with, 51
Mechanicsville arrival of, 116
Mechanicsville three miles from, 119
miserable conditions endured by, 35–36
mustered into service of, 20–22

New Kent Court House approach of, 78

officers not gentlemen in, 25–26

picket duty of, 82

Rebel Army attacks on, 143–146
Rebel Army skirmishes with, 102, 120–122
Richmond four miles away from, 118

Richmond twelve miles away from, 108
road building of, 123–125

second lieutenant in, 17
Ship Point location of, 73

target practice for, 35

Welling assistant surgeon for, 151
westward march of, 31. *See also* Army of the Potomac; New Jersey Brigade; Union Army

Titsworth, Edward B., 134
tombstone epitaph, 158
*Too Young to Die* (Keesee), 2
transcribed letters, xiii
transport ship, 71, 74, 94, 99, 130
troches, 65
troop miscount, 63
Tunstall's Station, 79
Tyler, Charles, 134

Union Army

Chickahominy fever suffered by, 82, 85
commissioned officers of, 3

Fort Monroe destination of, 33

Harrison's Landing base of, 153

McClellan, G., reorganizing, 79

Rebel Army bombarding, 74
Rebel Army casualties to, 83
Rebel Army skirmishes with, 145

Shiloh battle won by, 35
soldiers in, 2

Taylor, G., rallying, 147–148

whiskey given to troops of, 81, 110, 126

Vickers, David, 27, 53
Vickers, David, Jr., 69

Warren, Gouverneur K., 105, 136
Warrenton, VA, 70
*Washington* (balloon), 86
Washington, DC, 34–35
Washington, George, 71
Welling, Edward, 85, 116, 139, 149, 151, 160n49
Wessell, Henry W., 138
West Point, 74, 102, 117, 135
West Point Fishery, 4
Whig party, 5
whiskey, given to troops, 81, 110, 126
White House plantation, 79, 102, 105, 136
Whiting, William Henry Chase, 135
Wiley, Bell I., 3
Wilson, James M., 97, 135
Wistar, Caspar, 20
Woodbury-Alexander Bridge, 141, 148, 149
Wool, J. E., 68
wounded soldiers, 154–155

York River, 74
Yorktown, 71, 96, 98, 100, 102, 133
young men, 2

# About the Author

**James Scythes** is a tenure-track instructor of history at West Chester University of Pennsylvania. He currently lives in Mullica Hill, New Jersey, with his fiancée, Chere, and their two children, Isabella and Brady.